In His Time

Tim Mahn

Phil 4:13

In His Time

Tim Malm's Personal Road Back in the Saddle

CANDRA MARLETT

with journal entries
by Dixie Malm

CROSSBOOKS

CrossBooks™
A Division of LifeWay
1663 Liberty Drive
Bloomington, IN 47403
www.crossbooks.com
Phone: 1-866-879-0502

© 2013 Candra Marlett. All rights reserved.

No part of this book may be reproduced, stored in a retrieval system, or transmitted by any means without the written permission of the author.

First published by CrossBooks 03/27/2013

ISBN: 978-1-4627-2650-9 (sc)
ISBN: 978-1-4627-2652-3 (hc)
ISBN: 978-1-4627-2651-6 (e)

Library of Congress Control Number: 2013905580

Printed in the United States of America.

This book is printed on acid-free paper.

Any people depicted in stock imagery provided by Thinkstock are models, and such images are being used for illustrative purposes only.

Certain stock imagery © Thinkstock.

Because of the dynamic nature of the Internet, any web addresses or links contained in this book may have changed since publication and may no longer be valid. The views expressed in this work are solely those of the author and do not necessarily reflect the views of the publisher, and the publisher hereby disclaims any responsibility for them.

For Tim Malm, whose courageous spirit and Christian faith is the foundation for this book. He titled the book because he knows he will be healed in God's perfect timing, on this side of heaven or in God's holy presence.

Ecc. 3:11 "He has made everything beautiful."

"In His time, In His time,
He makes all things beautiful in His time.
Lord please show me every day as
you're teaching me your way
That you do just what you say
In Your time."

(Diane Ball—1941, Maranatha! Music 1978)

Acknowledgements

This book could not have been written without the journaling of Tim's mom Dixie Malm. From the very beginning of this journey, her daily devotional thoughts along with updates on Tim's recovery process are the inspiration for the book. The postings on Facebook and Caringbridge from hundreds of people across the country along with personal insights from relatives and friends also inspired me to tell this story. I thank each one of you for your thoughts, prayers, and words of encouragement. I thank Cheryl and Chuck Baber and Shirley Cooper for funding the publishing of the book. Profits from the book will go to the Malms for Tim's medical expenses and to support other cowboy ministries. I also thank the entire Malm family for inspiring us all to be people of faith. I thank God for giving me the ability to compile this information into a book that tells a story that needs to be told.

Table of Contents

Foreword - Steven Beer, M.D. FAANS	xi
Introduction - Tim Malm	xv
Preface	xix
Chapter 1 - Background	1
Chapter 2 - Day of Accident	7
Chapter 3 - Cheyenne Med. Center	17
Chapter 4 - Craig Rehabilitation Center, Englewood, CO	34
Chapter 5 - Home in Albin (2010)	118
Chapter 6 - Home in Albin (2011)	142
Chapter 7 - Home in Albin (2012)	217
Final Thoughts	249
Appendix	259

Foreword
by Steven Beer, MD, FAANS
Wyoming Spine & Neurosurgery
Cheyenne, Wyoming

"A Medical Miracle: Tim Malm's Recovery

A one in a million unheard of will to live driven by one of the most supportive families I have ever seen.

Calf ropers are rodeo contestants who compete to see who can lasso a calf and tie it up in the least amount of time and usually within only seconds. On June 6, 2010, Tim Malm, a strapping young man, found out that seconds can change a life. Although I wasn't at the event, I feel as though I could have been. We watched the video over and over to try to see what exactly had happened. On that day, after Tim was delivered to the hospital by ambulance in a deep state of coma, the degree of injuries identified on his cat scan made no sense. I explained that to his parents in disbelief as I prepared to mentally prepare them for what I figured would be the loss of their child. Boy, was I wrong.

As a neurosurgeon, I am the unfortunate medical recipient of some of the worst neurological problems imaginable. On the day Tim arrived, he was intubated and mechanically ventilated and in terrible shape. The trauma surgeon checked him from head to toe and then smiled as she handed him off to me saying, "He's all yours." She could essentially find no serious injuries aside from a punctured lung which usually heals after a tube is left in the chest for several days. Typically in the business of medicine, none of us 'providers' relish trauma. In cases like

Tim's, often the injuries are so bad it just doesn't matter what we do to intervene, mother nature gets her way and nature takes its course. Tim's case made no sense. His head CT or cat scan looked like a hand grenade had deployed between his ears. Literally every important deep brain structure appeared to have been injured with evidence of hemorrhage throughout. In my mind, mother nature would likely win and without thinking twice I prepared to share my nauseating assessment with his parents.

Not knowing his parents well, I started my discussion gently explaining how different parts of the brain are responsible for different things, emphasizing how some parts are much more important than others. We then looked at the cat scan together and I explained how all of the important parts had been seriously injured by whatever had happened to Tim. I spent probably minutes which felt like hours trying to explain quite simply that I did not think Tim had any chance of survival. Telling parents they have likely lost a child is perhaps the worst thing I ever have to do and on this day it was no different. I took the time to carefully explain what Tim was up against really expecting his parents would be overwhelmed by what I had to say but also realistic. I felt they would likely limit the lengths we would go to in order to keep this young man alive on life support. In this case the young man was clearly in excellent shape and if we wanted to we could keep him alive for years on life support, which may sometimes be the worst thing we could do as medical providers.

Well, I thought I had done a good job of educating his parents of how bad the situation was as I had literally convinced myself there was nothing I could do or should do for an injury that was that severe. I could almost hear my chairman, the guy that trained me how to do neurosurgery and his frequent voice of reason in my head saying over and over again how I would some day understand my limits as a healer, like this case was something he planned out for my future. This case was undoubtedly one he would have called unsurvivable. At that point in the discussion, I realized his parents had not really heard the true meaning of a word I had said and probably couldn't understand how bad the injury was, let alone accept what I was trying to tell them. And somehow by the grace of God their inability to accept what I was saying and Tim's amazing will to live ended up being the difference between life and death.

Tim's mother, Dixie, is without a doubt one of the most driven people I have ever known. At the time I was trying to say there was no hope, she showed me over and over the video of what had occurred. At some point during all of that discussion I guess the voice in my head became overwhelmed by Dixie and Tim's father, Howard's, insistence this was not happening. This was a nightmare and they would not accept anything short of giving it our all. At first I had not even considered moving forward with any treatment; then it occurred to me perhaps the injuries we saw on the ct scan occurred because of pressure. In this case as many times as I watched the horse get jerked down and Tim fall to the ground, I did not see what I had expected. There was really no significant whip lash and certainly not to the extent which would have been necessary to cause the damage seen. Against the voice in my head, against my gut feeling and also exactly what Tim's folks wanted me to say, I said we have to do something. To this day that remains one of the hardest decisions I have been faced with and clearly one of the best decisions I have ever made against my better judgment. Days later when the time came to send him off to Denver, I had no idea if and when I would see Tim again. I remember that call I had to make in which I had to explain to some doctor why I had chosen to treat what on the surface seemed to make no sense whatsoever. That voice in my head kept saying "See, I told you so," but I had to make the call and painted a realistic and only cautiously optimistic picture of Tim's injury and current condition. Almost as rapidly as he showed up and to my surprise, Tim was accepted at Craig in Denver for further rehab.

Almost a year after those nearly fatal seconds, Tim showed up at my office grinning ear to ear with Dixie. Howard even cracked a smile, concerned, but a smile. Tim was awake. His speech was tricky to understand but his comprehension was spot on. He had left sided weakness and his pupils still didn't work right, but he was able to say "Thank you Doctor Beer." I was in shock and even in tears. Finally that voice inside my head couldn't say a word. Dixie on the other hand just smiled. I think I heard the voice in her head say as they left that day,

"Come on Tim; we have work to do." I understand Tim is walking with assistance today and spoke recently at a local rodeo.

I am forever changed as I hope you will be too by miracles like Tim and his family. After all, they are "one in a million." I am proud to have been able to have helped them in their time of need. I will tell you, however, my effort pales in comparison to Tim's will to live and the tireless support of his family. God speed Tim Malm. I hope someday I will have the opportunity, as much as I hope I will never see another injury as bad as yours, to care for another amazing patient like you."

Introduction
A Word From Tim (Oct. 2012)

"For those of you who don't know me, I'm Tim Malm. On June 6, 2010, my life was changed forever. It started out like any-other Sunday. It was gonna be a good day. Emphasis on the gonna be. Now from here I'm just going off of what my family has told me because I don't remember. It was just another roping session except this was the first time tripping steers at home. I roped the first and last steer of the session really good and started off left and set my trip. The rope came from behind and under my horse's right front foot putting a half-hitch on that foot. Consequently when the rope came tight it jerked his leg out and jerked him down and the sudden movement of the incident jarred my brain. I didn't have a mark on me. It was God's perfect will.If you want details on what happened next, you will have to ask my friends and family that visited and stayed with me, because I have no idea what went on around me. I made progress every day, little by little. It might be slow and steady, but at least it's coming. PTL!

Growing up I was into tractors and the ranch. I'm 6th generation on our family ranch. I was started early in life and it runs deep in my blood. I was driving a tractor cutting hay by myself at age five. I can honestly say in my twenty-two years of life I've never had a job a day in my life because unlike most people I love to work and I cannot wait to get back. I've never had a job because work to me is enjoyable and I miss it dearly. I've been through a lot of wrecks in my life that seemed worse than this—Dad just thought I would be a little sore the next day. My greatest wreck was a broken bone in my arm in elementary school.

I mean I've had my share of bumps and bruises all over my body but nothing that kept me from what I love.

I will admit it—there's been times the devil has attacked and fed me filthy lies that God was upset with me or that I committed sin that was so bad that I deserved this—but God loves us so much He sent His Son to die for us. In Psalm 103:12 it says, "as far as the east is from the west, so far has he removed our transgressions from us." Now He knew what He was talking about! He didn't say north from the south because if you go far enough north you will be going south. So the distance is finite—that is it can be determined. But, the east from the west is infinite, it can never be determined. No matter how far you go east you will never go west. Now why would God say that if He didn't know what He was talking about, and why would He know that? Oh yeah, duh, He created it.

I cannot stress how important it is to make sure you're right with God. If you only take one thing from this let it be this—"Be Ready and Right with God" because you never know what tomorrow holds, so make sure you fully know and trust the Man that holds tomorrow! God is doing an incredible work through me and just like the song says, "Nothing, nothing, ABSOLUTELY nothing, nothing is too difficult for Thee. Now there is one thing that God cannot do. Do you know what that is? It is something I can do that my Savior cannot—SIN—and I am so thankful that my God cannot sin. If it wasn't that way, we, as believers, wouldn't have any hope. Did you know that this life is the worst that we, as believers, will ever go through and the best that non-believers will because this earth is the closest to Heaven non-believers will ever experience while it is the closest to "you know where" that we as believers will ever have to experience. Can you imagine if I wasn't a believer and didn't know without a shadow of a doubt I will see Jesus one day that this would be the best I would have? Now that would down right stink. It would be a bad deal. There have been times I'd like to just sit back and quit, and relax but that's not me. Rene Descartes says: "I think therefore I am". When people told me you can't do that my first response was always: just watch me. That's what has been the hardest thing about this injury is that I feel like I can still do anything and go to the rodeos. That's been the hardest part; I miss the rodeos so much.

I am so thankful for my memory and how I remember everything but at the same time I hate it, because I remember ever run I've made. I just so want to be back. Sure there've been times I've thought I could do it better but when I thought about it, no way.

    I still am yet to figure out how He brought some of the Facebook people into my life. Also who would want to be God and know what was going through 7,043 billion people's heads? Not this guy. That's really amazing how big our God is. That just amazes me that the God of the universe wants to spend time with me, and He loves us so much He sent His son to die for us. All He asks us to do to receive this is to ask him to save us and believe. Also if it wasn't for this accident I wouldn't know how much I like public speaking. At one of my speaking engagements at one of the cowboy churches, they usually average about 60-100 and at this one there was about 300. If that isn't God moving I don't know what is. It's a big God thing the amount of pull I have among the college rodeo contestants. I can relate with them because I've been with them and through the things they've been through. This might be wrong but I picture God as a calf roper and we are the calves. Now some of us are good calves and others are the eliminators and He has to tie us down. Some of us take the run pretty good while others thrash and fight it. If we would just take it, we would be a lot better off. I just know I'm gonna be completely healed and allowed to rope again. I have the faith, and if you don't know me—know one thing, I have the faith. I just know it's going to happen and He will give me the strength to stay strong in the faith and to persevere until that glorious day that I walk and rope again!

    This has been so tough, yet I wouldn't wish this on my worst enemy (I don't think I have any.) I've had people I love tell me if they could they would trade me spots but it's just me to not want that. Not that I am any better than anyone because on God's level I am just as bad as Hitler and only by God's grace I am reconciled and made whole. I am so tired of my situation, yet God renews me and gives me the strength for every day. Don't get me wrong; I'm gonna give it my all to be back this winter to roping because I really miss it. I heard a good line the other day. Not being able to rope is like missing a part of your body. Don't feel sorry for me because the Lord is using me in more ways than I know. I've seen God change friends' lives, but I'm not gonna be satisfied until all my friends know the truth. If you felt led to contact me and make the most important decision of your life, my email is skyhijordan@yahoo.com—many will hear this—few will take it to heart—and a select few will make a heart decision and change their lives. Be one of the select few and make the greatest decision of your life.

Thank you for your prayers and encouragement. Thank you for the purchase of this book. I pray that this book finds you well and that it brings God the glory. Plus, a big thank you to first and foremost my Lord and Savior, Jesus Christ, because this journey is 'all about Him'. I thank God for my parents (Howard & Dixie), and my sisters (Bethany, Cassady, and Jessica) for all they have done and continue to do for me. Thank you to the many other people I'm so blessed to call family. Thank you to all the friends who take the time to talk with me, have prayed for me, and have encouraged me in so many ways. I will never know or be able to thank everyone. Thanks to all who contributed their 'writings' to this book—I hope it encourages others to walk their life journeys with Him. Thank you also, to my aunts, Candra Marlett (for organizing and writing the book) and Cheryl Baber and my grandmother, Shirley Cooper ("Nanny") for their input and contribution to this book project. Thank you and God bless.

If you only take one thing from this book make sure you remember this, You never know what tomorrow holds but I know the Guy who holds tomorrow and I trust Him completely. Just remember, God has done so much for you; don't you think you would want to be around Him everyday. He doesn't ask you for much—Just all of yourself. Thank You and God Bless. Glory to God."

Preface

I am a retired English teacher from a small town in southwestern Oklahoma. Through my thirty-two years of teaching, I encouraged my students to read and journal throughout their lives. I know the importance of doing both. I have always wanted to write a book but could never really decide on a topic. One morning I woke up and God revealed to me that He wanted me to tell Tim's story through the daily journaling of his mom (my sister) and the prayers and thoughts of all the people on Facebook and Caringbridge websites. I wasn't sure where to start and where it would go, but I truly believed it was a real life story that needed to be told. As an example, my granddaughters (who are five and three) love for Paps (my husband Danny) and Ma (me) to tell them stories—some fairly tales and some real stories. In July 2012, they both saw Tim for the first time when he came to Oklahoma for a cousin's wedding. After the wedding, they asked me why Tim's neck was crooked and why he talked funny. I told them the story of Tim's accident. I also told them that we needed to pray for Tim every night and thank Jesus for making him better, like he was before. Now, every time we are around them they want me to tell them "Tim's Story." They also always ask me how Tim is doing and what all Jesus has done for him. Just like those two small children, I believe people of all ages across the country want to hear "Tim's Story" and follow his recovery.

    The journey that Tim and his family are going through is touching and changing so many lives. In the first few weeks they were in Cheyenne, there were over 2,000 Facebook guests to his page called Prayers for Tim Malm set up by Cameron Weddle. After they moved to Craig Rehab Center in Denver and the Caringbridge journaling site was begun, as of July 15 there were over 4,000 prayer entries there and growing every day. When they left to go home to Albin on Oct. 1, Caringbridge had around 18,700 visits on Tim's website. The last time I checked, there were over 37,000 visits. It continues to amaze me how many people are praying for Tim and his family, people from all over the US and even other countries as well. People have said over and over again how they continue to check on Tim's progress along with praying for him and his family. Most of them keep repeating the fact that Tim is such an inspirational role model and what an inspiration his family is to all those participating in this walk of faith—Tim's journey to recovery. Along with Dixie's weekly updates, Tim's page on Facebook is like a daily devotional book that one reads, ponders, and prays about. I am reminded of a little poem that says, "You are writing a gospel, a chapter each day, by the deeds that you do and the words that you say. People read what you write, whether false or true. Say, what's the gospel according to you?" People are truly reading the gospel according to the Malms—how they are going through this storm in their lives and what God is teaching them about faith and what he is ultimately teaching all of us as well. I am sure there are many people who read the journal and not openly respond on the website, but pray in their own hearts and homes. There are many people who possibly have never prayed before but are praying now. Many of them have never met Tim or any of his family, but simply want to pray for him. They are learning what the power of prayer is all about. People simply cannot successfully go through times like these without relying on God and through prayer.

Do you ever think about how you would react if your life were drastically changed in the blink of an eye? Do you ever think about how difficult it would be to go through a tragic event yourself, but how about watching your child have to go through it? How would you help them deal with the disappointment when their dreams are shattered? These questions and many more have gone through my mind since Tim's accident happened. I have always thought my faith would see me through something like this, but we never truly know until that faith is tested. Watching how Tim and his family reacted from the very beginning and now over two years later is a life lesson we all need to learn.

As parents, we try our hardest to protect our children. We are always telling them to be careful. We continually worry about them and their safety, but ultimately, we cannot protect them. We have to trust that God will protect them and keep them safe. There was nothing risky or reckless about what Tim was doing prior to his accident. He was doing what he loved and what he knew. It just happened. His family was right there and could not do anything to prevent it. Life happens. We are not in control; God is. One of the hardest things a parent does is let their children live. They need to experience life and live it to the fullest. We should not keep them locked up in a padded cell. That is no way to live. There are risks with everything. Howard and Dixie raised their children to really live each day that God gave them. I truly believe they would not go back and change a thing. They trust God with their children and always have. We have to trust in God and when the accidents do happen, He will see us through it.

I don't know a lot about rodeos, but I do know that most of the events are all about timing. One has to beat the clock. Events are won by the smallest margins of time. One second can actually be a long time. Throughout all areas of our lives, timing is important. Seconds count. In Tim's life, seconds counted. He lost the National Finals competition by only seconds. The accident that changed his life forever happened in just seconds. Healing can occur in seconds also—even in the blink of an eye. It can also take days, months, and years. God's timing is nothing at all like ours. One day to Him could be a thousand years to us. That is why we have to trust His timing-His plan. He is in control. Tim trusts Him. Tim will be healed "in His time." Just like the song says, "God will make all things beautiful in His time."

Chapter One

Background

"I have made you and I will carry you."
Isaiah 46:4

To truly appreciate this walk of faith, we need to understand who Tim Malm is. Tim Malm was born on July 16, 1990, in Kimball, Nebraska. His parents are Howard and Dixie Malm, who are from Albin, Wyoming. He also has three sisters. Bethany, Cassady, and Jessica are the sixth generation on a large, family-owned-and-operated farm and ranch located on the Wyoming/Nebraska state line.

Albin is a small community about forty-five miles northeast of Cheyenne. Dixie is from Oklahoma, where her family was involved in farming, ranching, and custom harvesting. Elroy Cooper and Daughters was the name of the harvesting crew. (Mom always said she was going to make a sign: SHIRLEY AND SONS-IN-LAW.) Every year, they traveled north for the harvest, and Pine Bluffs, Wyoming, was one of their stops. This is how Dixie met Howard and ended up in Wyoming.

Cheryl Baber, Dixie's youngest sister, said,

> The summer wheat harvest was our annual summer adventure and our family's main source of income when we were growing up. Our last stop on the trail was near where Dixie lives now, and that's how Dixie wound up in

what I sometimes jokingly called Siberia, or "that frozen wasteland" in reference to a song from *Fiddler on the Roof*. That's how she wound up "Far from the Home I Love." She had always wanted a big family and to marry an Italian farmer. She got everything she wanted, I suppose, except she married a Swedish farmer in 1986, and that seemed to suit her just fine.

Timothy was born four years later. I didn't see him much as he grew, but I remember calling him Hooch when he was very young for the way in which he seemed to tear up an entire room when he entered. Timothy grew into a lanky cowboy and followed in the steps of his father and grandfather, who all had a love for the rodeo event of calf roping. I remember, with a smile, the time Dixie had to get on him for roping his sisters as they rode their bicycles around the yard where they lived! He protested, saying, "But I didn't jerk them off!" My father was so proud of his grandson, Tim, and I know that the roping thing gave them a connection they wouldn't otherwise have had.

Every family has its own special interests and passions. For the Howard Malm family, it was God and family, with rodeo and ranch work consuming most of their family time together. They knew well how all of these passions could work together. Howard also had a background in roping, as did his dad, Gordon, and his uncle, Ken. Tim's granddad, Elroy Cooper from Oklahoma, was also a roper, so to say roping was in Tim's blood from the start is an understatement.

In 2005, Tim's grandparents, Elroy (Papa) and Shirley (Nanny), hauled up from Oklahoma to Wyoming a horse that Tim bought himself, a roping horse named DJ. Tim and DJ immediately developed a deep bond with each other. After Tim lost his granddad Elroy in 2006, he carried his inspiration with him in his rope can to every event. Tim's favorite verse is Philippians 3:14, which says, "I can do all things through Christ who strengthens me."

Tim also worked long hours on the farm and ranch, but every spare minute was spent practicing his roping. He had high hopes and dreams of becoming a successful professional roper. The family would travel all over Wyoming with Tim and Bethany in high school, and then Tim traveled to college rodeos and other rodeos across other states. It was something they were all involved in and truly enjoyed as a family.

Tim's honors included 2009 Wyoming State Champion Calf Roper, 2007 and 2008 State Runner-Up Calf Roper, three-time National High School Finals Rodeo Qualifier, and 2009 National High School Reserve Champion Calf Roper. He then went on to Northeastern Junior College in Sterling, Colorado, on a rodeo scholarship and competed throughout his freshman year, finishing fifth in calf roping in the Central Rocky Mountain Region division. He was a 4.0 student studying ranch management and agricultural business. He had filed his PRCA permit and was waiting to get his PRCA card and go for rookie of the year beginning in September 2010. He had started steer roping as a second event. Everyone knew of Tim's horsemanship, his knowledge of cattle, and his passion for calf roping. Tim was getting ready to start competing in the summer rodeo circuit by doing what all competitors do: practice.

One of the first posts on Caringbridge following his accident was from his rodeo coach, Brian Cullen. It gives a pretty good picture of the kind of young man Tim is and his effect on the rodeo team there.

> I know you have so much to tell us, Tim. I learned way more from you than you learned from me this year at school. Thanks for being the first guy to arrive and the last guy to leave practice. Your work ethic and drive to be the best is contagious, and it inspired not only your coach, but also your teammates. You are an incredibly strong man, in more than just the physical nature.
>
> Your family members are very special people. I knew your mom could cook after all the great treats she brought to the rodeos. Each member of your family has shown a faith and love that is incredible. From the first night in Cheyenne to today, their strength is an incredible testament to our Savior. You have changed my prayer life, Bible reading, faith in our Lord and Savior, and how I believe. Now I just don't

pray and hope, but I pray and believe. Your sister sent me your picture yesterday, and you are looking great. Keep up the good work. I have no doubt you will. I absolutely believe that very soon you will be reading this, and I wanted you to know how much we miss you.

Love, Coach

Tim is such a quiet, humble young man; the impact he has had on so many people would amaze him. He would just shake his head, grin, and give all the praise and glory to God. Whenever Tim speaks, you know he has something important to say. He is one of those rare individuals who really listens to people. He makes you feel that you are important and he wants to know what you have to say. I can't remember ever seeing him upset or angry with anyone, even his sisters. He was always so patient with them and was willing to help in any way he could. He is so kind and considerate of others, humble and never prideful, always giving God the credit. He leads by example and is a hard worker. I remember him helping his dad with the cattle and farming at such a young age. I never heard him complain about anything. His smile is so contagious. He has a way about him that makes people want to be around him. The irony in this situation is that Tim would be the very last person who would want people worrying about him or spending time praying for him. He would even be a little embarrassed with all the attention, but he would be so very appreciative and would do whatever he could to repay everyone for his or her support. He would be more worried about his mom, dad, sisters, family, and his horse than himself. That is just the way he is.

A friend, Britt Bath, wrote,

> Through all of this time together, I learned that Tim wasn't a typical high school or college kid. God placed no fear and an incredible amount of resolve in him, along with an unmatched friendliness, faith, and loyalty. Those qualities have been on display to the whole world since the first night of his accident, but I had seen those qualities on a regular

basis several years before. Not only was Tim not the typical high school kid, he has proven to not be the typical human. I think he might be Superman.

Family friend Sam McAdow wrote,

> As a Christian, I have often prayed that the Lord would bring godly people alongside my sons to befriend and mentor them, hoping that the Lord would fill in the gaps that I had not. I remember some years ago Dixie sought me out, at a roping our sons were competing in, to ask me about Northeastern Junior College and Coach Brian Cullen. Tim was planning on going to college there, and she was anxious to find out more about this place and the coach, who would have an influence on Tim. She was seeking reassurance because she was about to send her first born to a strange place, away from home, as I had done. She had prayed similar prayers for her children's spiritual and physical well-being. What I did not realize at the time was that I was talking to the mother of the one God had sent in answer to my prayers of many years. The Lord was faithful when Tim became my son's friend. I remember once my son told me, "Tim even prays before meals at Burger King." When I heard this, I silently thanked God for the gift of Tim Malm. Tim demonstrated what a true man of God looks like.

Long-time family friend Jim McNamee, who went to school with Howard, and has two boys, who roped and played basketball with Tim, told me in an interview over the phone,

> I have always admired Tim and the whole Malm family for their Christian example. They quietly believe and are never shaken. When the accident happened, they calmly got their son to a place where he could receive the best possible medical care, but they always knew their best chance was prayer and that God was in control of everything.

Throughout this whole ordeal, this sincere show of strength and faith in God has made everyone around them stronger in their own faith. There is absolutely no wonder what the purpose of this accident is—to bring people closer to God and to change lives."

CHAPTER TWO

Day of Accident

"Nothing is harder to heal than a broken heart shattered by experiences that seem so meaningless. But God's people don't live on explanations, God's people live on God's promises." Warren Wiersbe.

On June 6, 2010, a beautiful Sunday afternoon in his practice arena on the ranch, Tim was practicing steer roping while his mom was filming and his dad, sisters, and grandpa Gordon Malm were watching. Tim had used a breakaway rope warming up with the first few steers. He then had tied his rope down on the saddle horn and rode in the box. The chute gate opened and Tim was out and roped the steer . . . then something wrong happened and in the blink of an eye, Tim lay on the ground unconscious. Tim's life, his family's lives, and the lives of thousands of people around the country were forever changed in that moment, those precious seconds. The last thing recorded on the tape was Dixie's words, "Are you okay?" and then she dropped the camera and ran to her son. Tim quit breathing and Dixie performed CPR and had Tim breathing on his own when the Albin ambulance arrived and the EMT's took over. Howard and Tim were on the way to the hospital in Cheyenne. Dixie was on the plone, calling everyone for prayer. That was her first instinctive thought—prayer, because she and her family knew the power of prayer. From that very moment, prayers were begun.

Tim had gone home with Lee, his childhood buddy and closer-than-a-brother, after church where they had lunch and talked about their plans for the afternoon. Lee had come out to watch Tim practice and was in the arena when the accident happened. Lee texted his mom saying that Tim had been hurt and needed an ambulance. Chery, Lee's mother, wrote,

> "I pulled in as they were loading Tim in the ambulance. Lee was at the edge of the arena. Lee grabbed me as I told him to let me find Dixie to go with her as Howard was going in the ambulance. He hung onto my hand and said, 'No, don't leave me. I thought he was dead.' I drove with Dixie to Cheyenne. As everyone began to arrive at the hospital waiting room, they moved us to a larger area. It was then it all starting sinking in and as the tears came, we prayed individually and in groups as Dixie and Howard would come tell us the situation. At one time, Lee gave Dixie the cross necklace that Tim had been wearing. The EMT had cut it off and gave it to Lee, and they wrapped it in Tim's hand. Seeing Tim so lifeless was heart wrenching, when twenty-four hours before we'd been eating and laughing together."

Dixie later wrote about that day in her journal:

> "June 6th became one of those life shattering experiences that many of you experienced with us. After roping a few steers with a breakaway rope, Tim tied on to rope and trip. I was filming and then life changed in a second . . . For some unexplainable reason, after Tim roped the steer and was setting his trip, the rope got under the horse's right front foot and jerked the horse over on its side with Tim still in the saddle. It was not a violent fall, and while the horse was getting his front feet under him, he let Tim slide off the back of the saddle and on to the ground. Tim was unconscious but didn't have a red mark, bruise, broken bone, nothing on the outside. Later we learned the jerk caused the brain

to shake inside the skull and shear off nerves (brain shear) causing blood to clot on the brain stem. I asked God to help Tim come "out of it"—I thought he was knocked out. Howard and Grandpa had been at the 'box' but now they were beside Tim trying to get Tim awake. We checked for broken bones, cuts, etc. but didn't find anything. Howard then said, "He's not breathing!" so I switched places with Howard and gave Tim a couple of compressions then started mouth-to-mouth. After several breaths, he breathed back against me, but was still unconscious. I held my hand under his neck praying and hearing him breathe while I could hear the ambulance coming. Chery drove me to the hospital as we prayed and called others to start praying. Howard rode in the ambulance and met me outside the trauma room—I stood by the glass watching them work on Tim. It was one of those 'life times' you never want to experience—where the numbness is almost overwhelming! Thank you God for keeping us together, only by Your strength. So many people showed up—they moved us twice before finally moving us up to the ICU waiting room. We circled up and prayed on our knees twice begging God for a miracle. The doctor talked to us several times about the seriousness, telling us he was very critical. To have a nineteen-year-old come in with no bruises, scratches, broken bones, etc. but have a TBI (traumatic brain injury) was hard to understand. Howard was trying to describe the accident to the doctor when I jumped in saying that I thought I saw the rope get under the front leg. Howard had one of Tim's roping buddies that had just traveled with Tim to two rodeos on Saturday drive back out to the ranch to get our camera (120 mile round trip). The doctor told us that he was going to insert a tube in Tim's head (brain drain?) and that it doesn't always go exactly in the first try. I told him we would pray that it would. The whole ICU waiting room was on their knees as Tim went into surgery. When the doctor came out, he said it went in the very first time! I asked if this was a "glimmer" and he said "I'll give you a glimmer, but he's still critical!" We thank you God for the glimmer and ask you to let Tim live through the night. We stayed in a very little private conference room, so after we cried and prayed, Howard tried to lay his head on the little loveseat while I stayed with Tim. I stayed 'til 4:45 then Howard stayed with him while I tried to rest."

Sam McAdow wrote,

"When we heard the news about Tim's accident, we all had a sense of urgency that we needed to go to the hospital in Cheyenne. It was a long silent trip filled with prayers, hoping for the best, fearing the worst, not knowing what to expect when we got there. I was thinking all the time of how life can change in an instant—how this could be one of our sons. I remember how strong Dixie and Howard were trying to be, but at one point they had been in with Tim for a long time and we had gotten no news. Then they came out looking grim. The doctors were not giving them much hope for Tim's survival through the night. We all fell to our knees. I remember praying 'Father, you knit Tim together in his mother's womb. Please put him back together again.' I'll never forget Dixie and Howard's prayers. They thanked God for Tim and prayed for his healing but Dixie also said, 'not our will, but your will be done, Father.' What great courage it took for a mother to pray a prayer like that, knowing that the Lord might take her son home that very night. Sometime later a doctor came out and said they had done another MRI followed by 'I don't know what you people are doing out here, but whatever it is, keep it up because Tim's condition has improved slightly.'

Tim's coach remembered that first evening in the emergency room:

"When I walked in, there were lots of people in that ICU waiting room. But the thing that I remember most and changed my life forever was when Howard and Dixie came out and said the doctor said the next short period of time would determine if Tim was going to make it. Everyone got in a circle, got down on our knees and Howard and Dixie led us in a prayer asking for God to spare Tim's life. Prior to that I had never experienced that strong of faith, that intense prayer asking for their son's life but acknowledging that he belonged to his Heavenly Father. A short period of time later the report came back positive. That's the power of prayer and indescribable love.

Lindsy Booth remembered Dixie's face as she came out of the ICU the morning after the accident. She said, "There was anxiety on her face, but no tears, and a look of peace and hope that can only come from Jesus."

Lynette Malm Hunter (Tim's aunt) wrote,

> "A few months before Tim's accident, I had prayed quite frequently 'Lord please use Tim to bring honor and glory to you. Please guard his heart and life so he leads others to you and direct his steps to what you want him to do in life.' When I heard Mom's heart wrenching cries over the phone to pray for Timothy that his horse had fallen with him and he wasn't breathing, the world stopped. For the next twelve hours all I could do was cry and pray and pray and cry. I kept thinking the next update would be that Tim was awake and had several broken bones but he would be fine. Well that news never came. When my dad called at ten and said that they didn't give Tim much hope to survive through the night, I spent much time on my knees praying. My nephew is one of the most clean-cut, God-fearing young people I have ever known. He did not go through a rebellious phase like many of us have, so it was unthinkable that this would happen. Finally at three in the morning I told my husband Kent we had to go to the hospital. When we arrived, I met one of Tim's college buddies who had spent the night there and briefly introduced ourselves to Tim's college rodeo

coach who had slept on the other couch. Then I went in to see Tim. I wasn't prepared to see my Tim connected to all those machines and tubes running to and from his body. Howard and Dixie were amazingly strong, but all I could do was kneel by Tim's bed praying over him while tears streamed down my face. I had no words to help Howard and Dixie because in that situation there are no words. There was nothing I could do to change the situation so all we had was God Himself. The most amazing God thing took place through the first night and those first days and weeks. Our prayer routine quickly became Wait . . . pray . . . text . . . miracle—he made it through the first night. Wait . . . pray . . . text . . . miracle—the blood clot on the brain stem needed to dissolve. Wait . . . pray . . . text . . . miracle—friends recommended moving Tim to Craig Hospital where Howard announced that Craig works with traumatic brain injury patients. I remember Howard grimly adding 'Some come in and walk out of Craig and some don't.' For the first time since the accident I saw my brother cry as he walked back to Tim's room."

On the way to the hospital in Cheyenne, one of Dixie's first phone calls to request prayer was to her mom in Oklahoma. Shirley Cooper was on her way home from Sunday night church services and didn't have her phone with her. Dixie then called me:

"On Sunday evening, June 6, 2010, Danny and I had just returned home from church. The phone rang and Danny answered it. All I could hear was a frantic voice in the background. Danny wasn't saying much but his eyes said it all. Something terrible had happened. He then told me the voice on the other end of the line was Dixie, and Tim had been in an accident and was badly injured. She wanted us to tell Mom and start the prayer chain here in Walters. Only later did we learn what exactly had happened. Being fourteen hours away from all of them, it was very difficult to feel useful. We wanted to be there for them, but all we could really do was pray. Since Dad had gone through a similar situation four years earlier, I remember what it was like being on that side of everything. The last thing you want to do is have to repeat yourself over and over again to everyone who calls and wants to know what's going on. It truly wears you out so we didn't call Dixie and Howard very much. As soon as family and friends started arriving at the hospital and praying for Tim, they started posting updates on Facebook. We relied on those updates, which by the way, I was never a big fan of but don't know what we would have done without it during those first few weeks. It was truly a God send."

Dixie's sister Cheryl remembered,

"Mother called. She often does on Sunday evening. I'm sure it's just a habit from the days when long-distance fees were based on the time and day and the day of the week people telephoned each other. Rates were cheaper on Sunday nights so, when we left for college, careers, and families of our own, my sisters and I would call our parents, or they would call us, on Sunday nights, usually after church. Mom said that Tim had been hurt and told me the whole story, or at least what she had gotten from my sister, Dixie, about the incident with the horse. Mom was shaken, but steady, as always. She planned to drive there early the next morning, and hoped he would make it through the night. "Pray," she pleaded, "pray hard." I hung up the phone, told my husband, and tried to call Dixie. I don't remember if I got through, but I suppose I didn't or I would have remembered. Mother had told me how Dixie had been filming the roping practice when the horse somehow got tripped on the rope and fell with Tim. Amazingly, Dixie had performed CPR to get him breathing again. His own mother. Although tender-hearted, Dixie can be surprisingly and remarkably calm when an emergency happens. But Daddy had always taught us to never panic. "Never panic," he had preached, as we helped him with farm equipment, cattle, and the harvest. So, with these thoughts running through my head, I decided I would go to Wyoming with Mom to be with Dixie, Howard, and Tim's sisters. I knew I could help with driving the sixteen hours that my seventy-two-year-old mother would have to drive by herself if I didn't go. My sister, Shena, would be going as well, but her cancer had long since taken her ability to drive. She felt good enough to go and determined that she could lie down in the back of my mother's large SUV if she needed to rest.

We finally made it to Cheyenne the next morning around 2:00 a.m. Dixie and Howard were still awake, surrounded by a few friends who were in various stages of sleep, and sleep positions, on chairs in the waiting room. They looked so tired, worried, and afraid. Dixie was "holding up" but confessed that it was good to see family, knowing that she didn't have to "hold up" around us. "I just don't want to lose him," she whispered in my ear as we embraced. Mom, Shena and I were allowed to go in and see him for a short time, as he was still critical, but now stable in ICU. He looked so strong, Shena remarked, even with all of the tubes coming out of him and attached to him. Then we visited a while in the waiting room, and fell asleep ourselves still sitting up or reclining in chairs. The next day we tried to make ourselves useful. At one point, we convinced Dixie to leave with us to get something to eat and do some errands. She talked about how they had been recently to a place that sold modular homes nearby. We asked her to take us there and show us, and I think she welcomed an excuse to get away from the stress and pressure there at the hospital. We were all in a bit of denial at that point, and hoped or assumed that Timothy would be all right in a few days.

Dixie and Howard moved into an old, rented farmhouse when they married, and a few years later moved into a ranch-owned small house in Albin, the "little town on the prairie" near their ranch. Dixie and Howard would have to put their dream of building their own house on hold again. They have shown the difference between having a 'home' and having a 'house.'

Mother, Shena and I went to Albin to spend the next night, and get some clothes for Dixie, Howard, and the girls. We also felt like we could be helpful there by cleaning it, answering the phone, doing laundry, or whatever else needed to be done. We talked about going back to Oklahoma, as Tim's condition had stabilized. Shena wanted to stay an extra day. It was the first trip she'd been on in a while, due to all of the chemotherapy and surgeries that had consumed her the previous year or so. I think she felt useful and helpful as the focus was on someone in more critical a condition than she was . . . and she hadn't felt that way in quite some time."

Andy Malm, Tim's uncle, wrote about his experience during this time.

"I vividly remember getting that unbelievable call on Sunday afternoon and weeping and praying together as a family and with friends for the next eight to ten hours. I will never forget the realness of God and his hand of grace on Monday afternoon. I was sitting on a hill in the pasture to get cell service to call my wife for the latest update on Tim's condition when I scrolled to her number and the next one below it was Tim's. At that point my heart sank, I cried out to God, 'Please don't take him, Lord.' God heard mine and all of our prayers, our cries and the rejoicing of Tim and his healing. Today through God's grace and love, I still have Tim's number in my phone. Though I don't do it enough I'm blessed to be able to call or text anytime."

As a way of collectively posting updates from the family, the Malms were informed by people at the hospital in Denver of the website Caringbridge. I started saving as many of the posts and prayers as I could because I knew one day Tim would want to read through all of them that were sent in his behalf during those days and weeks. Maybe, just maybe, he would then fully understand what an amazing young man he is and the impact he has on people's lives.

Most of this book is a small collection of those posts, prayers, updates, and daily devotional thoughts through this journey with Tim and his family. I have paraphrased and summarized the postings because for the most part they all relayed the same messages of hope, inspiration, and blessings for the Malms. I have tried to separate Dixie's actual CaringBridge postings (with brackets) from her journal writings as much as I can. As we read the updates along with the scripture inspiration for that particular day, we become involved in the healing process of not only Tim's physical body but our own spiritual healing as well. I have also tried to include in the text with bold type just a few of the actual prayers from friends and family during those first crucial days and weeks. I believe we all can relate to these postings because as humans we share universal feelings. Even if we didn't post it, we share with the ones that did. We ask the same questions, try to understand the same situations, and express our thoughts and prayers with the Malms. We are all blessed to be able to participate in this journey as we watch miracle after miracle unfold.

Chapter Three

Time Line Journal Entries from Dixie

Cheyenne Regional Medical Center (June 6-June 21)

"Instead of asking why did it happen, think of where it can lead you from here. And as your pain is slowly easing you can find greater reason to live your life triumphant through the tears. When answers aren't enough there is Jesus . . ." *When Answers Aren't Enough* song lyrics by Scott Wesley Brown and Greg Nelson

Monday, June 7, 2010—Tim had a CAT scan around 5:00. He is on a ventilator via the nose but will change to mouth sometime, breathing some on his own and letting the machine help him at other times. Trying to learn all the lights, numbers, sounds, etc. Still sedated. Nurses doing some reflex tests and have had some response! People are praying everywhere. God, You are so mighty and we continue to beg for your total healing of Tim on this earth. Thank you for the pressure relief and drainage. We pray for his temperature to come down and for his brain stem to work as You created to work. Keep him breathing strong and keep the 'enemy' out of our thoughts and out of his room. Bring Your medicals angels around his bed to fight off any pneumonia or swelling. Thank you for another day of Life! Mom has left Oklahoma, coming up with Shena and Cheryl. Had so many visitors—the hospital's rule of two family members at a time is being stressed with us for Tim to have rest without stimulation, BUT we want Tim to hear his family and friends, so we are trying for a balance, but the numbers are winning out! We had our kids bring toothbrushes & paste, some clothes, cd player with praise & instrumental CDs, and other things. A lawyer friend (law office about 2 blocks from the hospital) is letting us use their shower/bathroom so it allows for a few minutes to walk in the sunshine and clean up—I use it to cry and let God renew and refuel me to be with Tim. About 5:00 they changed Tim's breathing tube from his nose to his mouth. They finally found a bruised lung on the inside that questions how you can have it on the inside, but not the outside? Howard and I prayed together and continue to beg God for His intervention. Love you, Lord, thank you for Timothy. We thank you for each of our girls, how you are holding them and our family together, for the many friends helping in so many areas. You are so gracious and good and I trust You with Tim tonight. Thank you for the daily miracles.

(1:30 a.m.) Mom, Shena, and Cheryl finally got here—so good to have them! Still can't believe Shena was able to make the long trip. Thank You for giving her the strength. They changed Tim from being propped up on his right to his left. Praying electricity stays on during these weather watches and warnings. God, we pray that You show Yourself in a HUGE way in healing Tim so all these young friends will see who Tim's God is and how powerful You are! They want less visitors and stimulation tomorrow and we pray that Tim's blood pressure to normalize so he can go down to have another CT scan. Thank you God, for giving me the strength to do that breathing for Tim—only You! In your Son's name, I stand on Your promises of healing! Had visitors that came through headed to Casper for the College National Finals Rodeo. Some prayed over Tim and with us.

During these first two critical weeks, time seemed to slow down while the family and friends were waiting and watching for all the signs for improvement from Tim and words of encouragement and hope from the doctors and nurses. People were praying constantly for Tim to simply open his eyes and wake up. "Prayers for Tim Malm" was full of people's words, Bible verses, and prayers. I've included some of those postings in bold print. These are just a few of the hundreds of prayers posted during those first two weeks.

Tuesday, June 8, 2010—Tim had a CT of his chest. He has developed a rash on his chest—maybe a reaction from the antibiotics or from the injury? They took another scan of his chest to make sure if he needed the side chest tube to control the air in/out of lungs. How he had a little tear in the bottom of one lung and not knowing how it tore is puzzling. We gathered everyone that was there and prayed. Lord, the tears I see from Tim's eyes (especially with his eyes closed) tells me that he's fighting and wants to live! To watch one his buddies wipe both his own tears and Tim's tears is quite a scene—what a heart! They had a special prayer service at our church in Albin this morning! The doctor finally caught up with us this afternoon and talked with us while showing us the scans; the small left hemorrhage had shrunk some from the initial one on Sunday night. PTL! The main concern was the blood clot on the brain stem—it needed to dissolve. The brain stem is your 'highway of life' (controls blood pressure, heart rate, oxygen rate, pulse, etc.), so that is our prayer! They started a feeding tube, praying he tolerates that well. Very little drainage, but will monitor it for about a week before they try to wake him. Would be great if You would wake him! Thank you for sustaining him, and we pray You will through another night and he has a great day tomorrow! Howard stayed with Tim while I went to motel with Mom, Shena, and Cheryl to sleep a few hours in a bed.

> **Dear Lord,**
>
> **You know Tim so much better than I do. You know his injury and You also know his heart. Lord, I ask you to be with Tim now, working in his life. Let your will be done in his life. Lord, I pray for Tim because your Word says I should pray for his healing. I believe you hear this earnest prayer from my heart . . . and that it is powerful because of your promise. I have faith in you to heal Tim, but I also trust in the plan**

> you have for his life. Lord, I don't always understand your ways, and why he has to suffer, but I trust you. I ask that you look with mercy and grace toward him and his family. Nourish his spirit and soul in this time of suffering and comfort him with your presence. Let him and his family know you are there with him through this difficulty. And may you be glorified in his life and also in mine. Amen (Tana Bahruth)

Wednesday, June 9, 2010—Slept from 10 pm to 2 am at the motel with Mom, Shena, and Cheryl. Let Howard go rest while I stayed with Tim and read from the promise book 'til they came to get Tim for a CT scan at 3:30 a.m. Numbers stable—a few minutes of silence without all the beeps of the machines. The silence is both good and bad: good to see improvements and almost "hearing' life, bad because it can wear you out and can drive you crazy waiting for the numbers you want to see. Praying to see the specific stem area blood dissolving and shrinking so the stem can start working fully as You created! 5:02-they changed Tim's drainage bag-thank You there's a small amount of brain and spinal fluid! Still giving him a little insulin to get his numbers down to around 120 (I think). They did some reflex tests around 5:30 and had some good response on both feet and left arm., right eye moves some, left eye still dilated—praying for true intentional responses! Blood pressure staying around 78-80 on the bottom, YEA! Reading and Singing! Ultrasound around 9—BP increase with bottom number (96) going to give some labetalol(?) Doctor did some 'lung cleaning', put in PIC line, x-rayed where it was put in and numbers are good. PTL! Mom, Shena, and Cheryl went to house in Albin. They took off some bandaids around where the pic is and Tim jerked when they pulled the hair! About 9 pm. I'm headed to go rest a bit so I can relieve Howard in the night. Tim's left forearm still swollen from the IV's, but hopefully will be absorbed. Temp up a little so I pray he cools off during the night. Have upped the feeding to '30'—almost half of the goal they want for him to get to! Tim put on an inflatable mat to lift him every little bit. They held an Albin community prayer service with everyone around the rock well (the one Tim and Lee built for VBS last week) on the softball field/track. Praying that the scans show the blood area on the stem has shrunk or dissolved to show Your power and amaze these doctors and nurses. Goodnite and thank you, Lord, for a good day and looking positively toward tomorrow to watch You work in Tim's room, his body, and his life!

Thursday, June 10, 2010—Tim weighs about 202 with all the tubes on the bed. They did an early scan at 3:40 and numbers are good! PTL! Feeding up to '40', hopefully will be at his goal of '60' by evening. Temp down to right under 100. They cleaned Tim with a bed bath and baby powder. Told his nurse it reminded me all the powder Tim used with his ropes and also when he would carry his rope can on the planes with all that powder on the ropes and in the rope can itself! Amazingly, he was always allowed on the plane with all that "whitestuff"! She washed off the betadine off of his head from surgery and he sure smells better! I am staying with Tim most of the day because Howard went home to help Bethany get things ready to go up to Douglas for a high school rodeo and ride/practice in the arena. Lord, we pray for her protection in the arena, to and from the rodeo. Thank you for taking care of all three girls with friends and family, what enormous love and support from them all. I pray for safety and protection for them all as they make hour-long drives from Albin, La Grange, and Hawk Springs to come see us. I thank you for Andy and Stacy taking our girls into their home-it's been good for them to have their cousins to laugh, work, and cry with. Food, clothes, CD music, prayer support from Lynette and Kent. Martha got home from J.D.'s. Now everyone helping Gordon and Fanny—keeping our family unit together really helps Howard and I. Mom, Shena, and Cheryl cleaning at my house with Candra keeping the 'fort' together in Oklahoma. Mom tries to keep Candra updated so she can be the 'headquarters' for everyone back home! I pray God You will turn any stress into energy and strength for Howard and I and keep everyone's immune system strong! With as many people coming and going, we have to rely on You and the hand sanitizer! I pray over Tim's body, bed, and room that there not be any germs or medical mishandlings. Day-by-night-by-day . . . we trust You! Can't believe they are having a Fire Drill!! CT scan showed everything stable, but doctor made mention that the eye reflexes and left arm movement is another 'glimmer'! Said that he would look at the whole situation and talk with us on Monday after the weekend with Tim keeping stable. Our hearts sank when he mentioned options like a nursing facility, but Tim would need a stomach feeding tube and a trach to even be considered for places. Howard and I decided from the start that there would not be any negative, medical, or uncontrollable emotion in Tim's room where he could hear. I'm so glad he didn't hear any of this talk. We had stepped out to the waiting room while another one of Tim's college traveling buddies was in with Tim. The doctor had come in, but the nurse hadn't came and got us, so the doctor came out and visited with us a little bit in between his other surgeries. Howard and I talked and prayed 'til about midnight—he stayed with Tim and I went to our little conference room/bedroom and prayed and cried for God to heal Tim—don't know what time it is now. Howard will come get me in a bit to switch with him.

Thank you Father for healing Tim, Jesus today we pray that Tim would wake up we know it is your will to do this and we know that you are the great physician and we are all so excited about the healing we are all witnessing!! Thank you for being our savior and thank you for your child Tim. What a testimony this is Lord . . . we are watching a miracle, and we glorify you Father thank you for Tim's healing!! We continue to lift him up to you! We also lift Lee up to you for comfort and Peace father we ask these things in Jesus name, Amen (Judy Sorenson)

Father God, please give Tim strength. Give him the power now to break through the sleep so overpowering him. His parents and sisters, grandparents, and aunts & uncles & cousins all want to see him awake! His friends are waiting to hear that he's broken through the fog and is alert once more. Thank you for loving Tim and protecting him every step of this journey. Thank you for the great big strides he's made in the last 11 days,

and we're praising you every step of the way. Thank you for all the lives and hearts that are being softened and drawn closer to you. Continue to use Tim and his family as you continue to heal him. We ask this in the name of Jesus—at whose name (Jesus) *every* knee shall bow and *every* tongue shall confess that He is Lord—Amen (Michelle Dutsch Childers)

Friday, June 11, 2010—Woke up about 4:00 a.m. shivering so I went up to the solarium (last place the hospital moved all our family and friends) and grabbed some blankets. Switched with Howard about 4:15. Worked on getting Tim's temp down using ice packs, ice mat, and Tylenol—wiping his forehead, arms, hands, shoulders, and stomach. Tim hated to be cold—he'd always take an extra sweatshirt, coat, hand packs, etc., and now I am rubbing his body with ice! Praying for Tim . . . temp and blood pressure. Then nurse talked about if the lung would self-drain at this rate, they may be able to take the chest tube out maybe Sat morning. Tim may have moved his thumb around mine while I was holding his hand . . . you so badly want to see anything and the nurses are careful to remind you that there is a difference between a movement and a reflex, but I choose to take it as a movement! Howard spent quite a bit of time on the phone with another doctor—we so appreciate him calling us back and talking with Howard about Tim. Started some papers for Craig Rehab in Denver. Doctors told us Tim would have to have his feeding IV thing, trach, and brain drain tube out. We're still praying for TOTAL head to toe healing!!! How blessed we are to have our pastor and wife as friends and they stayed with Tim and 'manned' the visitors in the waiting room while Howard and I slept for a bit on this fold-up twin bed that won't completely unfold in that little conference room. The rest was still good. They took Tim for an MRI while we rested. After all that they gave him a bath—temp down, BP good and he's calm! Lord, how we pray for that brain You created to fully function again the way You intended. Such a smart, bright, common-sensed guy with a huge heart! They talk to us about someday he'll hopefully be independent—we pray and know You'll decide to restore and continue to mature and develop him to be independent, but dependent on YOU!

Talked with Mom and they all made it safely back to Oklahoma—thank You for their safety on the road and for the strength You gave Shena to make the trip. Please watch over Bethany tomorrow as she goes to Douglas to the rodeo. Some friends of Tim's stayed with Tim while Howard and I took about 20 minutes to go to the hospital grill and eat for the first time both of us were away from Tim. I had a bite of the ice cream—sure wish I could take some to Tim's room and give him a bite! Tim's friends slept in the ICU waiting room recliners and a close friend stayed with me until 1 am. I sat by Tim's bed reading verses, praying, and 'talking' with Tim 'til I went and switched with Howard.

One person sent words to the family saying how unbelievably strong they were and how that showed their faith—how easy it is to be a Christian when everything is good but how amazing to be one when faced with difficulty. They hoped they would have the same strength if faced with such a trauma. Another wrote about Tim having the best two things in the world: Christ and a Christian family.

Saturday, June 12, 2010—Ken and Linda Malm (Howard's uncle and aunt) came early this morning. Several friends and Coach Cullen (Tim's college coach) came through on their way to Casper (College National Finals Rodeo). Hard to think that a year ago at this time, he and one of his high school rodeo friends left after the Douglas rodeo and went to Casper to watch the College Finals. Some friends brought in fajitas from Chili's—Tim will definitely take a raincheck from them! It's hard to eat some of these things knowing how much Tim would be enjoying them with his friends! Had a special nurse friend bring in some supper also—will have it tomorrow night! God, You are so good with these friendships. The doctor took Howard and I to read the MRI; it confirmed the brain stem injury, but PRAISE THE LORD it showed no complete stroke of any kind!! Prayer needs: that dried blood on the 3rd ventricle of the brain stem to dissolve. Flow and pressure of spinal fluid to become normal, temperature regulator to work properly, eyes to open, FULL brain power, strong heart, strong clean lungs, no pneumonia, and YOU to be seen in his room and his body. I pray the blood of Jesus, Your Son, on Timothy, over Timothy, and through Timothy, our son. Tim is Yours—flow living water through him, Lord—please, please, please. I stand under the Cross and on Your promises! We trust You, Lord.

> **Tim's aunt Lynette wrote: "The one statement that I began claiming over Tim shortly after the accident and continue to claim over him is 'Tim Malm will live and not die. He will declare the mighty works of the Lord.' Amazingly enough that is exactly what Timothy is doing today because God is who he says he is."**

Sunday, June 13, 2010—They are turning down the sedative halfway and will watch pressure, temp, reactions, etc. Some close friends feel like this is the day Tim will awake—we pray also for his personality to come with his awakening. You, Lord, have developed this young man to be Your vessel and we expect and beg to see what You've created to fully work again and anticipate great things from You through Tim's body and his life. Jeremiah 29:11 "For I know the plans I have for you . . ." Lord, might we see miracles today with Your plans. Tim has shown good vitals with the sedation off for these 2 hours. PTL and we thank You, Lord, for keeping the temp and BP relatively down, but especially for the ICP numbers staying down when they raised the 'thingey' to check the balance. I look at the dried blood on his brain stem as the Enemy, and I tell it to leave—it's in the wrong place and God didn't create that to cover that ventricle! Temp gone up a bit, so the ice bags are back on the job of bringing it down. Thank You for keeping the brain pressure normal. We tried to keep Tim's room quiet and very little stimulation from visitors for the afternoon to hopefully help with keeping him relaxed and all the numbers to stay where they want them. We shared in a time with some friends with anointing his forehead with oil and a time in prayer. Tim's temp didn't come down so they have put him on that cooling blanket (sounds better than an ice blanket)! They had to medicate him for an unbalance of sodium—another thing related to the function of the brain stem injury. I believe and know that You, Almighty God, can and will heal the brain stem, Tim's brain, dissolving the blood, and allowing the fluid to function the way You created! Again and again, all praise, thanks, and worship goes to You! Love you, Lord. The left lung is almost totally healed—Praise You!! I asked the doctor if Tim had taken a step forward—even if was a 'baby step'? He said yes, and that they'll raise the brain drain pressure tomorrow to 20 (don't really understand all the numbers or the ups and down?) Lord, You already know where that is and how You will walk with Tim and us through that to get the results needed so Tim won't need a shunt. Lord, we are still praying You'll dissolve that dried blood clot on the stem so all his bodily functions will function properly. My friend continues to stay every night with me until about 1:00 a.m. and I stay 'til about 3:00 a.m. then switch with Howard. What a God-send to have her to not only keep me alert, but help with Tim. Because of her time with me, it allows me the still have the energy and time with Tim for about two hours as I read, pray, and talk with the Lord and Tim. Again Lord, I thank You for all the many, many prayers warriors out there lifting and holding us up! One of Tim's friends whose has been in Tim's room almost every day went and picked up Bethany from Torrington after she rode there with another rodeo family, and brought her back to Cheyenne. Katelin had ridden along, so all three drove back to LaGrange to spend the night at Stacy and Andy's. Lord, thank You for the rest today and we pray for a good night's rest for Tim. We pray for Your hand of healing tonight and tomorrow to be seen, heard, felt, and witnessed by all who are praying for Tim and also the doctors! Prepare the day! We rest in Your loving hands!

Monday, June 14, 2010—Put Tim back on ½ of the sedative to allow BP to get to normal, I prayed and lay beside Tim 'til Howard came in a 3 am. Went and slept in our 'cozy' room 'til 8:00 a.m. Have to fold up the fold-away bed and set against the wall in case they would need to use the room for a private consultation with another family. Went and showered at our away-from-home (hospital) bathroom of which we are so thankful for! PRAISE the LORD!!—they have ventilator breathing 0 times for him!!! Probably going to do a tracheotomy tomorrow, maybe even the feeding tube (I think they called it a peg??) Still praying against any shunts. Lord, I want to see Tim's blue eyes open and communicate with us somehow. Talked with Craig Rehab and they will be calling back—we leave all that in Your Hands and pray You will guide us with all these decisions Lord, You have brought us so far this week! Sustainable—You have and continue to sustain us beyond food and sleep, but with family and friends' prayers and hugs!

> **Father in Heaven, we are lifting our Cowboy up to you today and If it is your will we ask that you help Tim wake up and be healed Jesus all to glorify you Lord!! Thank you for answering our prayers and thank you for healing our Cowboy Lord we love you, thank you for being our savior and living in Tim's heart and all of our hearts Father! WE ask these things in Jesus name, Amen (Judy Sorenson)**
>
> **Thank you Jesus for healing and taking care of our Cowboy! The miracles we are watching in front of our eyes is because of you Father! We pray that Tim progresses day by day Lord. We pray that in your time Tim will open his eyes and be fully restored Father! Wouldn't it be cool Father if tomorrow was the day you let Tim open his eyes and see his family and friends for his birthday Lord!! But we know it is all in your timing Father and we praise you for healing our Cowboy!! We love you Father, in Jesus name Amen (Judy Sorenson)**

Tuesday, June 15, 2010—Tim had a good night! Trach thing scheduled for 12:15 then they will also pull out the thoracic vent tube! The brain monitor and drain are all working the way they need to. I take all this as YOU—thank You for the miracles! God, You are so amazing with and through Your people, cards, gifts, food, etc., but above all the prayers and encouragement! Thank You! We pray You will guide and allow all "things" in the surgery room, hallways, Tim's room, the hands, and guidance in all the doctors and nurses to go smooth and accurate, and all his vitals from the brain and stem remain normal as You are dissolving that dried blood for full function and restoration! Tim looks so much better with the trach rather than all the tubes! They decided to hold off on the feeding tube today. Doctor talked with maybe Friday or Monday for transport if Craig can take us! Lord, we have learned to choose to see, hear, and listen all to Your ways with all the miracles You give! Had a full day of visitors! Tim's temp up to 102, so another fifteen minutes on cooling blanket—Lord, we need for Tim's temp and heart rate to come down—thank You ahead of time. From about 11:00 p.m. to midnight, my 'angel' friend who stays with almost every night worked with cold washcloths on Tim's feet, hands, and head, along with the cooling mat to help lower the temp. It lowered and he was breathing slower/relaxed so she was able to leave about 1:00—I held Tim's hand, prayed, and talked 'til about 2:00, then switched with Howard.

> **We are still praying for you and your family Tim! We are anxiously awaiting the day when the update comes out that you are awake and smiling! I know that God is beside you and your family's side day in and day out and that he will awaken you at the perfect moment. I read the comments and prayers on this page and am so . . . uplifted by the kindness and caring of so many people, you are truly blessed by God's love! (Tana Bahruth)**

Wednesday, June 16, 2010—Losing track of days and time . . . Got up about 5:00 a.m., checked in on Tim and Howard—they were both asleep. They had given Tim a bath, put on fresh gown, and he looked peaceful. As I looked at them, I also thought about Daddy—the three most important men in my life. Even though he's gone on Home, I asked the Lord to allow me to keep Tim and Howard here—they have a special bond far beyond most father-son relationships. I thank You again for the peace that You have given with knowing that You have all this and Tim in Your hands and I just feel that You know the plans and I trust You in that. When I have made myself "think" beyond that path . . . I have peace knowing that Tim would be with You and Daddy if You had chosen or choose to take him. Howard and I have thought back about how in our wedding that we had a special family/household vow time that our kids were Yours and we were just chosen to take care of them for awhile for You. I just pray for more time with them, all of them. Went back and rested 'til about 8:00 and then they came and got him to go do the feeding tube. They have the ventilator helping Tim while the surgery medicine is wearing off—he is sleeping well. Maybe today Lord, we will see those beautiful blue eyes? Praying for strong health for both Howard and I so we can be strong for Tim. They said chest x-rays look good! PTL! Tim's eyelids flickered, Yea, LORD! The doctor had started a statement that he would be amazed . . . well, I didn't hear the rest because I had this 'news flash' of the Doctor! GOD is amazing and you're going to be amazed!! So, amazed is going to be my word for him! Several visitors again today—what love and support. The doctor has come by twice and said if CT scan shows normal pressure, he's going to take out the brain monitor! Again, YOU, Lord! We used the cooling mat for a bit tonight. Prayed around and around Tim's bed—his "Jericho Wall" for God to break down this "wall" and heal Tim.

Thursday, June 17, 2010—I woke up about 7:00 and Howard told me they had taken Tim about 5-ish to do the scan. Long day, but another good day. Howard talked with Craig and they think everything is in place to transport on Monday! The gastro (feeding tube) doctor came by and listened to Tim's gurgling sounds and said everything sounded and looked good. Gave him stomach meds for acid and ulcers that were in there from the initial night of steroids, meds and from his own natural ones due to his body's stress. (No telling what our stomachs look like!) White blood count up a bit so they are doing some tests. Respiratory techs came in to do their 'thang'—I have come to appreciate that suction business. The doctor talked about the positives of taking out the monitor—praying this is Your sign of healing! They also said the scan showed some of the dried blood dissolving in the brain stem!!!Thank You, Lord! Went to clean up at our "bathroom" and had a good cry, celebrating what a gracious and loving Father and Great Physician You are! We now pray that You guide the doctor taking out the monitor and sewing him back up so he has no leakage. Tim has some infection and we pray that these antibiotics will take care of it. Had some trouble with checking the PIC line for infection and veins wouldn't take it—took about three different people and finally with helping them, we got one in and to accept the antibiotics. What an ordeal! Cassady and Karissa came in to spend the night here in the hospital (our "hdqrtrs" in the solarium) He's sleeping so I'm going to try! Praise You for dissolving the blood over the ventricle in the brain stem, IV finally working, strong lungs, BP becoming normal, cooling mat, restful sleep, showers, friends, and family!

> **One of Tim's family members wrote about watching Howard and Dixie's faith in the Lord and what an inspiration it had been to them as they were growing up. They know that in God's eyes Howard and Dixie are two parents that he knew, like Job, would not curse His name in a situation like this.**

Friday, June 18, 2010—Busy night in ICU with the admits! Woke up several times, but thankfully Tim slept well. Switched with Howard about 3:00, then slept 'til about 7:00. I kept Tim's door closed and pulled the curtains to try to let Howard continue to sleep in the chair with the least amount of noise and light. They put a pic in Tim's left arm because of all the trouble with the right from their ordeal yesterday! The tests showed infection in the GI tract. They will use pill form of antibiotics in his feeding tube! Pray that white blood count drops tomorrow! Tim is 'working' hard with this infection and his numbers are up and down. It's midnight so Tim and I are listening to some inspirational music and tapes with verses on Choose Life! (Jer 30:11, Deut 7:15, 1 Pet 2:24, Ps 91, Matt 21:22, Ex 15:26, Luke 6:19, Ps 107:20, Ps 112:7, Rms 8:13, Matt 8:17, Jer 33:6, Matt 15:30, Ps 116:8-9, Ps 119:50). Father God, I plead Your mercy over Tim's brain stem that controls the mechanisms of the breathing, heart, temp, eyes, etc. I place Tim's GI tract with the infection in Your Hands and ask You to clear that up and we see lower numbers in the morning. I pray all that enter this room will see You working.

A person commented how comforting to know there were so many brothers and sisters out there praying for Tim . . . even those who didn't know him . . . .

Saturday, June 19, 2010—During his late night bath, they shaved his head and beard—he looks clean and ready to wake up and work! He's missing all his haying! They are having any and all to "gown up, with gloves, and face mask" as precaution and for isolation of this infection. We all look so nice! His temp is sustained, so they think it is from the infection and not from the brain stem! We are leaning on You and Your Word! One of the many 'lessons' we are learning and re-learning is that God's delay is not always His denial. Also, His Word will bring nourishment to bones and healing to the body. Long day, but enjoyed the quiet time of reading and listening.

One posted a prayer for God to continue to heal Tim because they knew that Tim would continue to serve God as he did before. They also commented on how Tim had touched their lives in a spiritually wonderful way and knew that God would continue to grace them with Tim's presence here on this earth.

Sunday, June 20, 2010—Father's Day! Oh, how I'd prayed that this could be the day of awakening and healing for Tim and for Howard. Had a good drive just me and the Lord as I drove back to Albin to repack to head to Craig Rehab Hospital in Denver. We had lots of food and friends stop by as all the family came up for Father's Day. Good friends from Oklahoma came up and we shared some time with them. I stayed with Tim 'til about 2:00 a.m., praying over every inch of his body and his numbers. Thanked You again and again for how our family have so helped up! Bethany and Katelin stayed the night so they could ride down to Denver with me while Howard rode in the ambulance! Mom would drive from Oklahoma to Denver and meet us there. Tough for everyone for us to leave Cheyenne and be three hours away in Denver—but we all see it as Your plan!

During this time, my thoughts were also of Tim's beautiful sisters, Beth, Cassady, and Jessica. They are so close to their brother; I can't imagine what they were feeling. I was blessed with three sisters myself so I understand the special relationship that siblings share. Sisters and brothers grow up together. They are forced to share everything—toys, clothes, rooms, bathroom time, food, and time with parents. They have to get along with each other on road trips, even in the worst of conditions. They are forced to hug after arguments. Because of these special times in their lives, they form a bond that will never be broken. Even though they may be miles apart in the future, they are bonded together. When one of them hurts, they all hurt. Tim's sisters have been on this journey with Tim from the start and will ride it out with him until the end. They have had to make sacrifices but have done so gladly. There is no doubt they love their big brother dearly. Their term of endearment (Timmy) used in their posts cannot help but pull the heartstrings. These are just a few of the posts from his three amazing little sisters whom he loves dearly and whom he always took care of. Their love for their brother is evident in their postings.

Wow . . . Timmy's page has 2,000 members! That is truly amazing! So many prayers! God is so good! Timmy, you now truly have a "fan club!" I love you! You rock my socks off, Timmy! Keep fighting and stay strong! I have to tell you that we have an awesome dad. Today is Father's Day, and Dad is doing and has done so much for you! I know you appreciate that. He watches over you with such compassion . . . and I know he loves you and you love him. We're all here waiting for you to wake up. Love ya so much, Cass

It's amazing how much progress you have made, Timmy! You're so strong, and have so many people pulling and praying for you! There are so many things that remind me of you . . . the things we eat or the things we do! You're such a role model for so many, and sure are my hero! Keep fighting, buddy! Love you so much! I want you to know that no matter how many miles we're apart, you're always so close to my heart! It's not easy coming home like tonight, but the impact you've had on my life sure shines a light! Keep fighting, you're so strong! Love you so much! Cass

Keep up the fight Timmy!!! Love ya tons!!

Beth

After spending two weeks in Cheyenne, the decision was made to move Tim to Craig Rehabilitation Center in Englewood, Colorado for the next phase of his recovery. The doctors and nurses on staff in Cheyenne were amazed by Tim's recovery and were truly touched by the faith shown by the Malms and the Albin community. Tim's impact on others through this ordeal had already begun. (Paraphrased postings follow some of the journal entries.) [Bracketed sections are Caringbridge postings by Dixie]

CHAPTER FOUR

Craig Rehabilitation Center, Englewood, CO

(June 21-Oct.1)

Monday, June 21—Hustle and Bustle! Everything ready to go to Denver. God's timing and design always amazes me—the EMT/paramedic who rode with Tim in the ambulance was from Albin! Howard could see and hear and what news it was when we arrived in Denver and he told me that Tim opened his eyes on the way!!! Check-in was a whirlwind with his doctor being the "hub" of the wheel and the spokes would be all his therapists, nurses, techs, other doctors, etc. They have a camera above his bed so they can watch him (and us). Left Tim's room about 11:00 and went to our nice, little apartment provided by the Craig Rehab Foundation (paid for with some insurance and foundation assistance). It's right next to the hospital (about five—ten minutes to Tim's room on the second floor. First night in fifteen days that Howard and I both lay down together in a bed that was completely flat! Queen sized and very comfortable, but I think we could have lain on a bed of rocks—Howard even made comment about getting to sleep without his socks on. All the time at Cheyenne, he'd just taken off his shoes and slept in clothes and socks! The difference between being physically tired and emotionally tired really hit! Relying on You! Thanks for Your protection with the drive down here, Mom's trip and with Tim. We rest in Your arms as we also let Tim—I sure wish I could have the camera monitor in our apartment—gotta let You have that, I trust You! [This morning he had a fever indicating infection somewhere—they think possibly his secretions from the respiratory system and we should have that isolated and able to start antibiotics in the a.m. Three 'road trips'—from his room through the tunnel . . . underground between Craig and Swedish was tiring but he did well. We should know more on these entrance tests tomorrow, so everyone who reads this tonight, please pray for good reports, a good night's rest for Tim, and in God's timing—for Tim to WAKE-UP! Not only PRAY, but BELIEVE!!]

> **What a privilege to read these journals—yours is already a great testimony—We continue to keep Tim in our prayers and you as well. God is teaching all of us patience. We love you. It was so good to come and stay with you over the weekend! You're doing so good, and are looking better each and everyday! God is awesome! It's unbelievable what He can do! He's always watching you and loves you so much! Keep fighting and don't give up . . . God won't give up on you! I love you so much, and miss you tons! On Sunday, just before I left I re-did your marker board . . . the verse I put was Phil. 4:13 "I can do all things through Christ who gives me strength!" God will give you the strength you need! Can't wait to see you again! Stay strong, buddy! Love ya, Cass**

Tuesday, June 22—There is an underground tunnel between Swedish Hospital and Craig Rehab Hospital. We also found out this place is in Englewood, rather than Denver. This city-life will take some getting used to coming from Albin with our 120 people! Howard and I started right in with EVERYTHING concerning Tim. The second floor is for TBI's—can't believe they even have a neuro-pyschologist assigned for Tim! Tim yawned again today!!! He now gets to wear an external catheter! A cousin of Howard's (Deb—she lives here in Denver) came by and a female friend of Tim's and her mom came by(Emily and Rhea). Another God-thing . . . A friend of ours from Laramie told us to look up a friend of theirs who was also in Craig. He had been hit by a car and had a TBI and two broken legs. After meeting Tim's roommates—one of them was the guy of our friend we were supposed to find! We developed a friendship only God knew would be! [*BREATHE* by Michael W. Smith—those of you that know me know how very much music is in my life and this is one of the songs that could even come close to what my heart feels. Almighty God, loving Father, is our strength and through Him, His Word, and the prayers & encouragement from Him, family, and friends has allowed us to breathe when life took our breath away. God's grace is immeasurable, yet always sufficient for each day and through the night, He has shown us His miracles—even though the medical field might call them glimmers and little steps, there's no size to His miracles and we thank Him and give all glory, honor, and praise to Him. We continue to ask ya'll to continue and/or join us on our knees pleading God to show Himself in all these situations and completely restore Tim. Howard and I cannot express our deep, deep appreciation and thankfulness to each and every one of you Tim's favorite verse is Phil. 4:13 so everyone memorize it and proclaim it for Tim. Thanks, Dixie & Howard]

Wednesday, June 23—My writings are short on some days . . . so much for us to do. The doctor talked with us about some of the test results—I just listen and let You have them. I thank You for this place, all this technology, and all the people here, and however You choose to use it, that's great . . . but, we know and trust You! No HO (hetero ossification??). No blood clots (except for a tiny one from the pic lines, and fever has stayed down! Coach Cullen called and I held the phone up to Tim's ear—he held his eyes opened a bit! [Another day . . . Another breath . . . Tim sleeps and breathes so soundly. He does have several 'awake' moments where he is not truly awake from the coma, but will open eyes, yawn, blink, turn head, reactions, but not responses to verbal commands yet. With help (people and a machine) we did get him in a wheelchair for an hour to get everything to fit him correctly so he could be upright. He did well for the hour he was sitting! His temp and blood pressure remain good! Daily miracles—praise the Lord.]

Thursday, June 24—Walked over encouraged to see what the day would hold! Tim started throwing up, so we cleaned for about thirty minutes! Tim has hardly ever thrown up in his life! Had a bloody plug come up so they want to do a bronchial scope, look at his feeding tube, and do a chest x-ray about 3:00. An older friend (Frank W) who leads "Cowboy Up" Bibles study in Sterling came by, visited, anointed Tim's head with some oil, and prayed over him and with us. We all feel God has a plan for Tim and that He's going to give him a stronger testimony of power and passion for You! I'm watching beside his bed with my journal as they prep him for this scope and Lord, we pray for smooth going for this doctor and team that nothing irritated his lungs or trachea, please guide their hands, his coughing, and hold Tim in Your Hands! The doctor said they thought it was just some trachea irritation, but will send it in to be sure. Prayed with Tim then went to our little 'abode'. [Isaiah 40:29-31 "He gives strength to the weary and increases the power of the weak. Even youths grow tires and weary, and young men stumble and fall: but those who hope in the Lord will renew their strength. They will soar on wings like eagles: they will run and not grow weary, they will walk and not be faint." God renewed Tim's strength today after having a rough morning of vomiting and then an afternoon of tests. Tests all went well and they have him on a slow feeding so pray that his stomach accepts it. Pray for a good day tomorrow and that Tim will "rise up"! Thank you again for all the prayers and encouragement. PRAY & BELIEVE]

> **Timmy! Karissa and I are coming to see you tonight, and are going to stay there for a few days! I'm super excited! I miss you so much and can't wait to see how much you've improved since the last time I saw you! There are so many people praying for you and cheering you on! You've got this, buddy! Remember, God doesn't give up, so stay strong! "I can do all things through Christ who gives me strength" . . . . Phil. 4: 13! I love ya so much, and can't wait to see you! Love, Cass**

Timmy,

You have been such an inspiration in my life. I miss seeing your smile, hearing your voice, and watching you rope. I can't wait until you wake up. Stay strong! I'll be there when you are awake. Love, your baby sister always, Jess

Friday, June 25—Howard checked on Tim about 6:00 a.m. and then he left for Douglas to watch Bethany in the night performance at the State HS Rodeo Finals. Some friends even had a 'chicken ropin' and raise some money for Tim! It's still so hard to believe that this time last year at Douglas, Tim was a senior and Bethany a junior—our family had a great time at State Rodeo! Tim won the calf roping and was the State Champion and headed to Nationals for a third time representing Wyoming! Looking back at a year also allows me to look forward a year to dream about where the Lord could have Tim!?! Wheeled Tim down to have an EEG and Chest x-ray over (and under) to Swedish. Coach Cullen came in right as we were "fixin'" to go (Tim laughs at how us Southerners are always "fixin'" to go or do something!) I went and made some PB&J's in the family kitchen of the hospital while Coach had about thirty minutes with Tim. Again and again, we are thankful for God's directing Tim to NJC with Coach Cullen—it's an awesome sight to see him 'talk' with Tim even though right now there is no response, but there will be! Tim started throwing up a little, so I helped then started cleaning up the mess. I pray that You are cleaning out all the toxins, C-def, etc. from his body with this coughing and throwing up! Thank You for good responses during speech therapy, for wiggling his toes, his blue eyes, healing one cell at a time! Had some "Mama-Bear" moments with some nurses to day—had to apologize to them. I stayed in Tim's room rubbing his fingers and arms 'til Howard came home from Douglas about 11:00 p.m.—we talked about the day and prayed over Tim around his bed.[Tim had a good night, but a rough day of vomiting. Please pray for his stomach to settle down. Matt. 11:28 "Come to me, all you who are weary and burdened, and I will give you rest." Pray that Tim will have a restful night. Tim had a great therapy session with toe wiggling and other physical responses on verbal command. Thanks for all your continued prayers and support! Pray and Believe!]

Saturday, June 26—Day 20 of this journey. Can't believe it was almost 8:00 before we got over here! Been a long time, if ever, that we've slept in—guess we are more tired than we let ourselves think! Tim had a good night. He did have a little bit of throw-up earlier from coughing. Still on only IV fluids in feeding tube so he doesn't get sick and aspirate (?) in his lungs. Howard and I watched the suction/respiratory film because we are required to take this class at 1:30. We have to get "okayed" so we can take Tim like outside around the hospital or even around in the hospital. I'm praying this weekend to be a fantastic-a 'Godtastic' time of resting/healing and for Tim to wake up—but in Your time! Had to do all the suction exercises on a dummy and then we will have to suction Tim three times each before we will be 'certified'. That would/will be hard to do on Tim I think? We pray that God will restore his respiratory system fully soon so he won't have any problems. They are looking to change his trach to a smaller one on Monday. While we were gone to the class, they had put Tim in his wheelchair and the girls sat with him. The girls didn't know how or when to tilt him—we have to carry around a timer that every fifteen minutes we lay the chair all the way back to a reclining position for movement and get weight off areas. Had another "mother-bear" moment: This night was unbelievable: oxygen tube water spilled on the floor, problems with techs, nurses, etc. all built up and then to top it all off—Tim DSATted (which means his oxygen went dangerously low! Thank You, LORD, for an angel of a respiratory tech who really knew what and how to do what he needed to do—he stayed with us in the room 'til Tim was stable. It was 2:30 a.m. when we finally got in our apartment! Almost twenty hours—long day and night! I am so thankful we can be here with Tim because of our family and friends—there are patients here that don't have their family (spouse, parents, siblings, friends) here very often! Goodnight, Lord! [Tim had a good, restful day! YAY! He is still off of any food, only IV fluids. He didn't vomit any today! He sat in his wheelchair for about an hour, and even had clothes and his tennis shoes on! Tim also got to sit in the shower chair to have his shower. He has a KUB test in the morning . . . pray for good results! Exodus 14:14 "The Lord will fight for you, you need only to be still." Keep praying that he will completely wake up! God is good!]

Sunday, June 27—Came back over about 6:30 and prayed while watching Tim breathe so gently. While Howard and I went to the hospital church service, Cassady and Karissa stayed with Tim while he was in his wheelchair. We had about a dozen visitors today! Great to have Mom drive in from Douglas—she and I went over and took about a two-hour nap while everyone visited with Howard! I know he was tired also, and I thanked him for letting me rest a bit! Again, God is amazing who and when He brings people in our lives: some rodeo friends in Wyoming have a daughter who married into a family which they came to Craig to see one of their Texas friends who was on 3rd floor (spinal injuries). The sister of that daughter is good friends with Tim so they told the married daughter's in-laws to look us up while they were at Craig. They came by to introduce themselves (while I was sleeping!) They left their names and numbers. Their Texas friend's wife (Debby) came back down to Tim's room later on after everyone had left and I got to meet her. There's a special bond here—will be interesting to see where God takes this? She shared about her "prayer board" and we will get one! We got Tim ready for the night and had our prayer time then went over to the apartment—Thank you, Lord, for sustaining us these two days: Learning to fully rely and depend on You during all this—this is all about You! You've strengthened Tim, I asked-You fulfilled. We pray for the KUB (kidney, urinary, bladder) test comes back with good results and to have a good MRI tomorrow. [God is amazing and the people He is bringing across our paths is overwhelming us with joy and encouragement. Please continue to pray specifically for his digestive system to get back to functioning normally and continued healing of brain, but above all the God will be glorified as He fully restores and heals Tim completely and the 'world' will know that He is the Great Physician! Thanks, Howard and Dixie]

Cassady wrote this post to her brother: Timmy, I'm so proud of you! It was so cool to see you today in a wheelchair, looking so comfortable! To see you in shorts and a shirt, and even your socks and tennis shoes on, was awesome! Can't wait until we can talk to each other! Keep fighting, buddy . . . you're doing so good! God is so good, don't give up! Love ya,

Monday, June 28—4th week since accident/2nd week here at Craig. Resp Tech did a different way of treatment with the cleaning, misting, etc and it seemed to work great! We are currently sitting and waiting on the x-ray, metal test, and then the MRI. Praying for good reports and say 'Thank You' in advance. He was still sedated some from the tests, so they changed out his two-part trach (from Cheyenne) to the one-part type they use here in Craig. Got him in his chair and went down to therapy—Thank You for another good day of miracles and answered prayers! Love ya, Lord. [The beginning of week 2 here at Craig—it's still so hard to imagine that three weeks ago yesterday evening that one second changed our lives and many of you have told us how your lives have changed. It's not exciting to see one of your babies in this situation, but it is exciting to see God's hand of healing and teaching not only in our life, but to hear of those He is working in your lives—it's been such an encouragement! Tim went to the therapy room in his chair—it'll be interesting to see how he responds when he sees the basketballs and gets to swing a rope. I'm a goal setter and I've written down many as we take this step-by-step journey. We still pray, as we ask of you, for full restoration and healing! He knows we'd like to see it miraculous one complete healing, but we are 'learning to lean" (another song) on Him and His timing, so we take this journey step-by-step until He shows/tells us to run! Tim has a CT test in the morning on his midsection and if everything is okayed, then he will start on tube feeding! I told them chocolate milk in the tube would probably be his choice, but that may be a while! Please pray for nausea to not be a problem to and from the test room, test would be clear, and that his stomach/digestive tract would gladly accept the food properly the way God designed it all to work! He has been reaching and messing with the tubes and his

PICC line of which the nurses tell us that can be a good sign of waking up—timing . . . God's timing. We are doing 'just fine' (those of you know me can probably hear that southern drawl in the fine)—we thank you again for 'praying without ceasing' (1 Thess 5:17)]

Tuesday, June 29—Had an early CT scan over stomach/abdomen. The report from the kidney test showed enzymes up 1 point!-we'll take it Lord! In OT (Occupational Therapy) we learned how to stretch his neck and shoulders. Came back to room for Speech Therapy, but he was so relaxed and sleeping! Will have to get him up later on for the other classes. They have started the regular tube feeding up again! Went outside with the PT (physical therapist) and during her class Tim's external leaked, so Howard and I got him up to his room, cleaned, and changed for the next class. While waiting for the next class to start, Tim started coughing and burping, but the OT said he was throwing up! We got him suctioned for anything that might have been, cleaned up, and in bed. The schedule didn't work too well today! No results tonight—[Early morning CT abdominal scan showed good results, so they started tube feeding around noon. Tim had a very relaxed morning and early afternoon, until his schedule got busy and they moved him around. Too much moving caused exhaustion. As of right now, the digestive tract is functioning correctly. Please pray for it to continue! Prayer for tomorrow is . . . good day of therapy and to wake up! We should know MRI results tomorrow, pray they are good! KUB turned out great . . . PTL! Thanks again, keep praying and believing]

Wednesday, June 30—Everything looked good with his chest x-ray! He has kept his food down—still belching some—even with that Gas-X junk. Had some good verbal commands working with his speech therapist! After therapy, we strolled around on the bridge that connects the two buildings and is above the street. Tim got a bath tonight! Today was a goal date I had prayed that he would full awake—God's timing will prevail! Eph 6:20 "Be strong in the Lord and in His mighty power." Got to meet Bobby Bynum, the husband with the spinal injury from Texas—so thankful, Lord how You protected Tim from physical injury in his accident. We are suppose to give our Cheyenne doctor a call on

July 3—sure would be great if Tim could call him if that would be in Your timing? Had our prayer time then headed off to bed. [Full day and the feeding went well. Little bit of an elevated white count in his lung secretion, but they will just watch it since he hasn't been running any fever. Let's just pray that away!!! After all the respiratory therapists and nurses have seen him they all have commented on how strong a cough Tim has—good aspect toward getting any of that 'stuff' up! Had a good morning therapy class of following verbal commands again (I will remember this when we get home!) and in physical therapy they got him out of the chair and exercise/stretched his legs and arms on the exercise mat. All in all . . . a good day and very thankful and grateful for how God has and is working in Tim's body while we take these steps on this journey. Waiting and wanting to 'run' instead of taking slow, small steps is a daily struggle for us. Please pray for a good, full night of rest for Tim—he coughed and had a hard time last night around 3:30, so if any of you are awakened around that time, please pray! Thanks again for all the prayers and encouragement—we live on them!]

Thursday, July 1, 2010—Long day Tim sweated most of the morning (maybe getting all the extra toxins out?) He was very sleepy during speech—except when she would use this 'honker horn'! Had both PT and OT together and they worked on stretches and with him in the wheelchair-lots for us to learn about it all. Made a list of our questions for the doctor, nurses, techs so I ended up talking with the nursing supervisor. Tim had major 'results' with his 'program' tonight and we thank You. Prayed and went back to the apartment.

Friday, July 2—Big day! Tim was very relaxed this morning, had a good night! I did some laundry in our building washroom before I went over to Tom's room. Had several friends (pastors, wives, and families) come throughout the day. So encouraging hearing others praying for Tim's healing! OT and PT therapists spent their time working on adjustments with the wheelchair—I know I have to be patient, but I get frustrated with therapy time being used for the wheelchair. We only have three classes of about thirty good minutes out of about forty-five doing instructional things-one each of speech, PT, and OT. They had us watch these films on TBI stages from the most severe (I think the scale was 0) through the independent living stage. So discouraging and negative—I know we had to watch them for educational purposes, but we're not allowing fear, Satan, or anything about those films to cause us to look away from You—we believe that You are going to fully heal and restore Timothy and we thank You for that again. I pray that You show Yourself through Tim that he doesn't go through those stages and that You restore his brain, mind, heart, and soul and then we can work on the physical needs as You heal and restore. It was good to have Martha, JD, Esther, and little Tirzah come today—they took a picture of her lying beside Tim. [Tonight I sang at the Baptist General Conference (Converge) National Convention held here in Denver—the song was *God On The Mountain* by Lynda Randle—here are a few of the words.

> "For the God on the mountain, is still God in the valley
> When things go wrong, He'll make them right
> And the God of the good times, is still God of the bad times
> And the God of the day, is still God of the night"

That pretty much sums it up! Tim had a good day and not only kept down the feeding, but they also increased his amount. They were able to take him off of the fluid IV also . . . PTL!! Pray again for a full night's rest for Tim and FULL RESTORATION and HEALING!]

Saturday, July 3—Tomorrow will be one month from the accident! Candra called and so many people down there are praying, plus You have laid on her heart to some day put this journey into a book, so she will be compiling everything—I'll have to write neater to be able to read these tear-stained pages! We are supposed to do Tim's stretching exercises on weekends, so we did! Tim will never believe his flexibility—he has always been about a 0 on a 'flex' scale! The wheelchair changes with the head rest, elbow pads, etc seem to allow him to relax more. Sam and Kim came by. Here at Craig, they never have used "coma" with Tim—it's "levels of consciousness". Thank You for another day of strength for us and Tim-maybe the Miracle tomorrow? [Thank you for your prayers for Howard and I to stand strong—we feel your prayers! Tim had a relaxing day with Howard and I doing his exercises. Keep praying! We wish you all a safe and beautiful 4th of July! Every firework you see, may it be a reminder of our great God and his miraculous healing!]

Sunday, July 4—Howard and I went to the hospital church while Cass stayed with Tim. When we came back, two of our 'angel' techs and Cass almost had Tim ready to get in his chair. We went out on the bridge and read some from his 'green book' that people have signed from being in Cheyenne, from our church in Albin, and hospital visitors here. I believe in 'over-stimulation'—something he hears or sees might bring back memory or help climb that 'level of consciousness' ladder! About 12:45 our 'La Grange family' (Andy, Stacy, and all the kids) came! Visited a bit with Tim then put him in bed to rest while some of us went to the apartment to eat some of the food they brought! What a treat to share our Sundays with friends and family with food they bring in—Howard and I don't leave to go eat, so we are so thankful for all the casseroles, salads, sandwiches, veggies, and fruit we are given. Another tough time for everyone when they say good-bye to Tim. Lord, how we thank You for the many miles of protection You give to everyone. I talked with the kids about it's OK to have fears and tears—as long as we keep giving them back to God. They are really good about leaving the room when emotions start to take over! We all prayed together before they left. [Hope all y'all had a great Fourth! We got Tim in his chair twice today for over 1 1/2 hrs. each time. His eyes are clearing of the redness and his blue eyes are looking really good! We head back into the classes tomorrow and I am excited to see him work this week. We listened to a man at the 'church' here at Craig and then watched his DVD and one of the things he said was the 'test' is really hard, but the 'testimony' will be great! It is going to be awesome to see and hear Tim's testimony through and from this! Keep praying—maybe the miracle of waking up is tomorrow!]

Monday, July 5—Week 3 here at Craig and it's been a roller coaster of emotions and physical needs. God has sustained and provided daily strength for Howard and I, and we've seen the daily minute-by-minute at times—of the strength He's provided for Tim. Those suction times when he runs out of air from coughing and his eyes look scared and begging for help are the roughest times for me—but praise God that those are no longer and he needs less and less suctioning (sometimes only one or two times a day!).Thank You for his strong cough and lungs getting stronger and clearer—pray against any pneumonia! His digestive system is coming along and we are having 'results'. Tim had a first day in his chair over at the apartment with us while we ate with friends from Albin. Thank You for how we are seeing Tim pulling his own head/neck back into the headrest and relaxing arms and hands more! Little anxious about our 'family meeting' tomorrow with all the people on Tim's team (doctor, therapists, nurses, tech, etc)—I would love to see him fully wake uip fully healed! We pray for the strength to listen to them—but hear Your voice, Your report, Your Word. We will need to have on Your full armor tomorrow! We pray for You to raise Tim up to be Your vessel! [We need to pray that as they have reduced the amount of two medicines for his digestive system, that all of the system works! It's hard to imagine Tim's "steel stomach" could be a concern! We pray he gets chocolate milk soon! Continue to Pray and Believe! We are asking another challenge of you: Because of the meaning of the number "7" in the Bible, on Wednesday, July 7th (7-7) there will be several churches and people fasting and praying that day for Tim's Full Healing and Restoration by our gracious God. Please join us if you can.]

Tuesday, July 6—One of our 'angel'techs helped get Tim ready for OT therapy and then we went to our meeting. The doctors explained in detail of Tim's injury using word pictures with gas, fuel, filters, motor, etc. Hard to hear when all you want to hear is healing. They said every TBI is different for every person, and that's why you can't put on prognosis on it with time or how/where/what the injury consists of with healing and how all the areas (mental, physical, etc) have been affected or how they will come back. We learned that Tim's right side must have had the nerve ends shear (brain shearing) some even call it 'shaking-baby syndrome'? Seeing Tim go down on his left then he was 'out' when he came up and slid off the horse is hard to understand the energy inside the brain to do the damage it did and nobody could ever be certain if he hit his head on the ground or not! One of those life questions we will never know. Their release date is looking to be Oct. 1—we pray and believe that You, Almighty God, will heal miraculously in mental and physical ways that will astonish them all! Went to apartment to eat with Mom and the Peterson's. In speech today, they worked with Tim with the cuff down and put on the speaking valve. Tim uttered some sound, maybe even a soft "Hi"! He was able to have the cuff down for an hour before they came to go take his shower. Mom cut my hair—at least it feels good, even though I know this journey has taken its physical toll on my appearance. Howard and I were able to pray with Tim and he was sleeping by 10:00! [Ephesians 3:20 . . . God is able to do exceedingly, abundantly above all that I ask or think, according to the power that works within us! Continue to pray that God heals his stomach to accept more tube feeding to gain back some of his weight loss and to tolerate the cuff down and speaking valve. Like in His Word, He is able even beyond what we think or know how to ask!!!]

Wednesday July 7—Today is the Fasting and Celebration Fast and it has been great to hear how all the different ways family and friends are fasting! Computer, video games, food, etc. Talked with Mom while she was driving home—so good to have her here when I know it's double—tough looking through Tim and seeing/remembering Daddy's ordeal. Such a strong woman, wife, and mom—she'll never fully know how her example has been and is to me. We are enjoying our nightly prayer times with Debby—only You could have brought us together like this! [Tim has had his speaking valve in and the trach cuff down for 2 hours and has done really well! We are getting use to his "voice" sounds. No words yet . . . or rap, but it'll all come! Keep praying . . . . maybe today will be the day of waking up?!?! Fasting joyfully, Howard and Dixie!]

One post during this time told the Malms that some day they would know how many people they had witnessed

to through this trial. In John 16:33 Jesus says, "These things I have spoken to you, that in Me you may have peace. In this world you will have tribulation, but be of good cheer, I have overcome the world."

Thursday, July 8—Tim had a good night with the cuff down on the trach!! Our tech misread Tim's therapy chart wrong and we had Tim all ready for class an hour early so we went and sat on the bridge. While we were out there, Howard noticed Tim's left leg a little larger than usual and warmer—so the fill-in doctor called for a blood clot test for 1:00 over at Swedish. It's 2:10 now and we still haven't been called yet! Sug and Joe came over from Gunnison—really good to see them even though it's hard for them to hold back the tears 'cause this is the first time they have seen Tim. Hope they can stay longer next time they come! Coach Cullen came and held Tim's hand while the PT worked on his other leg. It's about all I can take seeing Coach talking with Tim. We circle up and prayed—I don't know how Howard was able to pray after Coach prayed. Again and Again, how we thank You for having Coach Cullen be Tim's rodeo coach and friend! The Subway sandwiches he brought were beyond great after skipping lunch waiting for the test! We walked some other friends out to the elevator and then took the stairs to meet Tim and the transportation tech down in the basement floor. When the elevator opened with Tim, one of Howard's high school classmates (Sandy, from Kansas) was standing with Tim! She went to Swedish with us—she and Howard go to visit while I went in with Tim to help the tech lady with the ultrasound test for any blood clots. You answered again with a clear test—no blood clot! Thank You. So many things to be thankful for!! [Thanks to everyone who took part in the 7/7 Fast: some did food, computer, electronic games, etc whatever you gave up to focus on God and His Word, we thank you. (Matt 6:17-18) They are talking possibly changing out this trach for the next one of which it does not have a cuff with it maybe tomorrow. He had several therapy classes today—daily miracles as he increases in strength and following verbal commands. Continue to pray for that and also that the increase in feeding would be accepted gladly by his digestive tract. We would love to hear how your fast went and any verses that you read and/or what God laid on your heart. We pray for good therapy classes tomorrow. Several people have been in today and it has been mentioned by several in person, on the phone, text, and email that there seems to be a 'feeling' that God's timing with His Hand of Miracles is around the corner! We thank Him because we see, hear, and touch miracles everyday, and we pray every night with Tim that maybe tomorrow he will wake up and be restored fully!!! Thank you again for 'praying without ceasing'! Love and Hugs to all y'all!]

Friday, July 9—[God is Good!!! Tim was downsized to a smaller and cuffless trach and did not have the oxygen on all day! They said he did extremely well! They put him on a tilt table and stood him up and his blood pressure adjusted well. There is still swelling in his left knee/thigh so please pray that it goes down—especially because Howard and I have to do his stretches Sat/Sun! Again, we thank you for all your prayers and encouragement through cards, visits, emails, texts, calls, etc. Pray also that Tim has a great night with this new trach. Goodnight, Howard and Dixie]

> **A post again reminded the Malms how their posted words were such an encouragement. They mentioned the fact that God was doing such a deep, deep work in Tim's soul that was a greater healing than anyone could possibly imagine. They encouraged them by saying they would see greater things in the days, weeks and months ahead.**
>
> **Another reminded Tim he was changing their little corner of the world and probably didn't even realize it. That is the great thing about Tim, he always worked hard and succeeded but had always been so humble about it. He is a great example to all.**

Saturday, July 10—[Tim had a relaxful day without the assist of any oxygen. We strolled around with him in his chair on floors 1, 2, & 3 for 2 1/2 hrs. His left knee/thigh area is still swollen, but I think has gone down some. We think he is just tensing those muscles so much for long periods of time that it may not be allowing good constant blood flow, but continue to pray for that area to relax more. Please start the week off by praying that God's timing of totally and fully waking Tim up will happen by Friday—it's Tim's birthday and wouldn't that be miraculous and amazing! It will also be 40 days since the accident and there are many timed events in the Bible with 40 days!!! 2 Tim 1:7 . . . power, love, discipline, sound mind!!]

Sunday, July 11—I pray that You will heal Tim's brain messages to that leg to relax from the tensing and will allow his increase heart rate to slow down. Working on the many thank-you's. Goodnight, Lord, thank You for another weekend. Today in the church here at Craig where about fifteen gathered in the chapel and who knows how many on the hospital channel, we looked at the passage Luke 24:13-35. Again the situation shows that Jesus is among us and we continue to choose to recognize Him and and His Hand. We see Him in the halls, rooms, MRI & CT rooms. We see Him in the hearts of the caregivers (nurses, doctors, techs, therapists). We see Him in the friends that we have met here, and in the visits, cards, texts, and food that have come to us. Whatever, wherever, whoever, and however God allows and crosses your path YOU and I have the choice and opportunity to see Him! We pray for daily strength and discipline to always thank Him that we can see Him. [Tim has had an even more relaxed day with very little "storming" (heavy sweating due to brain overload working with his body) and a great day on the stop valve over his trach that doesn't allow any air out the trach, but only up through his nose and mouth. More sounds which I know will mean more words! We are excited to see and watch how the Lord will be working on Monday in the therapies! Hope you were able to attend church somewhere where you can worship and praise God Almighty. As you pray for and with us, remember to thank Him for all your many blessings, but tonight we especially thank Him for all of your friendships and prayer support! Thank You!]

Monday, July 12—Week 4! Speech therapy in the bed @ 8:30 doesn't seem to work for Tim. He's use to getting up early—They don't know much about rodeos, farming, and ranching—I know they think we are from the 'sticks', but when asked what would Tim like to do . . . it involves rodeo, hay, or cattle! Tim didn't much care for even watching bball—he'd rather play it! Therapy had some tough moments, but Tim groaned through them! We prayed with Tim and left about 10:00. [Tim was in his chair for the morning with a tour of the therapeutic recreational area. They definitely don't have rodeos as one of their outings nor can they even comprehend rodeoing, ranching, or farming!! During speech therapy they are working on his sense of smell—I said we should have someone bring in some alfalfa—the lady did not know what it was! With lots of moans and groans from Tim, his physical therapist really worked his neck, back, and legs! We are praying for the LORD to really relax Tim's right arm—he's so strong and keeps it bent and he needs the extension. The doctor talked about increasing some of the brain stimulant and sometimes that can cause more toning (muscle overworking) so let's pray that away from the left leg and if it is to be—it can go to the right leg! They are also talking about taking the trach out so let's pray for the perfect timing (God's timing) for when that decision needs to be made. Looking forward to tomorrow! I don't know what tomorrow holds, but I do know Who holds tomorrow!!]

> **All of Northeastern Junior College were really "rootin', prayin' and hopin'" that Tim would come through this. They talked about how he had been an important part of this campus this last year.**

Tuesday, July 13—We saw Tim respond with lifting one finger and then the second finger! He repeated the response again—thank You for another miracle! He's resting calm and relaxed—it's hard to see him and really realize we're here. It's so much like a dream and you keep wondering when you are going to wake up? It took five of us, but we turned Timothy onto his stomach today—carefully checking tubes—I'm sure Tim was questioning what and how we were doing things! Also got him up on the tilt board and his BP did well. What a good day,—long, but good. [Jer. 30:17a . . . "I will restore you to health and heal you of your wounds says the Lord!" Tim has had a really good day. He has followed some more verbal commands, had a hard workout being rolled over onto his stomach on top of a wedge so he could bend his elbows for balance, and then he was upright on the tilt table! Continue to pray for the left knee/thigh area to loosen up to be able to stretch and bend more. More sounds today . . . more words coming soon! Again, thank you for continuing to hold us up while on your knees. Pray and believe!]

Wednesday, July 14—Therapies went okay—wish for more! Only having classes daily with each one hardly seems productive—but I have to be patient and work along with them. One of the many lessons You are teaching me is that I can't change or fix everything—I'm a 'fixer' and I can't fix Tim or this situation, so I have to leave it daily in Your hands! ("If you dream alone, it's just a dream. If you dream together, it's reality!" (Brazilian proverb)We received a card with this on it, and it's especially true when God is the answer to our dreams. [Matt. 18:20 "For where two or three have gathered together in My name, there I am in the midst!" Tim had a good day! We were able to bend the knee again with lots of moans and groans. Thanks for praying, we continue to pray that Friday may be the day?! We pray for a good night's rest for everyone!]

Friday, July 16—HAPPY BIRTHDAY #20 Timothy!! Howard shaved him and he looks nice. While Howard was gone with Beth a while, I stayed with Tim and prayed, cried, and 'talked' with him about his birthday, what we were going to be doing for his party, and told him how proud we are where and how he has come on this journey! Lots of decorations, hamburgers (Grandpa & Grandma), cards, my banana pudding, roper cake (Jillian Mc-brought from Albin), family and friends. Tim came over in his bball shorts so he looks skinny to many, but his eyes are opened—I can't imagine what he is thinking! He wasn't supposed to have any food, but I gave him just a little taste of banana pudding! After the allotted hour, we took him back to his room and then people came and visited him a few at a time! It was tear-jerking at times seeing Grandpa and Tim talking/praying forehead-to-forehead, friends and family having their 'moments'. Debby came by and we prayed through tears for Tim and Bobby. Tim was exhausted from the day, but did well. Lord, again IN YOUR TIME-we see Your hand every day, every hour, in all areas—so we will wait in YOU! [We just left Tim's room and the day has left him exhausted! In therapy class, three therapists created a "horse" with a large bolster, chairs, pads, and a rope—it was quite a scene! They even had some "reins". It was good for Tim, but the therapists had the harder workout and may feel it in the morning! Even though it was good exercise/therapy, it was hard for me to observe—those of you that know Tim and his horsemanship can understand. With the National High School Finals Rodeo starting next week, we look back to one year ago when Tim finished the finals in the #2 spot as the National Reserve Champion Calf Roper to where God has us for now here at Craig. He was with us there and He is with us now—just a different arena and definitely a different horse! Continue to pray for rt. bicep and lt. thigh/knee muscles to relax, wake up fully and TOTAL healing and restoration. Again, we "wait on the Lord" and remember it's green in the 'valley', even though I'm looking to the 'mountain top'!]

Numerous postings and prayers were sent the Malm's way on Tim's birthday. They all voiced the same sentiments about how thankful they were for Tim and what a blessing and inspiration he had been and would continue to be in their lives. Happy Birthday, Tim!

Saturday, July 17—The '40' day was yesterday, so we will continue to trust and wait—he's in our hands. We had further movement with his right arm today! It's hard to hear well-meaning medical people tell you that we need to learn to do 'this and that' because Tim will need this when he goes home . . . like when our nurse whom we think the world of tell us how to use this feeding tube! She means well, but 'this is just a season' and Tim will eat normal again! We pray for continued focus on You and Your healing—we're going to walk out of here! [Heb. 10:24-25 . . . Let us consider how to provoke one another to love and good deeds, not neglecting to meet together, as is the habit of some, but encouraging one another, and all the more as you see the Day approaching. Today's devotional dealt with planting flowers close together to withstand the wind, rain, and sun. Closeness works—living things need each other to survive and grow. The strength of fellowship, friendship, and community helps encourage and motivate each other—and as believers in Jesus Christ, He is that Strength! When the winds and storms of life hinder our growth, it's that strength and closeness to one another and to God that grow us! One of the songs on a CD of Tim's is *I'll Praise You in the Storm* by Casting Crowns. We praise God for Tim's day—it was relaxful without any therapy sessions—only Howard and I do his stretches! He was able to relax his right arm more! PTL! Please continue to pray for the left thigh/knee area. He seemed to enjoy watching the Greeley Stampede short round on tv tonight! We thank everyone again for their prayers and hope you have a great day in worship tomorrow!]

Sunday, July 18—We pulled the tv around and in front of Tim so he could hear and see the church service while we went to church. While I ran back to his room to get our CD player because the one in the church fouled up, I ran into Mike (S) in the hallway—he stayed with Tim for the service. Mike and the nurse that was in here said Tim started mumbling words and watching the tv when he heard and saw me singing on the tv channel. Hopefully the sounds were singing joyfully unto the Lord and not moans for Mom! In the afternoon, Howard and I did Tim's stretches and exercises on the big mats in the therapy room. Concerned with his tightness—but we keep praying that You take that swelling, tightness, inflammation, or whatever it is and make it function properly again! Pray for a good night's rest for us all! Prayed with Tim. [Luke 10:38-42 . . . the Mary/Martha story was our theme for our Craig worship time this morning. Makes you look at what the necessary few things are and to stay focused on being with Jesus! Howard and I again had him out in his chair and stretching his legs and arms today. We saw a little more relaxation in his left arm today—keep praying for full extension of that arm! His left thigh area is about the same, and Howard did as much as he could bending and stretching with it—hopefully therapy will show improvements tomorrow, plus he will be standing on the tilt table tomorrow. Continue to pray for 'regularity' with the end of the digestive system—never knew all the medical decisions that were based on that! We're starting Week 7—and you know what 7 can mean with God and His Word so let's all pray that we see, hear, and PRAISE GOD for His healing this week each and every day!]

Monday, July 19—What a GREAT day! In speech, Tim responded quicker to her verbal commands of different fingers and with swallowing! In OT, he got to do a computer-video game with a control switch that he would squeeze to 'shoot' things in the program! In his neuro-psychological therapy he responded correctly and quickly to simple addition and subtraction problems answering with his fingers!!! We were so surprised and excited-again. God encourages us with His surprises! In PT, it was decided to have a HO test in Tim's femur—I think they said they'd only had two other cases in the hospital history because it is usually in bones where there are joints like the elbow, hip, or knee. Lord, we pray that You will show none there! Our pastor, wife, and her dad came by this afternoon—such encouragement as they prayed with us! Another friend from NJC (Stormy) came by and they all watched Tim on the tilt table! Thank You, Lord, for sustaining BP, strong HR, strong and clear lungs, good stomach! Thank You! [We asked God to start off the week with some big eye-openers . . . They are doing a 48-hour test with Tim his trach closed off and then will make the decision whether and/or when to take the trach out in the next few days so please pray for all of that. We just thank God for a great day and ask for daily "manna" (strength) one day at a time! Have a great night and thank you all for your prayer support and encouragement!]

Tuesday, July 20—The doctor talked with us during OT therapy-which Tim got to suck on a cherry tootsie pop! They had to put in some medicine into Tim's feeding tube for that HO test. Tim had a good day and was asleep about 9:00. We prayed over his bed like we do every night. Hope he has a good night! [Hebrews 12:3 . . . Just think of him who endured bitter hostility against Himself in comparison with your trials so that you may not grow weary or lose heart and faint in your minds. One of today's devotionals reading was titled "Today I Wait and Rest." It talked about knowing God has put dreams and desires in your heartthings you are hoping for, praying about, and believing in. When you have the promises of God deep in your heart, the Bible says you will "enter into the rest of God." That's the place of total trust—a place where you know, beyond a shadow of a doubt, that God is going to see you through. It's a place of faith, knowing that God is in control, and at the exact time, right time, His time, He will bring your dream. Today, may we all choose to confidently trust God and wait and rest in Him while He is directing our step and path. Tim did not have the best of nights last night and this morning the nurse said he had some 'throw-up' so today they took away the Ibuprofen and one dosage of another medicine, but kept with the other new one and hopefully and prayerfully his stomach will adjust to the change and accept it—we just left him and he was comfortable and sleeping well. He stood on the tilt table for almost an hour and a short physical therapy time. They did one test on the thigh area this morning and the other test on the leg is a bone scan tomorrow around 7:00 & 10 a.m. (Mtn. time) so please be in prayer at those times. The chest x-ray showed all clear so the trach is scheduled to come out in the morning—Tim has been picking and pulling at it so I guess he's ready for it to come out! He did some more different responses today—God keeps us going on all the daily miracles! Again, we thank all of you for all the prayers, cards, visits, food, and gifts ya'll have graciously given in the name of Jesus—thank you, Dixie and Howard]

Wednesday, July 21—[Proverbs 20:24 . . . since the Lord is directing our steps, why try to understand everything that happens along the way? After the day we've had, the Lord led me to this verse and devotional. Trials are never wasted, nor does God ever give them to the wrong person. Trials are growth hormones for our Christian walk in developing perseverance. We are stronger coming out of the situation than when we entered. God did not give this accident to us, but allowed it, and He does give us the opportunity to grow as a people during this adventure. Through all the pain, tears, hurts, and prayers, we're learning to lean on, grow, and depend on His Word. Tears and prayers water our hearts for growth. (from Emilie Barnes' book-*More Faith in My Day*) Tim had a slower day than yesterday. His thigh area looked a little less swollen, but seemed to give him some pain today. They are doing a test tomorrow and Thursday for any trauma injury that may have developed in the femur area—please pray for these tests and that the outcome is clear. They also have changed some of his meds—so let's pray that his body accepts the changes. We will possibly know in the morning about whether and/or when he gets his trach out. Yes, Lord, we trust You—even if we don't understand everything!]

Thursday, July 22—Tim had a good night! Went to Sam's Club to print off some pictures-was gone almost three hours! It was hard to see and print the pictures from Nationals—just about a year ago! We're looking forward to the day we get to see you rope again, TIM—IF that is where God wants you or wherever He wants You! Took out trach—Pray for a smooth night! [1 Peter 5:7 . . . "Cast all your anxiety on Him because He cares for you!" I had a little anxiety this a.m. with the trach being taken out and the tests. At those times, I have to take in a breath and quietly give my worry, anxiety, care, whatever to Him and really let go! The trach was out in about three seconds and a clear patch was placed over it! He did well throughout the whole day—PTL! We headed out at 7:15 for the 1st and 2nd phases of the bone scan test, then back again at 10:30 to finish the 3rd phase. They never reported back to us today so we hope 'no news is good news'! While Tim was in the bath/shower room, his nurse assistant (they call them 'techs' here) said when she told him she was going to tape over his trach cover, he said "No!" We will be excited to hear even a 'No' tomorrow! How we are so thankful for that! God has really relaxed Tim tonight and he is sleeping well! Please continue to pray for restful sleep, alert times to lengthen, thigh/femur area to relax, and strength for therapy sessions. Pray for tomorrow's still in the 7th week!]

Friday, July 23—You lose track of time—a week ago we had Tim's birthday! Stacy and Martha brought the kids down for a visit. What a blessing they have been and are for us to leave our girls with Andy & Stacy and how the whole Malm family and so many friends are taking care of them! Jen brought our "Cajun" friends and they brought their BBQ Ribs and Red Beans & Rice! I bet Tim can smell them on our breath! They know how much Tim loves their ribs!! Ken and Linda came by and visited and are spending the night. What prayer warriors, support, and encouragement they have been and are to us! The doctor said that even though tests show no HO, he thinks Tim might be in the early stages of it in his elbow—God, we pray You dissolve any extra bone, if any, and heal Tim in the way You created his body to function. [Psalm 118:1 "Give Thanks to the Lord, for He is good; For His love is everlasting." We continue to give Him thanks for all the daily miracles we see. It is also so encouraging knowing that His love is everlasting even if we aren't lovable, He is still there! What a God—what a Father! He followed some more verbal commands, 'answered' some math problems, stood on the tilt table for an hour, and it looks like he tried putting his small rope in his mouth (I'm sure unusual for the nurses to understand that, but not for ropers!!). Howard got a little of a "hi" out of him we think! We are overwhelmed with the Tim Malm Benefit Roping scheduled for Labor Day weekend in Cheyenne. (ropin for tim.com) All of the people involved with it have huge hearts and we are beyond grateful and thankful; know you are being used by God. Tim's HO test with his joints came back negative. They think he has the very early beginning stage of HO in his thigh/knee and a little in his left elbow. HO is a condition that is caused by trauma from an injury that sometimes can cause bone/joint fusing or even new bone to grow—medicine will stop it from progressing and we have to keep those joints stretched and limber. We all know that God can have a different report and He may well just take care of it—we will leave it in His Hands. Again, pray for Tim to have another great night and for Howard and I to be good 'therapists' on the weekend.]

Sat, July 24—Ken and Linda came this morning and we took Tim out to the North patio and did some stretches out there while we visited with them. The hospital is amazed how many visitors Tim has! We are thankful and grateful! Jerry and Andrea (M) came and we prayed over Tim and his room—very meaningful and encouraging! Siri (S) from Rodeo News came by to visit with us and Tim—she has watched Tim all through Wyoming high school and his first year at NJC (college). She has and is so supportive of Tim and we thank her for her kindness and support! Gordon, Fanny, Lynette, and Kent all came while they were there. [Mark 1 . . . "I say to you, all things for which you pray and ask, believe that you have received them, and they shall be granted you . . ." What motivation when He said to believe—He didn't say 'hope for' in this version. We have had a great day in His Word and praying with and for Timothy for God to fully heal and restore him. We are so thankful for Tim's regularity, his swallowing mechanisms, and his withstanding his 'personal' assistants' stretching his arms and legs! God is Good—please worship with other believers somewhere tomorrow proclaiming His Word and thanking Him for the week ahead for Tim and yourself. Tim's main doctor is away for the week on vacation and we're praying that God really shows His awesomeness through Tim, and when the doctor comes back and sees his progress, he'll stand in awe of the Great Physician! God bless.]

Sunday, July 25—It's hard to believe that the 2010 National HS Finals has ended! One year ago-we were coming home from Farmington, NM as a family—I had gone home with Mom to have a "Sisters Week" with my three sisters and Mom in Oklahoma and Howard with all the kids were traveling behind the trailer hauling Tim's horse with his friend, Dalton, and his family and his horses. "TIME"(2010) from then to June with Tim at college (NJC with Dalton as his roommate), Bethany a senior, Cassady in 8th grade, and Jessica in 6th grade! "TIME" (now) here in Craig with Tim. The girls are two weeks away from FAIR of which Tim was a HUGE part of it, all working together getting the steers ready to show. Beth is struggling with going away to college with Tim here. I told her it's a "Leap of Faith" and we all will trust You for the strength You'll give to her and to us! So thankful to have my Missouri, Arkansas, and Oklahoma family close and within driving distance! After we all went to church, we took Tim out on the basement patio and did some stretches out there. Tim had good 'results' and was resting well, so Howard and I made ourselves leave for an hour to go eat together at "The Black-Eyed Pea"—we enjoyed the food, but we both had our minds on Tim. We have rarely, especially without kids, ever gone out for dinner in twenty-four years, and we were so tired, but at least we made the effort!) Prayed with Tim!

[Luke 11:2-4 . . . The shortened version of the Lord's Prayer. Today in the hospital church we see where He taught His disciples to pray powerfully, and confidently, for all of us who are His followers. We thank all of you and the many, many others who are powerfully and confidently praying for Tim and our family. Another relaxful day for Tim (except for the time he has to put up with us doing his stretches!) We are so thankful and amazed at how well he is swallowing which may mean a little closer to maybe adding some banana pudding in his diet soon! We are excited for the upcoming week and please join us as we thank God in advance for all that He will be healing and restoring this week!!]

> **There was a personal posting to Dixie, encouraging her by saying she was lighting the world those reading her daily journal, mentioning how nothing grips a mothers heart more than watching her child's journey toward healing whether it be physical, spiritual, or emotional for the journey is not without its struggles and its heartaches.**

Monday, July 26—Started out anticipating a good week! The morning nurse said the night nurse had a long night with Tim and he had kept his roommate, Chris, awake! (Wouldn't that have great if Tim really woke Chris up!) She pushed all day with the doctor and everyone to have Tim change rooms. It was a 'mama-bear' day when the fill-in doctor wanted to give Tim a medicine to help him during the night if he awakes or has anxiety about being here because they think he may be "waking' up more! YEA, LORD! Seems odd that we want him to wake up more to a higher 'level of consciousness,' but yet want to give him something when he does to keep him calm? We told them to call us and we will come over if he is having a 'loud' night! In PT, they had us practice using this portable lift with a sling you put Tim in for when we need to go home . . . Again one of those 'we aren't using this when we go home' moments! I expressed that we feel this time is using our PT time up and needs to be a separate time, not a therapy time! We change rooms tomorrow and the night nurse will be fine! [Eph 2:10 . . .

For you are God's own handiwork, recreated in Christ Jesus that you may do good works that God has prepared for you; you should live the good life which He prearranged. One of today's devotional readings that I read to Tim was this one. It was also mentioned that Ps 139 says that He knew you before you were formed in your mother's womb and he has given unique gifts, abilities, & talents—God has a special plan for your life. You are the person who God says you are! We are praying that our moans and groans turn into words so we can communicate rather than guess as to what he needs and wants. Please pray that his voice and words come soon, that if there is any pain that it will subside, a good, comfortable night's rest for Tim, and for continued weight gain for strength. Above all, we continue, as we know many of you do also, to pray and plead in Jesus' name for His miraculous total healing and restoration soon!]

Tuesday, July 27—It was almost like a fire drill moving all our 'stuff' to Tim's new room. IF they had shown us this one instead of all the other ones we'd seen, we probably wouldn't have been upset yesterday! We had a commode/shower chair demo today, but luckily got in some PT time. Prayed with Tim and thanked God for his night nurse he had and has again tonight! (2 Tim 2:1 . . . "You therefore, my son, be strong in the grace that is in Christ Jesus." Grace is what our holy and loving God gives that we, as sinful people, don't deserve. In Acts 17:25, we learn that "He gives life, breath, and all things." Those gifts include our very next breath . . . I truly believe that and thank God for His design of our respiratory system. From when Tim quit breathing in the arena, while I was breathing for him until I got him breathing on his own, through all the breathing tubes and treatments, and to now leave his room watching him breathe so relaxful and to hear him snore!—I praise and thank God for that gift and will never take it for granted. I will also add that anyone and everyone reading this to please learn CPR and I thank God for giving me the strength during that time. Even in our darkest hours/days, our strength comes by the grace of God. Continue to pray for his left thigh area—it seems to be less swollen and bending a tad more. He is relaxing his right bicep more and more every day!!!

Regularity is beginning to look like Tim's freethrow percentage—7 days with "progress" Thank you Lord! Keep praying for words!]

Wednesday July 28—Another great night! Tim got to chew a little ice today and swallow! Visited with Sandy before she left to go home. What an amazing woman! Had an hour of stretching in OT-very good! In PT, Tim rode the pedals, stronger with the right, but did some with the left! We had to help hold them on and turn them, but he did it! We had twelve people (Andy, Stacy, three K's, our girls, Stormy, Sam, Kim, and Emily) with us during therapy! After a bit, they all went to the room while we worked with him on the tilt table! Lord, how we thank You for strong breathing, good/steady bowel movements, stronger muscles, eyes tracking more, stronger swallowing and smoother—so many blessings we are grateful for! Forgive me for showing my frustrations (inefficient usage of time, nursing changes, etc) Thank you for my devotional—"Guard Your Heart". [Prov 4:23 "Keep and guard your heart . . ." plus Lamentations 3:21 . . . "This I call to mind, and therefore I have hope: the steadfast love of the Lord never ceases, His mercies never come to an end: they are new every morning and great is your faithfulness." The last one we wrote on our white board for our verse of the day. I really don't know the words to describe the feelings of security, comfort, peace, encouragement, etc to be able to go to sleep at night (usually after some 'let down' time and prayer) and rest in the Lord knowing that He holds tomorrow in His hands, holds Tim in His hands, and His love and mercy never ends. Staying in His Word guards against worries, fear, anxieties, etc . . . Stand strong, Faith, and Joy is how we stand in Him. Tim had 1 1/2 hrs. today of stretching overall, muscle isolation, pushing a stationary bike pedal, and standing on the tilt table. Arms moving and relaxing, and he had a great night of sleeping through the night!! Again, we rest in the Lord and look to the One who holds tomorrow for that healing and restoring with Tim!! Thank you again for the cards, calls, and visits that are so encouraging!!]

Thursday, July 29—I think that people, including even our girls, and those that don't know You or haven't trusted You are scared to 'Let Go and Let God"—to allow You to totally have this situation. We pray that You take away negative and doubting thoughts and replace them with positive affirmations and promises from You and Your Word. We pray that people will see You through Tim's life. We pray BIG because we have a BIG GOD who is all-powerful, loving, healing. We plead for Tim so that You will be honored and glorified in a magnificent way so all will know it's YOU! [Romans 15:13 "May the God of hope fill you with all joy and peace in believing, so that you may abound in hope by the power of the Holy Spirit." Many of you have personally told us of the peace God has given you about Tim's healing and restoration thank you for that encouragement! It's that addition to the 'tank' that God fills and refills nightly and daily that allows us to abound as we wait for Tim to abound in God's timing. Tim had another great day in therapy sessions. He was on his stomach some and also got to shoot some nerf dart guns. Please continue to pray for muscle isolation and words to come, and total healing and restoration!]

Friday, July 30—HOBIE DAY here at Craig! The whole hospital and staff all go to Cherry Creek for a day on the water, food, and music, etc. They've done this for about thirty years. The doctor and nurses really encouraged us to go and with Tim's feeding tube we will just go for a couple of hours. They load up everyone on their buses. For the outing—Debby and her sister, Marion, rode with us in our car! Howard and Tim rode in a pontoon boat while Sam/Kim/Emily/Rhea/and I rode in a speed boat beside them. Tim didn't have much response—he never was much of a 'water-rat'. Food was good, but would have been better if Tim could have eaten with us! Went back to the hospital behind the first bus that took both Tim and Bobby back. We were tired, but Tim was exhausted! [Proverbs 3:8 . . . "It will be healing to your body, and refreshment to your bones." Pray for the upcoming weekend when Tim has to put up with Howard and I pulling and stretching him! We get our weekly schedule for the next week every Friday and it looks to be a busy week!! They are looking to put Tim in the therapy pool maybe even next week! Continue to Pray Believe!!]

Saturday July 31—Tim sat outside with us 'til about 12:30—he's able to be in his chair longer and longer! Some relatives of Howard's came by and they are both PT'S (Charlie & Pete) and they were encouraging and thought Tim had come a long way since Cheyenne! This is our 8th week (six weeks in Craig) since the accident—almost too hard to believe! We pray that August will be a big miracle month that You glorify Yourself through healing and restoring Tim! Mentally-full brain/body functions, personality, laugh, voice/words, cognition restored, eyes aligned! Physically-muscles stronger, walking, arms full relaxed and strong in bending, bathroom functions, head/neck strong, upper-body strength, weight gain (Tim weighed 140 lbs in junior high—needs to be back up there on his way to 190 and strong! [2 Tim 2:1 . . . "You then, my son, be strong in the grace that is in Christ Jesus!" We're starting a new month tomorrow and expecting great things and big steps as Tim is strengthened every day by God's healing hand! Our God is an Awesome God (one of the many choruses I sing a lot through out the day) and we thank Him for all He has done and is doing! Tim spent sometime outside with some friends and their dog, and trying to relax for most of the day—(Howard and I did get some good stretching exercises out of him), but is resting very well when we left his room tonight. Continue to pray for restful nights, regular routine (bowel), strength for therapy sessions, and total healing and restoration! Hope everyone 'makes' the opportunity to attend somewhere tomorrow where you worship God with other believers of Christ—let us know of songs and/or messages that touched you!]

> **As your Aunt Donna said in an earlier posting, Tim's angel has been with him and along with the Holy Spirit has been whispering to him from the very beginning of this journey. Who can even imagine the spiritual dialogue and groundwork that is being wrought this very minute in Tim's heart, mind, and body to prepare him for his awakening and for the ministry and testimony his life will be to others? I know Tim is praising Him in the storm! You and Howard have given him the spiritual foundation he**

> **needed to weather this storm and now God is building on that very foundation to bring about His perfect will in Tim's life, to fulfill the purpose that He has ordained for Tim's life. His purpose is greater than the pain you are now walking through and I look forward with great anticipation to watching how God's plan for Tim's life, for your life, for your entire family's life, unfolds in the coming days! What Satan meant for harm God will turn into something more amazing than we can even fathom! And to Him we will give all the Glory! (Sam and Donna Burnett)**

Sunday, Aug. 1—Hospital church was very good this morning. Had a special prayer time with several who were there at the end. Took Tim out on the patio for lunch and then listened to the CFD Finals on the computer. So encouraging for friends to take the time to stop by even if just for a few minutes. ["We are CONFIDENT that God listens to us if we ask for anything that has His approval. We KNOW that He listens to our requests. So we KNOW that we already have what we ask Him for." (1 John 5:14-15) This is where we start August with in our faith-walk-confidence and trust in knowing Him, not knowing His timing or ways. We pray that you have that confidence and trust in Him as you continue praying and believing!!! Tim again was sleeping very relaxed in his room when we left tonight. We have a busy week and ask you to pray for daily strength and big steps of progress by God's healing hand!!! Sorry we're late with this—try to do better and earlier this week!!]

Monday, Aug. 2—Still hard to believe we are almost two months on this 'journey'! Eagerness and excitement still fills my heart and mind for each new day. Cimarron B. came by after being at CFD and spent time eating with us and going to therapy—hard for him seeing Tim, when the last time was when he picked him up at the DFW airport, then went directly to a roping where he was 1st and Tim was 2nd! Tim will always remember that week he spent with them! Tim a little uncomfortable tonight—pray You dissolve any HO if there is any in that leg. They talked with us about injecting a medicine onto Tim's arm muscles to relax and numb the muscles for about three months and they would use casts along with it. We have to make the decision by the 19th. We got Tim up in the new lift chair. He also did toe-kicks two times with a ball with each leg—we helped the left leg some. Prayed with Tim and for all our friends here. [Psalm 33:20 . . . "We wait for the Lord. He is our help and our shield. In Him our hearts find joy. In His holy name we trust." The verbs here are wait, find, and trust with the nouns being help, shield, and joy. Sounds so easy . . . and we're trying hard to totally follow His Word. Thank ya'll for the daily strength and with your prayers, comments, cards, etc—that keeps the 'fuel' in our hearts. Tim had a full day starting with two mornings sessions and three sessions in the afternoon. He followed verbal commands and muscle isolation with toe-touch kicking a ball with each foot twice and we also used a different chair that 'stood up' with Tim for balance and strength. Please pray for the right arm to completely relax and straighten because they are looking at possible muscle injection and a series of different casts for the arm. We're praying that pool therapy will loosen and relax, but wholly that God would relax that arm. His left thigh/knee joint area has bent more, but again, keep praying that if there is any bone ossification that He would just dissolve any for full range of motion. Tim is sleeping well through the nights so praise and thank God, and continue to pray for total healing and restoration! BELIEVE]

Tuesday, Aug 3—Speech was the tops today! Tim kicked the ball four times today in PT, and also worked wearing his cowboy hat and keeping his head up for it to stay on. We pray for healing of that neck teneness and for him to say "Beth" before she leaves next week for college. Lord, we believe in Your 'Big-ness'—we even prayed for Tim's to be restored so he can go back to school this fall! Prayed with Debby again tonight-especially for Tim to have a good night! [.Matt 11:28 . . . "Come to me, all who are tired and weary, and I will give you rest. Place my yoke over your shoulders, and learn from me, because I am gentle and humble. Then you will find rest for yourselves because my yoke is easy and my burden is light." This verse is so energizing for us-to know that His rest and His yoke are what we can trust daily. It also extends our patience when we are helping Tim to relax his shoulders and neck muscles and trust us and his surroundings. I really try to be gentle with my voice and massages! He had a great afternoon session and sat up on those exercise balls with the therapist only holding his head/neck! We exercised his arms again and had some good range of motion, but continue to lay this whole right arm situation (bicep muscle relaxing with full extension) before our Great Physician to heal or work the way He created it with full range of motion! We continue to ask God to heal his left thigh/knee joint area. He is starting to move and place his tongue in the different places of his mouth so we are looking for words to come soon! Have a great evening! Howard and Dixie]

> **One person thanked the Malms for their words of scripture in their postings. They commented on how the Malms are the ones encouraging and supporting the readers instead of the other way around.**

Wed. August 4—Busy day! It still amazes me (and I am so thankful) that You rest me and wake me up with excitement to come over thinking this might be the day we get "Tim" back! He swallowed five times in speech within a two minute time period!! Hopefully, we can do ice chips over the weekend! We had a positioning clinic today and some friends from LaGrange (Barry and Bailey W.) went with us. Again, it was during our PT time and we felt like we lost out on the therapy good in exchange for the clinic time. Praying we won't need these wheelchairs, shower/commode chair, lift, extra 'stuff' when we go home. [Ps 91:1-2 . . . "He who dwells in the shelter of the Most High will abide in the shadow of the Almighty. I will say to the Lord, My refuge and my strength, my God, in whom I trust!" Because of Him, His Word, friends, family—we are a 'dwellin' and 'abidin' here at Craig and He is our strength and we fully trust Him. Tim had a full day with doing well in the morning sessions—he will be able to have ice chips to chew and swallow this weekend!! (Banana pudding around the corner!) He was able to use the standing table today again, so keep praying for the strength to stand soon! We're praying for continued relaxation for the arm and leg, also hoping that the pool will help. Pray for Tim to start gaining weight back for his strength! Words—we pray for words! We are hearing different tones, yea! Have a great evening!]

Thursday, August 5—The day turned out to be my most frustrating one so far here at Craig. Without calling us during the night, some 'new' (not on Tim's team of nurses) nurse gave him the medicine, Adavan (anti-anxiety) at 4:00 a.m. and it knocked him out so hard that we couldn't do our morning devotional, feet massaging, not even get ready for speech! We couldn't even do his oral care (teeth brushing) 'til noon! Major 'Mama-Bear'—I talked with the nurses, techs, PT, and OT—maybe some changes will happen! The doctor came by when the speech therapist was in, but he must've talked to our nurse and found out we were frustrated, so he didn't come back by! [We so appreciated Amy's post on Tuesday of II Corinthians 4:8 and then Sam's the next day Psalm 62:5. II Corinthians 4:7b caught our eye, "that the surpassing greatness of the power may be of God and not from ourselves." Also take a look at the three verses following Psalm 62:5. God is the only thing that we can hold onto right now "the rock of my strength, my refuge is in God." Tim did manage to have a productive day in his PT and OT therapy sessions.This was one of the toughest days for us for some time now. Satan is working overtime to steal our joy and cause depression. We continue to covet your prayers for Tim's right thigh and knee area and for our physical and emotional strength as we care for him. God is so good and faithful and continues to give us what we need for each day. Bethany, Cassady, and Jessica, we miss you dearly.]

Friday, Aug 6—Thank You for giving Tim a good night! Were able to do our morning reading, pray, oral care, and get dressed for our co-therapy with speech and OT. Tim has been cleared for the ice chips, even though we've been doing the water-thing for a week! Tim did well with the arm-skateboards in therapy, stretching exercises in PT—and then we had to go through with the wheelchair ordering ordeal! I never have liked roller-coasters and this emotional one we're on, I would really like to get off it! I could tell all the talking was upsetting him, so I just got out of the discussion and stood by the bed in between Tim and where Howard was talking with the guy and just talked into Tim's face and ear while I was hugging him, telling him that I knew he had heard them talking—but we had to listen and do this, but we aren't planning on taking a wheelchair home with us! We got some extra time to stand in the standing table! We will do stretches this weekend. [2 Thess 3:3 "But the Lord is faithful and will strengthen you and protect you against the evil one." As Howard mentioned yesterday that we had a "hospital" day of frustrations that the devil wanted to drain us of our joy, trust, and faith, but as usual, God was faithful and as we talked with nurses, therapists, techs, etc—some frustrations turned into positive changes and stronger commitments between everyone on Tim's team. Today Tim was able to work hard during the sessions and then relax very comfortably. It's tough to imagine today has been two months to the date since Tim's accident and this faith journey began—how we thank God for all He has and is teaching us and for each one of you walking alongside with us! It was so good to have Tim's college rodeo coach, Brian Cullen, with us today.]

Saturday Aug 7—Prayed with Tim-sometimes he is 'awake' and sometimes he's asleep, but we always leave his room with praying and usually a CD left on with praise or instrumental Christian music. [1 Peter 5:7 "Cast all your cares on Him because He cares for you!" What a relief this is when we truly 'Let go and let God!' It also greatly helps the stress level to remain low. Tim had a relaxful day, had a good stretching session, and had visitors. Thank you, Lord! We continue to pray, believe, and expect God to totally heal and restore Tim; we are thankful for the daily miracles He gives everyday! Thanks again for your prayers and belief with us—it's such an encouragement!]

Sunday, August 8—Thank You for another good night's rest! We all went to church. We have added pool therapy next week so we pray that he can relax in the warm pool! We see our monthly 'family' meeting scheduled for Tuesday and oh, how we want to hear encouraging words! God—we thank You for where we've come—we're just excited for Tim to see progress, for all the people praying to see You in all this, and for the young friends of Tim's looking to see if the God that Tim walks with is really big enough to heal Tim! I'm excited to see and hear Tim's testimony of YOU! [Everything written long ago was written to teach us so that we would have confidence through the endurance! Romans 15:4 It still amazes me how His Word was not only God, but it was, it is, and will be, ETERNAL! We always think of eternal or eternity as in the future, but it was eternal when it was written. Because Jesus is the Word, it is the same yesterday, today, and tomorrowand because of that it is what gives us the confidence in our Lord and Savior. Tim had another relaxful day with family visiting! Pray for continued relaxing of the leg and arm, a week of progress, and a restful night. Thank you and have a great evening!]

Monday, August 9—Tim got to eat applesauce today! (He'd like it better hot with a little cinnamon & sugar over some buttered bread!) That's the high side—the low side is he was uncomfortable and had both PT and OT sessions in his room. We are praying for pool time tomorrow—also for the 'family' meeting! In Your Hands, and In Your Time! [Ps. 95:6-7 "Come let us worship and bow down; Let us kneel before the Lord our Maker. For He is our God, and we are the people of His pasture and the sheep of His hand. "Ever wonder about God's 'pasture' here on earth? We would have never dreamed of this one . . . but it is His pasture because He is here with His hand over His sheep (us)! I don't know about other pastures, but the ones we've been across are not smooth and can have some big rocks and ruts. Alongside the bumpy ride you can choose to see the beauty of the pasture with its grasses, wildflowers, wildlife (hopefully you see/find all your cattle, too), and water. Tim had a 'bumpy ride' today is physically moving more and more, it causes more muscles to fire and overwork to the point of being very used and needing some extra Tylenol at times. Please pray for an extraordinary soothing and relaxing time in the therapy pool in the morning and also for our monthly family meeting with his team in the afternoon.]

Tuesday August 10—In Speech, Tim got to eat Strawberry/Banana yogurt. Pool time went great for the first time. I got in with him and the instructor—and they keep the pool about 95-96 degrees! He took a noon nap! I would have liked to, but our meeting was 1:00-2:00, so just have to 'keep on ticking'. The doctor discussed some options for us to think (and pray) about! One was the muscle injections in his arms and the other was this baclofen pump that is surgically put in your body and then it send messages to release the medicine to the spinal fluid in your back. The OT had taken Tim on to his therapy and when we got there, she was having a great session with getting to respond 'yes or no' with crossing his right leg over his left knee (high for yes) and then at the ankle (low for no). [Isaiah 43:2a "When you pass through the waters, I will be with you; And through the rivers, they will not overflow you . . . ." God's timing amazes me—this was one of our devotionals today and only God knew Tim was going to be in the water today! We also claim this promise verse because this journey has been and continues to be through some deep and fast water. After a major rainstorm in NW Arkansas which had the Buffalo River at flood stage and only allowed experienced canoers on it, my aunt and I put the canoe in. She is very experienced and I think she took me along because I could use an oar, balance the canoe, and swim! I found out what "experienced" meant! We did fairly well in the fast-moving currents, but hitting big rocks finally flipped us and I swam with the current until I could swim close enough to the bank to grab tree limbs or whatever. I sat on the bank and hollered upstream to let her know where I was and then I saw her come around a bend after she had found the canoe and floated downstream where I was on the bank. I've thought about that adventure and this journey has been dangerous and fast, and now we're sitting on the bank looking 'upstream' to see Tim healed and restored. This verse promises He will be there . . . and we know He is upstream with Tim and He is on the bank with us! Continue to PRAY & BELIEVE!!]

Wednesday, August 11—Had good therapies. Had a late bite of supper after we prayed with Tim. [With God all things are possible! Matt 19:26 During the early update time tonight I went for a few groceries and items for Howard since I'm headed with Bethany tomorrow to College of the Ozarks (Branson, MO). I bought this matted poster that says, "Faith is not knowing that God can, but that God will". So with that and the verse today it encourages us to continue praising and thanking

God daily (sometimes by the moment) and praying our hearts' desires and cries to Him. We thank all of you for being on our prayer team as we all honor Him and hang on tightly to His Hand! Tim's Occ Therapist today said that today was even better than yesterday in his session with her following commands more consistent and able to work longer! We ate more yogurt and worked with a straw in speech therapy. Continue to pray for vocal/verbal progress and relaxation to continue in big steps! Again, thank you for your cards, Caringbridge posts, and visits, and we know and feel all your prayers and 'spiritual' hugs. Please keep Bethany and me on your prayer list for tomorrow as we travel—I'll be flying back to Denver on Monday. Goodnight!]

Thursday August 12—Beth had some private time with Tim while I put things in her car. I had told Tim that I loved him and that I would see him in a few days—really hard to leave him and Howard. Howard, Bethany, and I held hands in the parking lot and he prayed while we cried! Left Denver at 1:15 p.m. headed to Branson! About sixteen hours later, we drove in my 'kinfolk's' carport (Donnie & Bonnie's) about 5:30ish a.m. their time! After cleaning up, moving in her dorm, a Walmart trip, a few other things—I took a nap and slept 'til 8:00 p.m.! After being up since 6:30 a.m. yesterday morning (thirty-three hours) I needed it and God, I thank You for keeping me alert and awake—praying, talking, singing, listening! Talked with Howard about 9:00 p.m. and he did a great job doing the Caringbridge! [Howard had to write a few of the daily posts while Dixie was traveling. What a day. We cried when Tim uttered his first clear words since his accident. Then we cried when we said good byes to Bethany as she left for her first year of college and then I cried when I heard how well Cassady and Jessica did at County Fair and knew that we had missed it. Tears for all different kinds of things. God is good. Jesus was accustomed to tears. In John 11:35 we see the deep emotion of Jesus as he wept for Lazarus and his family. And just after that reminds Martha that "If you believe you will see the glory of God." We continue to believe. The morning started off with Tim telling the speech therapist "more" when she asked him if he wanted more pudding. It even brought tears to her eyes. He repeated it a few minutes later. There was no question about these two words. A hard but good day. We continue to ask for specific prayer for more movement in Tim's left leg and would love to hear God's voice calling Tim to come forth. Thanks to everyone for their prayers and generosity.]

Friday, August 13—[Another good day. Dixie and Bethany drove all night and arrived safely in Point Lookout, Missouri. Tim was cleared for a full diet, only problem is, it all has to be pureed (not sure if that is spelled correctly). He seemed to like his spaghetti, pears, mashed potatoes and gravy tonight but I didn't even make him try the spinach. In PT he rode the bicycle (to the delight of his PT therapist) with only his right leg for five minutes under his own power and had to be physically stopped. In OT he worked on the word no and seems to be getting much closer to being consistent. I continue to be amazed at your strength at the times when it is most needed and was struck by the fact that in Matthew 9:2 it was the paralytics' friends faith that moved Jesus to action, so keep praying and believing.]

Saturday, August 14—Talked with Tim a little on the phone-Howard held it up to his ear. Hard to not be there, but thankful I got to bring Bethany here. [Psalm 5:11 "But let all who take refuge in Thee be glad, let them ever sing for joy. And mayest thou shelter them, that those who love thy name may exult in Thee." In times like these, it is only by taking refuge in a God that we know loves us, that we can experience joy. Today Tim experienced a combination day. At times somewhat upset at times very comfortable. The right side of his neck seems to be firing more and if you can imagine having a cramp in your neck that pretty much says it. However, when he was in his chair it was much better, which many times is just the opposite. We spent about three hours just strolling around, inside and out in his chair. Another hour or so of stretching and that was pretty much his day. God blessed our girls with very good prices for their steers at the County Fair 4-H sale. We were overwhelmed with the continuing generosity of all those at fair, may God richly bless you. Looking forward to tomorrow and our little worship service here in the Chapel at Craig.]

Beth posted this entry about this time: Timmy I've been wanting to get on here and write ever since mom set it up, but I couldn't find the words that I wanted to say. I can't believe that it's been over two months since the accident, by the way my side is perfectly fine now I just have a tiny scar. After your accident I went home to practice the poles, and going into the arena was one of the hardest things I had to do all summer, next to actually having to go to rodeos. The summer went by so fast. I think about you all the time. Sometimes it still doesn't seem like this all happened, like it seems like you're just at a rodeo and we are waiting for you to call home and let us know how you did. There is nothing that I do that I don't think about you. I miss seeing your big blue eyes, and hearing your voice and "brotherly" advice about some things in life. Going to the rodeos was hard, but the hardest thing will be me having to leave you, mom, dad, friends and all of our family on Thursday when I head to college. I can't wait till you're fully awake and restored and I can see you rope calves, and ride horses."

Sunday, August 15—[Isaiah 26:4 "Trust in the Lord forever, for in God the Lord, we have an everlasting Rock." In church here at Craig this morning we looked at Hebrews 11. All those named and referred to in this chapter were there because they lived out Isaiah 26:4. Tim had another laid back day of just getting outside and over to the apartment for a few hours plus some stretching. The right side of his neck continues to provide significant discomfort at times. Other than that he had a pretty good day. Dixie will fly back into Denver tomorrow afternoon. Thanks for your continued prayers.]

Monday, August 16—Bonnie took me to the Branson Airport after we visited at their house for a bit. The flight took one hour and forty minutes! Howard told me that during one of the therapies, Tim said "rope, purple, and brush when asked to identify or questions about objects!! More and More!! The 2nd floor staff still is so excited that Tim is speaking! They truly are sincere in their care so when the word went out that he was speaking, we had and still have different people stepping in to either hear him and/or congratulate him. [Romans 12:12 Be joyful in hope, patient in affliction, faithful in prayer! We have joy and faith—it's the patience in God's timing that He has and is working with us. In therapy, Tim said more words today!! He named items and read a few words off cards!!! He gets to go to the pool in the morning so we hope for more and easier range of motion in the left leg and arm! I (Dixie) made it home safely from Branson in time to help with Tim's dinner—did you know you can puree beef spare ribs? Thank you for praying for Bethany and myself with the traveling and all of the emotional time. I truly felt God's presence driving and physically keeping me going for almost thirty-six hours with a short hour nap that morning in the car before we could move her into the dorm! Restful nights have me caught up and am excited to watch and hear God's miracles this week with Tim! God Bless All Y'all!]

Tuesday August 17—[We so enjoy all the cards—they are and have been such an encouragement and I have saved every one of them to read and reread! One of the cards really fit for today . . . Everyday of treatment and recovery deserves a trophy. Some for courage, some for just hanging in there . . . Keep fighting the good fight. It also brought us to Exodus 14:14—"The Lord will fight for you while you keep silent." Tim had a really good day yesterday and today was one of those 'hanging in there' days. He had a fill-in therapist for speech and he mouthed the word 'bye'—guess that spoke of the session for him! He had a great time in the pool—really stretched out his arms and had good movement with the left knee! The afternoon sessions were fair, but the pool time was exhausting and it showed in the sessions. He ate club steak (puree)! We continue to ask for restful nights, comfortable times in his chair and bed, big steps of progress, more words, clear vision, and just overall—a total and full healing!! Thank you all again for being such encouraging with your cards, calls, and visits! Sorry for the lateness tonight. Try to be earlier tomorrow!]

Wednesday, August 18—Tim is saying more and more words—we have him say anything and everything—probably going overboard! We even have made word cards with everybody's names, even his horses! We have colors, rodeo/roping words, addition, subtractions, etc. and etc.! He is working with a straw for drinking! We did the standing table today in PT. [Mark 11:24 "say to you, all things for which you pray and ask, believe that you have received them, and they shall be granted you!" Now that's a big rock to stand on! If you notice though, the verse only mentions the 'ed' endings in any form of a time reference. My English background tells me that means it has happened!! When, where, and how we 'see it' is only in His timing—so we continue to wait on Him. Tim had a good day—worked on using a straw, identifying objects (mouthed and/or verbally said pen, brush, glasses), and three therapists with our help also turned, lifted, and had Tim on his stomach on top of a huge exercise ball with his knees on the mat. He did really well, even though I can imagine what he thought of this circus of people he had around him! He also had his best day using the standing table; pray that his left leg shows progress in bending! We go to the pool tomorrow! Please pray that the changes in medicine will go well—taken away some and added some! Also pray for Tim's right side of his neck muscle to relax more!! We thank God for so many miracles we see daily and weekly—what a privilege, because of the Cross, we can come before Him with thanksgiving for He is our very breath of Life! Pray and Believe!]

> **Dixie, you always thank everyone for their prayers and words of encouragement, and I appreciate that. However, I have to confess that I look forward to reading the Caringbridge update for two reasons. First and foremost, I anxiously await the culmination of God's Plan for Tim and your family. Secondly, and very selfishly, I have found your postings to be so important to me personally. I work with Candra and can't wait to share with her what it has meant to me to connect spiritually with her family on this mountain that has been placed before you to climb (or rather**

> this valley through which you have been with Tim). Either way, God has such tremendous plans for all of you and, through your trial, you have touched my life and the lives of the women in the Women at the Well Sunday School Class in Devol. We continue to lift up your entire family and the staff who works with Tim. God is so good every minute of every day. Thanks you and God bless. (Laura Booher)

Thursday, August 19—Our "LaGrange" family came down and got to see Tim work in the pool. Did really well today! We had this 'spasticity clinic' and had to listen to all this stuff—Botox injections for this and that, Phenol for this and that, and also that Baclofen pump thing. We pray for Your guidance for all these decisions. We really pray for You to completely heal so we wouldn't have to make any decisions—is that "copping out" or "totally relying" on You? Tim got chocolate milk today! [James 1:2-4 "Consider it pure joy, my brothers, whenever you face trials of many kinds, because you know that the testing of your faith develops perseverance. Perseverance must finish its work so that you may be mature and complete, not lacking anything." JOY and COMPLETE are the two words we concentrate on out of this verse because when you are in the midst of the trial—the trials are all around! Also notice again there is no time frame—only that it develops and it must finish its work! Praises include many, but especially the eating and swallowing pureed foods, little improvement with bending the left knee, little more relaxation in the neck area, and more words! Another prayer request would be for Coach Cullen, Coach Taya, and the whole NJC rodeo team as they start school and rodeo practices this next week. We prayed with all belief for God to have Tim ready for school, but we are still as the verse says, waiting with joy for the time, His time, for Him to make Tim 'mature and complete, not lacking anything'. Thanks again for all of your prayers, cards, and visits!]

Friday, August 20—The first session in speech, Tim said, "banana, more milk". Had a fill-in for OT and she really stretched his arms and worked again with a tootsie pop. In the afternoon speech session, Tim was able to finish phrases like–'it's raining cats and _____." He also said Dad, Mom, Cassady, Jess, and Beth—so it will be great when she hears him say her name tonight! I ran and got some ice cream to make Tim some milkshakes-he's been cleared for thin liquids! Tim added 'back' to his word list—said it in PT, kind of uncomfortable with some of the stretches, so he let us know! Thank You for more words, interaction with his sisters and friends, and ice cream! [Col. 3:17 "Whatever you do in word or deed do all in the name of the Lord Jesus, giving thanks through Him to God the Father." Oh how we have prayed for more and more words and Tim said quite a few new ones today—We are so thankful as we wait for the Lord to bring back his speech and vocabulary. Please pray for a great weekend with us as his therapists and his sisters as his speech therapists!! Tim didn't have a restful night last night so we pray for him to have one tonight! Thank you again for your prayers; they support our daily fuel!]

Saturday, August 21—[Col. 4:6 "Let your speech always be gracious, seasoned with salt, so that you may know how you ought to answer everyone." We're so thankful for the answers (words) we are hearing Tim say. The nurses and techs are also so excited to hear their names! Continue to pray for his right hip/lumbar area to relax as well as more relaxation in his right neck area. We look forward to worship tomorrow and pray each of you have a wonderful day!]

Sunday August 22—After church service, we took Tim out on the basement patio where Cassady and Jessica could have their "speech class" with Tim! Grpa, Grma, Kent, Lynette, and Kaden all came, and Tim said all their names! After we all prayed and the 'Amen' was said, Tim moaned something and Jessica told him to use his loud voice . . . we all could hear Tim's 'Amen' and what joy! Cass and Jess went back home with them. Thank You for letting us have these few days with our girls down here, Beth's calls, more words, Tim's blue eyes, family and friends. [Jer 33:3 "Call to Me, and I will answer you, and show you great and mighty things, which you do not know." Again another verse to continue to stand on—we have called and He has answered!! We continue to call knowing He will answer and show us things in a great and mighty way that only He knows so we wait with great expectancy and belief daily. Tim had a very good day after a restful night (slept 'til 6:00). When asked by one of the techs this morning what he was doing when he slung his right leg over the bed's siderail—he said, "I getting up!" maybe he is just tired of being in bed! PRAY & BELIEVE!!]

Monday, August 23—They really stretched Tim's arms for measurements and he was a bit sore during the day! In speech we added new words, said some sentences, and spelled Albin, Wyoming, Kenworth, etc. He knew his birthdate, address, college, etc. Praying for more words, clarity, fluency, just to talk again like he used to—he so enjoyed visiting with people of all ages about so many subjects. We pray You will restore all his agricultural, ranching, and roping memory! We pray for boldness with his testimony! They are going to do night feeding (with their cans of 'milk') and do day trays of a soft diet. (Tim and soft diet don't go together!-but it's a start!) ["After you have suffered for a little while, the God of all grace, who has called you to His eternal glory in Christ, will Himself restore, support, strengthen, and establish you." 1 Peter 5:10 This verse of promise is one of my 'big-breath' verses! Again, it doesn't state a definite amount of time—it only states for a 'little while'! (Kinda reminds me when our parents and also ourselves as parents respond to our kids . . . in a 'little bit'! But the 'deep breath' doesn't come because you have held it in for that 'little while', but because of the enormity of the grace and the promise to restore, support, strengthen, and establish because of God's love and salvation plan (the Cross)! We have been and are in that 'little while' time—but above all, we're in that grace of the Almighty God! Tim will have his lower lumbar/area tested tomorrow (CT Scan) so please pray for that to go smoothly. Continue to pray for restful nights—so important for the next day! Goodnight!]

Tuesday, August 24—His CT scan came back clear of any spinal/lumbar area problems—so don't know why his back hurt? The doctor caught Howard out in the hall and talked with him about Tim had some injury to his right side of his brain so that's why we see the left side affected. God, I know You are healing and we will see more movement on his left side! We're getting closer to our Oct 1st dismissal date and we are praying for bathroom abilities to come about and the feeding tube to be gone! Please, please. We still believe and totally trust You for TOTAL healing and restoring Tim to full health—back to the young man You had developed. I so badly want to feel that big hug, hear that laugh, hear his real voice, see that twinkle in his eye, along with TIM, we want to have him back—to be a walking, talking testimony for YOU! God, we beg Your willingness, we plead the blood of Jesus, Your Son, over Tim for his total restoration. Thank You, Lord. ["He gives strength to the weary and increases the power of the weak. Even youths grow tired and weary, and young men stumble and fall: but those who hope in the Lord will renew their strength. They will soar on wings like eagles; they will run and not grow weary, they will walk and not be faint." Is 40:29-31. Such a refreshing verse! I'm not sure of the age of the youths, but remember the ages in the Bible! It encourages us all to remain youthful at least in our attitudes. Keep praying and believing!! Howard and Dixie]

Wednesday August 25—Tim slept well, thank You! After breakfast, he had his left leg cramp up! Took us about fifteen minutes of rubbing, stretching, and massaging to get it calmed down. His neuro-psychologist was very pleased at Tim's quick responses to questions and directions. Had a great speech session! Had a really good pool time! Sam (M) came by—been forever since we have seen him! Went in to the vision clinic today and they still tell us Tim has good vision in both eyes—his right eye is still low and the misalignment may cause some double vision. We pray that You will strengthen that muscle and nerve to lift and hold that eye up. ["Be strong and courageous! Do no tremble or be dismayed, for the Lord your God is with you wherever you go!" Josh 1:9. We find it important that in this verse He said how to be and what not to do and then because He is with us wherever we go—we know that includes here at Craig in CO, with Bethany in MO, and with our girls in WYO! His omnipresence is such an encouragement for us! We also know that all of you are with us in prayer support and we thank you. Tim had a great speech therapy session where he answered many questions. One was "Where you put a tractor and hay?" The therapist was looking for barn but Tim said outside because that is correct for us. Howard then asked him where your horses go—and Tim said horse barn! I then asked where we put our feed truck and loader—and Tim said quonset! So we had to describe what that was to her. He also named several people in different pictures! We are asking for bigger physical steps, continued memory recall, increase in words and fluency, and muscle relaxation God's healing and restoration. Have a great night!]

Thursday, August 26—Very Full day! We like it that way than some of the really slow days. More and more improvement in speech! In PT, we got to stand up!!! (with help from the PT, Howard and I—but we're up!) Sat in a rocking chair! He had these Quick tests for the Pre-Test on Monday for the Baclofen spinal test. I think those tired him out as he was tired in the pool. Went to the spasticity clinic and visited with the doctor. He was very good to talk with and asks questions. We thank You because Tim was comfortable the whole time! After about an hour, we decided to wait 'til after Monday's test. Lord, we need guidance—shots or wait to allow You to be the Great Physician here. [I asked Tim what an object was and he said "Bible". I asked him whose it was and he said "mine". We were reading in Luke 8 when the storm was about to overcome the disciples and Jesus calmed the storm and he asked, "Where is your Faith?" Our faith is in Him because He is in control of this 'storm' and is in our 'boat'. Please pray for us as we talk with them and gather all the info and then make a decision that is clearly guided by God. Have a great night!]

Friday, August 27—BUTTERFINGER!! Now everyone knows Tim's favorite candy bar! Tim asked one of the nurses, "What are you doing?" Said a few words on the telephone to Grandpa and to Sam (T). Had really good PT and OT therapies. Drank two milkshakes today—will be interesting to see his weight tomorrow! Gaining some back. We pray for answers and direction with all these tests, and the doctor wasn't thrilled with us that we made the decision to wait on the Botox shots. Weekend prayers!! [God's Word is a big mouthful to fill you up and chew on—it's your choice to spit it out or digest it and let it be your health. Tim has eaten very well today and we read to him every day from God's Word. He had the hardest workout in his physical therapy class today that he has had here—and he told the therapist "too much!" He mouths the words pretty quick, sometimes they're muffled, but most are becoming very clear! Continue to pray for fluency and sentence structure with thought. Pray very hard that over the weekend God really shows Himself by relaxing the muscles in a way that is not understood by the doctors or nurses. Seeing progress in those areas, but would like very evident signs so future decisions pertaining to medicines and procedures would be easier to decide. We would love to be at the Albin Benefit on Saturday night, but we send our 'hugest' (biggest no-word I know) thanks and hugs to everyone involved with it and those attending; ya'll have a blast! Dixie and Howard]

Saturday, August 28—Tim told Grandma and Nanny "I Love You!" on the telephone. Said "Hi and Bye" to Rhea and Deb. Weighed 152- YEA!! Bill and Shirley came by with butterfingers!! We broke one up into very small pieces and he ate it! Tonight is the Albin Benefit for Tim; hope it is a great night for all who attend and sent a thank you home for the girls to read from us. Did some exercises with Tim. Prayed again with Debby. [Romans 15:13 "Now may the God of hope fill you with all joy and peace in believing, that you may abound in hope by the power of the Holy Spirit." This is a verse we have held on for 12 weeks now and one we've been asking each of you—fill yourselves with joy and peace in believing . . . all by His power! Every night we have and continue to ask God to 'refill' Tim and ourselves and He is faithful. Tim is saying more and more words by the day. He rested outside in the morning and had a better day with fewer left leg cramps! Continue to pray for his neck relaxation as we are seeing a little more every day! We pray for a great day in worship time tomorrow and maybe Tim will want to physically go with us. Again, we thank you all for the prayer support—we have so many things to be thankful for and look forward to watching God work this week! Goodnight!]

Sunday August 29—Almighty and Gracious God! Gordon called to say they fed around 420 at the Benefit! I didn't know it could hold that many! They made a video so we will able to see it—so many stories of how our community pulled this off! People we haven't met from other communities came, donated items for the auctions, donated money for their meal, they even sold some of the decorations! Howard shaved Tim and we all went to church. I can't believe after the night last night that Andy, Stacy, and the 'crew' came down and brought us some of the roast beef from the Benefit! We are still overwhelmed with the whole thing! Later in the afternoon, Sam, Stormie, and Brittany (from NJC) came by! Had a good visit with another patient's mom about knowing You, Lord, we continue to ask You to meet so many of the needs of the Craig family. Prayed with Debby and Tim tonight! [Phil 4:6-7 "Be anxious for nothing but in prayer and supplication, let your requests be made known to God; and the peace of God, which surpasses all understanding will guard your hearts and minds through Christ Jesus!" Another one of the 'pillars' of His promises for us. Many of ya'll know how much I enjoy cooking and recipes and this is a great Biblical 'recipe'(Preheat) Be anxious for nothing(Ingredients) prayer, (Supplication) thanksgiving) (Directions) let your requests be made known(Finished product)God! Tim had a full day—went to church with us! Had family and friends for a visiting afternoon and ate very well. Please pray that relaxation shot test will go smoothly in the morning! He can read the time on the wall clock and finished telling Howard the last four numbers of our phone number! We enjoyed some of the Chuckwagon Benefit (Albin) food from last night—We are overwhelmed and greatly humbled by the "hugest" acts of friendship, kindness, and support from all of you! May God bless each one of you and our communities! Excited for the week—how, where, and when God will be healing and restoring Tim! PRAY & BELIEVE!!!]

Monday, August 30—I got over here about 7:00 after doing putting in some laundry and picking up the apartment. They'd already done his IV and Howard was massaging/rubbing his leg while I fed him ice chips for an hour (no food after midnight for this test). Went over to Swedish to have the pre-test shot (about a twenty-minute procedure) then he had to lay another hour before eating, another hour before the two-hour test after the shot with the PTs who did all the measurements with their pre-tests. They did see improvement. Went to PT/OT time together. Right leg has quietened down and no left leg spasms to speak of yet! The doctor was pleased. Timothy had a neck massage today! He talked with Bethany on the phone and told her he loved her! [3 John 2 "Beloved, I wish above all things that thou mayest prosper and be in health, even as thy soul prospereth." We had some "prosperin'" today with the relaxation pretest shot—Tim' right leg didn't jerk and kick as much because his left leg relaxed with no muscular spasms and the knee bending a bit more. He was able to have some therapy sessions in the afternoon and did well with them. One of the therapists asked Tim the names of his three sisters and he named all of them—then she asked if he were to have a wrestling match with one of them, which one might win? I'm sure most of ya'll can guess what Tim said! He is getting a massage tonight from one of the therapists so we are hurrying to get back over to his room. He has been sleeping well so continue to pray for his restful nights! Until next time . . . Dixie]

Tuesday, August 31—WOW, the TIME amazes me how you lose track of it! In our 13th week! Tim told Lindsy on the phone that "he was great!" The doctor talked a little with Howard about yesterday's baclofen test—I'm still unsure about the risks vs benefits, and that we want and have asked You to heal & restore Tim so he won't need or use this thing! We have that injections appointment on Thursday?? We might have had the best PT therapy session today so far—Praise and Thanks! Talked on the phone with Grandma today, and we heard more words (marvelous, great, plus many others as we had several visitors through the day! A HUGE act of friendship came when Britt drove through on his way to Pueblo—he got one of his horses out while we had pushed Tim over from the hospital and Tim was able to smell 'that smell', and feel 'that feel' he so badly misses with his horses! [Psalm 66:1-3a Shout joyfully to the Lord, all the earth; Sing the glory of His name; Make His praise glorious. Say to God, "How marvelous are Thy works!" One of the highlights of the day was when after having the best session in PT the physical therapist (pain terrorists) asked Tim about what he thought of the session? Tim replied, "Marvelous!" The therapist gladly took that response. He is putting more and more words together and gaining strength in his body, plus relaxing his neck/head more—he even asked today if he had his head in the middle! That's so important for balance when sitting and standing. It is also so encouraging to hear nurses, techs, and therapists say things like 'prayers are working', and 'keep praying!' We continue to pray that God really shines in Tim's room and His presence is both seen and felt in these halls and rooms. Pray that the Great Physician continues to show Himself in this medical facility! Continue to pray for Tim's neck to continue to relax, more movement in his left leg, and to continue progress in all areas of his body toward the restoration and healing the way God created. Goodnight!]

Lynette (Tim's aunt) wrote: "Those summer days passed slowly; then weeks passed and friends from our small community held a benefit with a huge turn out in August. Albin's town population is 120 and over 435 people attended. In September it had been three full months of caring daily for Tim and yet he still wasn't considered fully conscious. Howard and Dixie were understandably physically and emotionally tired but God sustained them with his daily strength. One of the toughest tests Tim faced was when they began putting his limbs in corrective casts and while no one will ever know how truly tough Tim is, we watched as he struggled with the pain as the healing process began. We've all dealt with the grief so seeing Howard and Dixie suffer incredible heartache while watching Tim endure intense physical pain in regaining his strength and healing of the brain connections. We are so grateful that he continues to improve, yet incredibly sad at times to see him work through incredible milestones which once were so easily mastered by this highly and gifted young man. In referring to Hallmark moments, none can compare to the picture of Tim's first smile of recognition at his parents in the hospital."

Wednesday, Sept 1,—Been three months on this 'journey'! Tim had some 'real' food today, some ham and chicken (also a butterfinger mini)! With help from us and his PT, Tim stood up in the parallel bars today. We were all sweating! Highlight today was hearing Tim reciting John 3:16 and Phil 4:13—reminded me of the verses about what we put in our hearts, memorize, ponder on, etc! Howard talked with the Cheyenne doctor and said it brought a tear to his eye and wants us to check back in with him on Oct 1. I went to the Mother's Support Group meeting—Thank You, Lord for Your faithfulness and graciousness again today.—[John 3:16 For God so loved the world that He gave His only begotten Son that whosoever believeth in Him shall not perish, but have everlasting life! You've probably memorized this as your first verse, seen it on posters at pro games, and it's probably the most well-known verse . . . but when I heard Tim recite it today verbatim and then his favorite verse, Phil 4:13—it was a highlight of this long journey! While I was in a mothers group meeting, he and Howard were outside and Howard was just visiting and Tim answered him with the verses. When I came back, Howard asked Tim if he knew the verses and what a surprise and gift from them and God to hear him! Tim also stood up easier today than last Thursday in between the parallel bars, and with only one therapist and us—it was harder on us than Tim, but he did well!!! Tim also beat one of his therapists in a card game (War) where he had to say the cards then with help drag the pair off the edge of the table. He gets to go to the pool tomorrow! Please pray that relaxation shots go smoothly and be effective for Tim! Continue to pray and believe because everyday we see God's hands in Tim's mind, body, and life!]

Thursday, Sept 2—Tim slept well. OT started late and we worked with Tim on a bolster in PT. Went to Spasticity Clinic where Tim had botox injections into specific muscles (wrist, pects, fingers/knuckles, & neck) Lord, we thank You for this technology and pray that it will help Tim, but we totally trust in Your healing with and/or beyond injections or pumps. Still unsure about the pump—need some confirmation from You. [2 Cor 9:8 "And God is able to make all grace abound to you, so that in all things at all times, having all that you need, you will abound in every good work." Is that not powerful? To have security in Him, knowing and trusting in the "all's"! Tim did extremely well today with this round of relaxation shots—we should see results within one-two weeks, but seeing what and how God relaxed his muscles in the preceding days—we are anticipating God's timing in this matter. Tim had a great day in pool therapy—it will be about ten days before we get to go again because they are doing some cleaning and maintenance work. He was also cleared for his entrees to not be pureed!! He was asking for fried chicken tonight! We asked him several of his menu choices for next week and he told us so it will be great to see real food! Continue to pray for daily progress for Tim to see, hear, and feel himself getting stronger every day! Goodnight!]

Friday, September 3—Had a fill-in for Speech and she had made copies of pictures with different cattle breeds of which Tim knew all the names of them and identified them! She then had lots of questions about Malm Ranch Company and all our cattle and Tim answered most all of them! It was great to see and hear Tim's memory! Sug and Joe came in for the afternoon with all her 'goodies'—we are so blessed with having them close (Gunnison) to us during the summer! Mom, Shena, and all the Baber 'crew' are on their way up for the big Tim Malm Benefit in Cheyenne. Lord, we pray for safe travel for everyone coming for the weekend. Howard and I prayed with Debby in Bobby's room tonight! [Ps 145:13-14 "The Lord is faithful in all He says; He is gracious in all He does. The Lord helps the fallen and lifts up those bent beneath their loads!" Beyond all the promises of what He does, what catches our eyes and hearts is the plural of loads—He knows each and every load and He is always there to listen to each one of them, and places their importance as if there was just one. With His sovereignty and His timing, we have the choice and blessed assurance to give the load(s) to Him. What a life lesson! Tim's appetite is coming back . . . The speech therapist asked him whether he wanted a Butterfinger or play a word/card picture game? You can guess which he chose! Then the physical therapist asked what he wanted to do and was just beginning to give him a couple of choices when he said "a malt!" The latter two sessions did not contain food. He was questioned by a new therapist (originally from a Kansas farm) to identify the breed of cattle by the pictures. He got them all right, plus with further question could tell her all the different breeds we've used on the ranch. He also remembered several things about his horses (ages, names, etc). It was great hearing him recall them. The 'real' lasagna was really good tonight and he enjoyed it! I hope he has a weight gain tomorrow! Please continue to pray for continued relaxation in his left leg/knee and neck area! Have a great Labor Day Saturday! Be ever so thankful for the gift of labor.]

Saturday, September 4—The Oklahoma 'crew' got in about 2:30 a.m. to their hotel room where Sug and Joe stayed also. Mom cut my hair (try anything to help look decent—one of the times you feel better than you look! I now know what emotional stress can look like!) So good to see and hear how Tim recognized everyone! Shena brought in a red Mountain Dew and he asked 'What pop can I have?" We gave him a little bit. Drove out to the DIA and picked up Bethany—of course she was wearing pink! Tim really smiled when Bethany walked into his room. Linda and Ken drove up for a visit and we will all be at Cheyenne tomorrow. What a great day—You lifted my heart especially when we were in the chapel this morning and I sang two songs for my family and of course, Joe took pictures! [John 14:1 (Jesus said) "Don't be troubled. You trust God, now trust Me." We really felt this as a question and have prayed many, many times—Lord, we trust You! We've had to and continue to verbally say what we have truly felt with that trust. Tim had a huge day with his family from Oklahoma, Arkansas, and Wyoming. What a big smile when Bethany surprised him when she walked in the room! Tim "skyped" with Cassady, Jessica, and other family members. Excited to see the Lord's healing and progress starting off week 14 (I think)! Have a Great Day worshipping with other believers tomorrow!!]

> **Cheryl Baber wrote, "My husband and I decided to take our two sons out of elementary school and spend Labor Day weekend in Denver. My mother and Shena decided to come with us, so we borrowed my in-laws' large conversion van for the trip. I was impressed with the facilities at Craig Hospital in Denver, but I wasn't prepared to see the dramatic changes in Tim since I had seen him lying serenely, albeit heavily sedated, in Cheyenne just days after the incident. My uncle,**

who lived nearby in Colorado and had seen him at the hospital several times over the summer, tried to warn my husband and I before we saw him, to no avail. Never one to let my emotions get away from me, I struggled not to cry, or to let him see me cry, when I saw him in his specialized wheel chair for the first time. He looked much thinner and his movements were that of people I had seen with cerebral palsy. He had difficulty holding his head up; his eyes were no longer aligned, his left hand was bent into an awkward position, and the sounds he was able to make were barely intelligible. It was heart-breaking. Over the course of the next twenty-four hours, we watched as Dixie and Howard cared for him, listened as they spoke of all the progress he had made, and learned how difficult the road ahead would be for them. He had come out of his coma and was slowly beginning to remember. We were there to hear him say, "What happened?" We saw him take his first few bites of pudding. We observed how the apparatus hanging near his bed allowed nurses and his parents help lift him and get him into his chair. I felt helpless, and I didn't really know what to do or say to make him or his parents feel better. I hoped my presence was enough. Shena knew, however. She had spent the better part of the preceding seven years in and out of hospitals. Ever outgoing, personable and compassionate, she talked to him, touched him, and spent time talking with nurses, visitors, family and friends. At one point, she even went searching for, and found, another patient who was somehow related to friends she knew back in Oklahoma. All of us there to see Tim had dinner together on Saturday night outside near the apartment where Dixie and Howard were staying near the hospital, and the next morning Dixie led us all to the chapel in the hospital for a time of prayer. Then a friend of hers who is a nurse came to stay with Tim while we all went to Cheyenne for the calf-roping event their friends had organized to benefit Tim and help Dixie and Howard with his medical expenses. That was the first time that Dixie and Howard had been away from Tim since the accident. The calf-roping was a much bigger deal than I expected. People in the rodeo world came from "near and far," and it was obvious that the organizers had put a lot of time and effort into it. There was a silent and public auction for various items people had created and/or donated. Dixie sang, and a cowboy presented the gospel. I thought her voice sounded better than I had ever heard it. The rodeo world is its own sub-culture or community into which Dixie and Howard fit. Howard had roped, and Tim's involvement had put them deep into the heart of it all. And now that community was giving back in a big way. It was comforting to me to know that they were so well-loved, and that my sister and her family would continue to be supported in the days ahead."

Dixie and Howard . . . I work with Candra at WHS. Candra had issued a charge to her English classes to look for the little things in life that might make their heart leap (from Emily Dickinson) referring to the change life's path can take in a blink of the eye, such as for Tim. I decided to expand on that a little during my time with my small group (it is called homeroom). I found a picture of Tim on the internet and shared the events of the day of his accident and summarized the events that have transpired since then. Like Candra, I want them to relish and treasure today, open their eyes to the blessings God has prepared just for them, and build on the present for a future that is all it can be. In short, thank you for doing this for me through your daily messages about Tim's progress and your

daily walk through the valley. God bless you and your family. (Laura Booher)

Sunday, Sept. 5—After asking Tim if he thought we could go to Cheyenne while Rhea and Emily stayed with him, we left for Cheyenne. Great friends, but I was still uneasy leaving Tim—not with them, but with the nursing situations. Thank You, Lord for allowing me to feel it, then feel myself give that uneasiness to You. They had a great day—watched a little movie, rode around Craig, etc. We arrive at the Tim Malm Benefit Roping in Cheyenne about 10:15. OVERWHELMED and so amazed with You, Lord! So many people and contestants in the indoor and outdoor arenas, so many tears and hugs, so many memories—it was almost hard to breathe at times! Had about seventy calf ropers, sixty barrel racers, thirty-five breakaway ropers, and so many goat tyers! One guy we don't even know had a huge heart that he paid the entry in Tim's name so they drew a name each of the ten rounds to rope in Tim's name! Thank You for getting me through the three songs I sang at the Rodeo Church that Jerry Martin spoke at and many, many attended. We pray that many decisions were made for You—Tim will not want this 'journey' to be in vain. Tim was glad to see us and they had a wonderful twelve-hour day! Our hearts are still numb, we can't get a grasp on Your amazing love and how unbelievable so many people we don't even know, and our many friends are and have been with us, the Albin Benefit, and this Benefit Roping . . . Thank You for allowing our Okie family and our Wyoming family to be such a huge part of today! [Ps 103: 1 "Bless the LORD, O my soul; And all that is within me, bless His Holy Name!!" There have been and are so many times that we find ourselves wordless (is that a word?) and after being beyond descriptionclosest we can come is totally numb from being emotionally overwhelmed with these past two weekends, Albin Day, the generosity of so many with cards, financial gifts, visits, food, acts of kindness, but above all the prayers, time, and love all ya'll have encouraged us with! May the Lord bless each and every one of you! Tim had a full day of visitors! With the graciousness and love of two friends, he was well taken care of for the full day! Howard and I went to some of the Tim Malm Benefit Roping at Cheyenne—for our church time I had the privilege to share three

Candra Marlett

songs that have been strength. We truly are are numb with our families, friends, communities, and God himself—you will never know what you all have done to show God's power and His love! Thank you!]

Monday, Sept. 6—We heard the Roping lasted into the early morning (2:00 a.m.!) Tim asked for the first time, "What happened to me?" Howard told him he had a fall with his steer roping horse and it hurt his brain, but that he was getting better every day!—knew that had to be hard on Howard, 'cause it was hard for me to hear and watch him tell Tim. Mom, Shena, and the Baber Bunch were in the room also and Howard handled that so well. They left to go back home to Oklahoma about 10:00—was hard hugging everyone, but especially Shena, knowing the physical strength it took for her to come. She looked really good and said she enjoyed the weekend—how she loved to watch Tim rope! Seeing her smile and hearing her say that familiar, "I'm fine" or "It'll be alright" encourages me. Thank You again for bringing them safely out here and I ask You to watch over them on their way home—I also continue to ask for her healing miracle in her battle against cancer. Heard off and on from Cheyenne with the Roping Benefit—a Texan won the calf roping! Debby came by and we all prayed together in Tim's room. It will be hard for all of us to have Bethany leave tomorrow. [Isaiah 12:2 "Behold, God is my salvation, I will trust and not be afraid: For the Lord God is my strength and song, And He has become my salvation." I want to share some of the words of one of the songs I sang at the church service at the Tim Malm Benefit Roping and want to thank the group (or person) Kutless who sings this popular song—*What Faith Can Do*

> "Everybody falls sometimes; Gotta find the strength to rise
> From the ashes and make a new beginning
> Anyone can feel the ache; You think it's more than you can take
> But you're stronger, stronger than you know . . .
> That's what faith can do"

Enough said! Tim had a good day with us and we are looking forward to a full week of progress!!]

Tuesday, Sept. 7—After breakfast, we all sat downstairs while we talked and said goodbyes—Bill (B) came by and took Bethany to the airport. She called back when she landed in Branson—thank You for her safety. Tim had a really good day in pool therapy! The warm water felt good, but sure didn't help my emotionally exhausting day! Pray for a full night's rest for all! [Isaiah 41:10 "Don't be afraid because I am with you. Don't be intimidated; I am your God. I will strengthen you." Pretty plain and simple! We are praying this verse for the upcoming days of progress now with Tim trying extremely hard to physically do things as he watches himself—for him to stand behind this verse and rely on His strength as he is progressing within God's timing, healing, and restoration of Tim. Tim had a very busy day with sessions and pool therapy—of which he had the best session in the pool today with really stretching legs, hips, and arms! We get to try a real (Malm Ranch) hamburger tomorrow in speech therapy—it won't be the size Tim normally would eat, but at least he'll enjoy the taste! Continue to pray for upcoming decisions that need to be made concerning medicine changes and possible procedures to help him relax certain muscle so he can really strengthen other muscles! Praise God and Thank Him "hugely" (probably not a word!) for the progress by His Healing Hand with Tim. Thank you Lord God Almighty and we give all praise and glory to You!!]

Wednesday, Sept. 8—Tim got to eat some Malm Ranch beef today! After eating his hamburger, he was cleared to have any and all foods! What a HUGE blessing—especially when they told us that Tim might go home with a feeding tube! Thank You, Lord! John (H) came by and brought fresh Colorado peaches of which I sliced one up and he ate it! Tim said "thank you" to John. Lord, how we prayed from when we had to watch those awful tapes that Tim would 'skip' over that bad language level—so far he hasn't said a bad word or had any kind of an outburst—that's all You! We told them we'd never heard him say a 'bad' word, they said to be prepared that it would probably happen—YEA, LORD! They changed out the regular bed for a 'Craig' bed—it is a huge (2+ twin sized) wall-padded big bed about a foot off the floor—reminds me of a huge playpen! Tim can now roll around, sleep catty-corner without his feet hitting the end, and we all can lay around him. He went to sleep comfortably and Debby came by and we prayed around the 'big' bed. [Ps 34:8 "O taste and see that the Lord is good; How blessed is the man who takes refuge in Him!" Timothy had a good night and awoke at 5:00 a.m. with some muscle spasms. We went over and massaged his legs and feet until about 7:30! He ate a good breakfast; then in Speech about 10:30 he had about five bites of the 'Malm burger'! He was cleared to the complete diet level—PTL! Hope we see weight gain this week! He had really good sessions. We look forward to his pool time tomorrow! Please pray for the Lord to hold us tight tomorrow—we have our monthly family/team meeting, another round of relaxation shots in his right arm, casting of the arm, plus decisions that will have to be made so pray for God's guidance! We still believe that at any moment God could totally heal and restore Tim, but waiting for and in His timing draws us to rely on Him, His word, and His guiding us with decisions. We thank God for the daily miracles we are seeing, so continue to thank Him with us! Goodnight!]

Thursday, Sept. 9—Tim had a great session in the pool-he was so relaxed and rarely had any spasms! PTL! We had our big 'team' meeting and discussed the baclofen pump—close to the end of our discussion, Howard asked him if he would do the pump with his own kids? Dr. W said he would with his own, but not with Tim; the room was very silent and we felt You had given us our answer! Thank You! What a relief—especially when almost everyone, including the doctor, was leaning opposite of what he replied. They are still shooting for October 1st to be the release date to go home. Went to the Spasticity Clinic for the phenol injections if Tim's right side (arm, shoulder, chest areas) Tim did so well with all the sites. We then went to the cast room to have his right arm casted as to help extend it. Tim went all day without any pain meds—what an answer, Lord! Thank You! [Ps 145:15 "The eyes of all look to Thee, And Thou dost give them their food in due time." This verse hit me today in two ways: first, His faithfulness—like the right amount of 'manna' for each day! Secondly, His timing—if we could only trust Him all the time. One of the many lessons we are learning is to stand with trust in His timeframe. This verse also shows the dependence on Him and today Tim had his first full day of all meals of real food! Plus, they took away the tube feeding! PTL! Please pray that the kitchen can keep up with his calories and appetite, and that Tim gains weight! He also swallowed all his medicines today so we are praying that his g-tube in his stomach will not be going home with us! He did amazingly well with the relaxation shots to his right arm and shoulder area and has a cast on it tonight—he sleeps well again tonight! He has not taken any pain meds all day—what a HUGE step at least for the day! He had his best session in the pool and will be able to get in next Tuesday. We will be standing tomorrow so pray for added strength for this cowboy to "Rise Up!" Please pray for emotional strength for Tim as he told his early morning tech, "I remember, I remember". When she asked about what—he said he remembered his accident! His speech therapist asked him more questions and he does remember to when he was in the tractor moving his chute from the calf roping side of the arena to the other side to rope the steers. Class was over so we will wait for another time to carry on . . . Goodnight!]

> **A posting repeated the fact that the Malms' faith encouraged them and built their faith. They commented on how this ordeal made them realize that every day "problems" are really nothing and how this journey is one that many were on with them**

Friday, Sept. 10—Again, a huge blessing to have a whole day without any pain meds! Blood pressure doing great—Big God, Big Blessings! Kim, Jim, & Jenny came by! Cassady staying the nights 'til Sunday. God, You are awesome and amazing—I thank You beyond words. [Ps 145:149 "Hear my voice . . . ; Revive me, O Lord, according to Thine ordinances." Tim had a good night and another day of no pain meds!! Please continue to pray for God to continue controlling any pain. He has also allowed some relaxation to the neck, arms, and legs whether by His Hand or His choice of technology, medicines, and/ or his big bed! We thank Him and praise Him for all His healing and blessings! He did a great job of standing with help from us and the therapists, but he really used his legs well. He is eating well and with a cast on the right arm, they may wait until Tuesday to get a true weight! Please continue to pray for physical, emotional, and mental strength as he continues to progress daily. We would really enjoy hearing him laugh, especially at his humor, and see his dimples when he smiles! Goodnight!]

Saturday, Sept 11—Cassady stayed in Tim's room and she woke up at 3:45 because they gave a pain med to Tim and he wanted more water. Cass asked, but they didn't want to give him any so she called us. Howard came over and Tim drank almost three little cups of water! Emily and Rhea surprised Tim with a Sonic Banana Cream Pie shake—we had to hide it in the family fridge at Craig 'til he could have it at 5:00! Deb came by with Scott and Cindy—WOW What a visit with them. Garrett is making some improvements! Tim is taking his pills "just fine"—sounds like Shena! Talking more and more! We are praying for BIG, BIGGER, and BIGGEST with Your miracles these next few weeks with standing/walking, strength, bathroom 'facilities', hand controls, G-tube out! Etc . . .

Sunday, Sept. 12—Psalm 145:9 "The Lord is good to all, And His mercies are over all His works." How true, how true—when you look you really see Him and His Hand! We see and thank God continually for His works—His healing and restoring and give all glory and praise to Him! PTL! Tim had a good day with visitors, five milkshakes, and a haircut from one of the nurses (he is also a licensed barber)! He has adjusted well with the cast and his forearm/hand has relaxed quite a bit so he can drop them out of that part of the cast to continue working them. Please pray for greater bend in the left knee and progress with working the arms, hands, and fingers this week! Some of you may wonder why Tim has physical issues when he didn't have any broken bones, bruises, cuts, etc.? It shows how awesome our Creator, Almighty God, is when He created the brain—the control center of the entire body! Tim had brain shearing where now those nerve endings are reconnecting and healing. Please continue to thank and ask God to continue to heal and restore all those nerve endings back to the way He created them. We are seeing His Hand and give Him all glory and praise! Have a great day tomorrow in your place of worship! Goodnight!

Monday, Sept. 13—Tim had a fairly good night! Went to an Orientation Class with this folder where you are supposed to remove a sticker from a page to finish the sentences for the date, day, etc info; Tim went and was mentally ahead of this game! He told us he didn't need that! Tim is eating everything (except green vegetables!) that we order! He'll have his weight back probably sooner than we want, but Lord, it is so great to see him eat 'normal' foods! [Exodus 16:4 "Then the Lord said to Moses, "I will rain down bread from heaven for you. The people are to go out each day and gather enough for that day." We have shared the last few days with several people about God's faithfulness and provision of that daily bread from Him! We've heard that story over and over, but when you live on that 'manna'—the story becomes even more real! God has been and is so faithful to give us the amount He knows we need, not the amount we think we need. Tim had a busy day with visitors, a massage, good food, some skype time, and telephone calls! We are excited to see how God is going to work this week with Tim—the pool time on Tues/Thurs and all the therapy! Please pray for Tim's 'daily bread' and therapy sessions to be super productive in his eyes! Tim mentioned during one of his visiting times today that "he wasn't expecting this summer to be like this" and I said we didn't either, but somehow, someway God knew all about this summer and we're getting better everyday—we just keep believing and trusting Him! Tim answered as usual, "Yep" We thank each one of you for walking with us during this unexpected summer.]

Tuesday, Sept. 14—Ps 5:3 "In the morning, O Lord, You hear my voice; in the morning I lay my requests before you and wait in expectation." God's humor is sometimes hidden in His Word and maybe it just hits me when we need laughter! The reason this verse hit me as humor is that Tim has asked every morning since he got this cast on when it was going to come off or he asks one of us to take it off! Well, he has made his requests known and he has waited. Tomorrow he gets at least this one off! Plus, he gets to go to the pool! He did 'just fine' (a southern phrase) in his sessions except we could not get him comfortable in the standing table today so we'll try something different the next time—he does show us great patience when we try all we know to do! They are lowering his blood pressure medicine and we no longer have to turn in what he ate for them to count calories—he was averaging around 4500 a day! Pray that all goes smoothly tomorrow with taking off the cast and movement with the arm, more strength, a relaxed time in the pool, and a great day of progress! Pray and Believe that we will walk out of here!!! Our dismissal date as an inpatient looks to be around the first of October so we are praying September is full of bigger and bigger miracles of God's hand of healing and restoration. [2 Tim 2:1 "You then, my son, be strong in the grace that is in Christ Jesus." This and the verse of His grace is sufficent . . . both remind us to stand in that grace which He strengthens us in all areas of our lives! This is a verse for Tim we pray over and with him for that strength in his therapies especially tomorrow when he will be standing. We're praying that God shows Himself and His mighty power to and through Tim as he and others watch the actions and reactions in his therapies. We saw great improvement with Tim's right arm when the cast was taken off today!! Pool time went "great" as Tim says and the day was ended with ribs and potatoes!! Continue to pray for more movement in the left knee and left arm. We also pray for emotional strength as Tim is remembering more about the accident. Our God is big—pray big! Goodnight! Tried that orientation class again, but Tim said his elbow was hurting, so we left—his speech therapist decided that he didn't need to go anymore! He has good memory and I didn't think it was challenging him. Tim had the cast cut off today and it went well. We see improvement in the arm. We thought we had another OT session, but even though it was on the schedule, we were told "no"—thank goodness we had pool time with Matt. Tim did well and the warm water feels great! We had speech outside! Another one of the times when our OT time is taken up with a 'class' that needs to be offered in addition, but not in place of—we had to go to a transportation class. Messed up the nurse's schedule with being gone, so needless to say, one of the "Mama Bear" frustration days! Lord, help me in all these areas . . . Our prayer with the transportation issues is for Tim to be able to travel sitting and 'fitting' in our vehicle!

He has grown a couple of inches and that left leg/knee doesn't bend very well right now, and we don't want to have to buy anything "handicap". We leave it in Your hands.]

Wednesday, September 15—We had our visit with Dr. B (neuropsychologist) and Tim did well. Being very honest in speech class when asked about what he had done for the day, Tim said "Absolutely nothing!" They filmed Tim eating/holding a fork, stretching his arm, etc. Frustration level is elevating and we are only in the middle of the week! The fill-in for our OT didn't have any plans so we had to 'wing it'. Thank goodness we had a good PT time with Tim on the bike and working with the big yellow ball standing up and sitting down. Thank You for the blessing of talking with Mom on the phone today-even though it's almost every day we talk, but I needed a little more outside 'air time'. [Prov 16:3 "Entrust your efforts to the Lord, and your plans will succeed." We knew Tim would be asked to try some new and different challenges today in physical therapy so, we told him to repeat his verse when things got hard. He did extremely well with the new standing positions and exercise machine, and yes, there were times we just repeated the verse over and over to get through some of it. He really enjoyed his supper tonight because they made his grill cheese swandwich the way Tim makes his! (Not on weight watchers!!) He is looking forward to the pool tomorrow! The brace on his arm will be replaced with another cast tomorrow for Fri-Mon. We are seeing the knee bend more today so keep praying we see more and more pain. No pain meds today!! The speech therapist asked Tim how long he had been at Craig? Tim answered, "Way too long!" Continue to pray that with Tim's questions come acceptance without understanding and complete confidence in knowing God has the 'big picture'. With the sovereignty of God, He asks us to accept, not understand. Thank you again for your continued prayer support. love, and encouragement. It is what we live on!]

Thursday, September 16—Worked on balance and posture strength. Without the lift, Howard was able to lift Tim's left leg up, around, and off while we held him on his right side! We then went to the parking lot where our Navigator was—we transferred Tim and he fits in the front passenger seat with the seat all the way back and tilted back!! What an answer to prayer, Lord! Not the usual way of getting in, but Howard and I together can steady Tim while he puts his right foot on the running board and pushes us on the count of 3! We're thankful, Lord! Had speech and then went to the pool! Today, they put on a full cast, straightening the arm even more—so glad they will do this on the weekend so Tim can have pool time on Tues and Thurs! Tim did well since he had to be off for food for four hours because of the HO med—we pray You will dissolve any, if any, in that left knee so it will bend and heal back to 'normal'. [Psalm 34:3-4 "Oh, magnify the Lord with me, and let us exalt His name together. I sought the Lord, and He heard me, and delivered me from all my fears." We sought the Lord with the issue of Tim being able to ride in our vehicle with his knee until God fully heals that to bend fully—and today we were able to get him in! It took some time and effort, but he/we did it!! Thank you Lord! He had a surprise awaiting him from the therapiststhey found they had a western saddle in storage and had it all ready for him. We got him in it and held him with both feet in the stirrups—he was able to stand with help on his right leg while we lifted the left leg off! The saddle was on a stand tall enough for him. It was a gracious and kind gesture even though it was 'hard' to watch and help this cowboy . . . we pray and believe that he will be in his own saddle soon. He had a great time in the pool—was able to stand against the wall with help. We are continuing to see more bend in the knee and relaxation with the leg muscles! He did get a full arm cast today and we pray for full extension when we take the cast off on Tuesday. They have taken off three medicines and added a little more to one so pray for all the changes. We were told they are considering taking out the g-tube (stomach) since he has been eating on a full diet for almost two weeks and swallowing all medicines be great! Continue to pray for strength—we are believing that we will walk out of here! Have a great night!]

Friday, September 17—Prov 16:9 "The mind of man plans his ways, but the Lord directs his steps." There are number of words in this verse, but what it speaks to us today is of the trust in the faithfulness of God for that direction driving home the point for us to be walking with Him so our mind is of His direction! Our plans should align and meet with God's plans—where we can go wrong is trying to justify or make His direction fit into our plans. Tim had a very good day. Plenty of food helps keep him fueled for his therapies. He rode on the recumbent bike and got some really good bending movement out of his left knee!! We also did another vehicle transfer and were cleared to go on a fifteen-twenty minute drive on Sat/Sun—if the parents have the energy!! He slept very well last night and continue to pray for that, please. We are excited to watch next week for God's healing of Tim's muscles for he is sitting better and hoping for more standing time and better balance. He is fully aware of the college rodeo fall season . . . and after hearing about the calves last week he said, "I should've been there!" We just say, "God willing" you'll be back! We thank all ya'll for the prayer support and ask for specifically that you ask God to allow Tim to walk out of here! Have a great weekend!

Saturday, September 18—Tim started hollering about 5:00 a.m. after eating eight applesauces and popsicles during the night! We have told them to call us and we're here in five minutes if Tim is not sleeping well. Howard went over and brought him back over to the apartment for Tim to greet me with a "Good Morning, Mom" about 6:00! Psalms 71:5,8 "For You are my hope, O Lord God; You are my trust from my youth. Let my mouth be filled with Your praise and with Your glory all the day." One of the books we draw from also had the following with this verse—Your faith in Christ is bread for daily use, not dessert for special occasions! Oh, how we have lived on that 'daily bread' and have so appreciated all the verses and encouraging words you have shared with us! We've helped each other to grow in this journey and all praise and glory go to God! [He had a pretty restless day, but had about a dozen visitors through the day that helped move his day along. We left around 10:00 and he was asleep so we pray for a restful night! (for everyone). We think the day might have had something with all the therapy on Thur. and Fri.—we will stretch and exercise him some tomorrow! We pray each one of you enjoy your worship tomorrow and will share what God lays on your heart with us! Like Tim answered yesterday when I said, "God is good" and he said "All the time"! We then say "And all the time . . . God is good!" Goodnight!]

> **One posted and reminded the Malms that when they get discouraged they should look back at the journey through the postings and see how far they have come.**
>
> **Another put into words some of my thoughts by saying what a really good book the daily postings are—so good that they hate to put it down. They can't wait until the next day to see Tim's progress. Thanks to God there are so many pages and that the story keeps getting better. Couldn't have said it better myself.**

Sunday, September 19—We tell people that we truly live on their prayers—that's the 'food and fuel' when you are emotionally wore out! Praying BIG (Believe In God) for Tim to walk out of here, ride comfortably in the navigator, and only need a simple wheelchair to get around 'til he's stronger! Tim's friend, Lee, called on the phone—good to see him using the phone! [2 Cor 5:7 "We live by faith, not by sight." Sight can encourage our faith, but it does not determine our faith! Faith has its own eyesight that's why we have the choice and need to train our eyes to see as God sees. (*Father's Eyes* by Amy Grant.) Tim rested well last night, but his heart rate has been up a bit and has made him rather tired today. He was comfortable in a regular lounger chair and ate his meals today in it—wonder what the therapists would think if Tim rolled in the gym in that instead of his wheelchair?? We are excited to stand more this week and Tim is saying he wants to stand! Please pray that God grants him extra strength and balance to stand this week! In our church service we looked at Romans 5:1 . . . suffering-perseverance-character-hope. Lord, how we thank you for that development even when we are at different and/or combinations of those stages! Hope you had a wonderful day in God's house with other believers! Goodnight!]

Monday, September 20—1 Peter 4:16 "Yet if anyone suffers as a Christian, let him not be ashamed, but glorify God in this matter." When you read this verse, you might have to check the reference and writer—you know Peter . . . the one ashamed to even be recognized as 'one of them' or that he knew Jesus!? The little comment that went along with this reading said to stub your toe doesn't mean you are walking in the wrong direction. God doesn't promise a path without trouble—He promises a journey worth the trouble. We add in that not only does He promise to be on the path/journey (whether ahead of us leading or beside us walking, but we know He sometimes just picks us up and carries us!! This has been and is our plea—that God would be and will be glorified through this journey!!! Tim answered mult/div problems in one of his morning therapies. He pushed his knee to bend further because we said to continue to push a little more everyday and God would give him that strength! For those of you that know Tim, his giving a little more (shooting more freethrows, tying more calves, roping the dummy more minutes, etc.) is part of his personality! He is excited to have this full cast off tomorrow to not only be able to go to pool therapy, but maybe not have to have another one—they will work through Tues & Wed and decide on Thurs. Keep praying big for continued strength, balance, control, movement, etc. God is big and we continue to bring before Him big requests, but above all—big praise and thanks!!

Tuesday, September 21—In speech, Tim told his therapist all about how the cow dogs work! They took off this full cast then went right to the pool. Tim had an extra fifteen minutes working with Matt. I've noticed a difference when I'm in the pool with Tim helping hold him however the therapists tell me that he is more relaxed and improving with standing in the water. Denise (PT) worked with Tim standing with the ball in front on his chest. Kim came at PT time and got to help us with Tim. Amy (OT) fiddled with a brace for Tim's hand—praying for more function and activity with that left hand/arm. When we pray at night over Tim's bed, he now will say "amen" at times agreeing with us and/or in closing. [Isaiah 41:10 "Fear not, for I am with you; be not dismayed, for I am your God, I will strengthen you, yes, I will help you,

I will uphold you with My righteous right hand" What a verse just to lay back and feel God's arms around you!! The tidbit that came along with this in our devotional makes you sit up and chew on it—'Pray as you ought, and you will live as you pray! Praying, along with all the prayer support from all of you and the many, many others is and has been our 'daily bread'. The Bread of Life has been so faithful every minute along the way sustaining and as we totally trust and believe in Him. He was wide awake after his night meds last night so we stayed up 'til midnight read the Bible, sang songs (Tim even sang several of the words to the songs!), listened to music, watched tv, and talked. One started with him telling us that he loved both of us So much! We told him that we loved him so, so much, but what was so amazing was that God loves Tim and us more than we love each other—what a God!! Pray for Tim's left elbow to relax and let him move it, for more bend in that knee, and strength for tomorrow! He had x-rays on the left elbow, hip, and knee to check up on those areas, plus a test for any bladder infection so we ask for God's healing in those areas as well as total healing and restoration of Tim for God's glory! (Also pray we have a FULL night's rest!]

Wednesday, September 22—Very little PT because once again it was one of those times that should not have taken up our PT time, but schedule in as another time . . . we had to 'try' out this new take-home wheelchair with all the head rest, leg brace, etc attachments. Know this had to be discouraging to Tim. Along with all the adjusting, he had a different speech therapist trying to work with him . . . not good timing at all. I went to the Mother's Support Group and was able to let off some of my frustrations along with the other caregivers (mothers and wives). We had a new night nurse and they tried the other pill that kept him awake for an hour so we didn't leave until about 11ish! I called back later and found out there was a new night nurse—26 nurses total in this 'team' approach! God, we thank You for protecting Tim through all the nurse changes—we respect them and their very hard job, but you have to stay on top of everything and everyone so even the slightest medical mishap might not happen. I'm probably way beyond protective and I've told most of them that I'm not 'questioning' them, but with my experience with my grandmother and my daddy, I know and have seen medical mishaps. I try to balance trust in You throughout the day and night, but I also believe You expect us to be good stewards and parents to stay alert and on top of things during our stay here. ["Therefore, having been justified by faith, we have peace with God through our Lord Jesus Christ, through whom also we have access by faith into His grace in which we stand, and rejoice in hope of the glory of God." Romans 5:1-2 What a verse to stand on and state when people ask how we get through this journey? Faith gives you peace for the past, grace for the present, and hope for the future—thishope isn't the 'wishy' hope, but the excited, anxious awaiting and assurance that only He gives and is! Tim had a good session in his therapies and is looking forward to the pool tomorrow morning! He is also scheduled to have the stomach tube removed tomorrow. Continue to pray for God to move, correct, bend, heal, restore, but above all be glorified and magnified as only He is worthy. Goodnight!]

Thursday, September 23—Started with a pool session—not Tim's best, but Matt did some good stretching with him. We had busy and challenging times in PT and OT! So glad to have one of our 'team' nurses back from her three week hiking adventure! She was so excited to see Tim's progress. Prayed with Debby, but Tim still stayed awake for a while—I layed beside him and tried to sing him to sleep. I would fall asleep and he would say "sing some more, Mom". [John 15:13 "No one has greater love than this, to lay down one's life for one's friends." This verse brings me again back to the Cross—God's great love for me and each one of you. I have often said that I might give my life for someone, but as a parent, to ask me to give my child's life for someone's hard for me to even think about. During a recent discussion, I stated that even with all Tim has gone through, he would choose himself instead of his sisters, family, cousins, and many of his friends to ever walk this journey. This journey is incomparable to the pain and agony of the Cross . . . but it gives a glimpse of God's great love! Tim had a good pool therapy and speech time. They then took out his stomach tube!!! He had one relaxation shot in his left bicep and then during physical therapy, he was put on the saddle and it drew a crowd and there were tears in the eyes of nurses, techs, and others in the gym! He was very comfortable and more relaxed even though he still needed some balancing and help. Pray for continued progressive therapies tomorrow and a restful night! Keep praying and believing for total healing and restoration!]

Friday, September 24—PT time had us in the lounge area trying to transfer Tim from his chair to the floor and back. Again, thank You for our strong backs, but especially for Howard—his hip needs surgery and everyone asks him about it. So far, You have kept him from having pain with it! Tim is bigger and taller than either one of us and he is catching up with his weight. We will weigh again tomorrow! I think it was 160 last time? Getting closer to our release date! [2 Tim 1:12 "I know whom I have believed and am convinced that He is able to guard what I have entrusted to Him for that day." (NIV version) I have also been reading through an old hymnal and the song from this verse always gives strength and emotional relief knowing and reminding us that He will "keep that which I've (we've) committed". This also reminds us that during our wedding we also made home vows and committed our home and children to Him. The song starts off every verse with "I know not . . . . why, how, what, when"—we don't know, but we do know who we have believed in and continue to believe in. Tim had a busy day learning with us how to get down to the floor and back up in his chair! He stood for ten minutes against a new standing frame!! He also had a wrist/hand cast put on his left hand until Tuesday to help relax those fingers. Pray he understands the worth of the cast and time! Continue to pray for urine test results and restful nights! It was special tonight to hear Tim pray asking, "Lord, help me" and to know he places his trust and confidence in Him. Weight will be taken in the morning so, we hope for a gain! Also pray for us as we take Tim for a couple of outings in our vehicle and that all goes smoothly! Thank you again for the prayer support!]

Saturday, September 25—Heb 10:35-36 'So don't lose your confidence. It will bring you a great reward.' You need endurance so that after you have done what God wants you to do, you can receive what He has promised. This is a 'breather' verse that encourages us with that endurance—leaning on Him and His promises. Tim had many visitors today and we see all his visits as 'rewards' from those who haven't lost confidence or endurance in God and with/for us in this journey. That goes as our thanks to all of you and the many others who have sent cards, visited, called, emailed, wrote on caring bridge, attended, donated, bought, etc, but your confidence in God and your endurance with prayer has also been our encouragement, we say thanks! Goodnight and have a great day in your worship time tomorrow!

Sunday, September 26—Howard and I went to church while the girls stayed with Tim. Afterwards, we took Tim and the girls in our navigator to Goodtimes for an ice cream sundae and a Walmart trip. The absolute best jelly doughnuts were brought all the way from Albin by our friends, Dwayne and Chaurisse—plus, she gave Tim a massage! No telling the miles they have driven Albin-Denver! God, we want a step . . . but we trust in Your timing! [John 15:7-8 "If you remain in Me and My words remain in you. ask whatever you wish, and it will be given you. This is to my Father's glory, that you bear much fruit, showing yourselves to be my disciples." Some devotional thoughts from Joni Eareckson Tada ask a question and really gives a good picture of this verse. The question is have we really grasped the link between getting our prayers answered and steeping our minds in Christ's words? Her picture was the longer the tea bag sits in the cup, the stronger the tea. More time in the Word—the stronger our walk and our prayer life. This journey has been and is a prayer walk with the Word keeping us fueled for the days and resting in the nights! We are so thankful for the many Sunday schools, vacation Bible schools, Bible studies, youth group meetings, boys club, acteens, Wednesday night prayer meetings, revivals, etc. that the word was presented, taught, memorized, and hidden in our hearts! PTL!! We are excited for this week—we are so praying for one step—please pray with us for that. Hope you enjoyed your special time in worship today! Goodnight!]

Monday, September 27—What a night—Tim couldn't get his left leg and arm comfortable, so we stayed 'til midnight. They called us back about 2:30 a.m. and I came over and worked with massaging, singing, reading, talking 'til about 3:20 when he finally went asleep! Not too long ago, we were told that there was a nurse who seeing Tim's room with the Bible verses, crosses, Bible, and hearing the music we would leave on in his room, would sometimes come during the night and pray/read verses to Tim while he slept. She was always gone by the time we would get over, was on her day off, or gone on vacation. I thought this might be a night I would meet her, but not. Thank You God, for that angel! Tim was too sleepy for speech, and OT had a fill-in. They cut Tim's cast off! Went to the pool and he did great! In the afternoon, he got to sit on the saddle again, and he's looking better and better, but it is still really hard for me to see him in a saddle like this when he was such a gifted horseman and loved riding his horses not only for roping, but ranchwork. Lord, please let him ride and rope again. His doctor filmed him on the saddled 'rolling horse'. Tim almost stood up with the help of therapists and a grocery cart!! Rhea came and sat with Tim while we took his wheelchair to the Navigator to see how it would fit. Shallini and Avy said goodbye with laughter and tears! We prayed for Shena's meeting with her oncologist today and waited all day for any report—Cheryl called and said the cancer had spread to several places, not the report we had hoped for. We're praying for decisions they need to make. We know You cleared her before, and we sure would like to have some more time with her here. You're a big God and this cancer is not too big for You. Thank You for the time You allow Mom and Shena to be together. She is such an inspiration to her community, church, school, family, friends, especially Tim—thanks for making us sisters! We pray BIG for her and Tim.

Tuesday, September 28—Ps 56: 11, 13 "In God I have put my trust; I will not be afraid. Have you not kept my feet from falling, that I may walk before God in the light of the living?" Tim had a very good day in the pool with standing and stretching . . . amazing! It always reminds me how amazing the Living Water is when it flows through our minds, hearts, and bodies. Tim also spent another session in the saddle and he has a little more balance and strength which each time. He also did some more standing today!! (with help) He is off his shot for blood thinner—one to mark off the med sheet! PTL!! Tim was really stretched yesterday for the measurements they took and we're not sure if that is what affected his sleep last night or what—A saying that came in a devotional today. You won't know the peace of God until you know the God of peace. So true and we are so thankful we all know the God of peace and can lean on Him, as we have, with supplying that daily!! Thank you, God! Goodnight!

Wednesday, September 29—Isaiah 55:8-9 "For my thoughts are not your thoughts, neither are your ways my ways," declares the Lord. "As the heavens are higher than the earth, so are my ways higher than your ways and my thoughts than your thoughts," declares the Lord. Ever wonder why He said this verse back to back? Probably because it takes many of us more than once to get the message, plus He added a word picture (heavens) to emphasize it even more. This speaks of His Sovereignty where He states HIS thoughts. He doesn't state any time table that we might understand or if we will even understand any of it . . . He just states the truth and we accept it because we have accepted Him and His Sovereignty. There are so many situations in the Bible where questions were asked—we just can't ever let it become doubt. Tim had good sessions in his therapies in his bed on his side then was helped onto his stomach and elbows to start learning to 'army crawl'. He is looking forward to the pool tomorrow. We had our last family/team meeting with the doctor, nurses, therapists, etc. as we will be leaving Craig in a few days!! Continue to pray for full healing and restoration, and especially in his left leg and elbow. Pray as we prepare for our next chapter in the journey of going home!! PRAY and BELIEVE!!

> **Jeff Chapman, PRCA Calf Roper, NFR Qualifier, said, "Tim always looked at the glass half full instead of half empty, but it is easy to do that when everything is going good. When I heard about Tim's steer roping accident I was heartbroken knowing Tim had a long road ahead of him. I was worried that his positive spirit would be crushed. Man was I wrong. I found out just what kind of man Tim Malm is. He is in short**

> one of the most amazing people I've ever known or heard about."
>
> Tim's coach was amazed by the Malm's strength and said, "Every time I left Craig hospital I cried like a baby. I am glad it is downhill to that parking lot, because I don't know if I would have had the physical strength to make it back to my truck, but during this whole time, I never remember Howard or Dixie not being at Tim's side."

Thursday, September 30—Schedule still crammed a bit trying to get in so much this last week! I have spent time over at the apartment and in Tim's room packing up everything while Howard stays with Tim, feeding him, doing paperwork, etc. Pool time was his best ever, will miss that the most just because he does so well in the water. We will be able to use our little community center pool when we get home! Jack (T) stopped by on his way with the steer roping horse that Tim had the accident on and he will be taking it to another steer roper. A good friend taking a good horse to a good home. Kim (T) stopped by—such a good friend through this journey with us. [In the margin of one of my Bibles, Dr. John Piper gives a viewpoint on why in Scripture that God is described as grieving over affliction, and in other verses it doesn't seem to bother Him? God has the capacity to look at the world through two lenses, one narrow and one wide-angled. When looking at a painful event through the narrow lens, He sees the tragedy for what it is in itself, and He is deeply grieved. Looking at the same event through the wide-angle lens, He sees the tragedy in relation to everything leading up to it, as well as everything flowing from it. The connections form a mosaic stretching into eternity. Joni Erickson Tada concludes that one day you too will put on that wide-angled lens and see a beautiful mosaic. We write tonight concluding our stay here at Craig with Tim's favorite verse . . . Phil 4:13 "I can do all things through Christ who strengthens me." So with that, we thank God for the narrow lens which we have learned and grown through, and continue to pray for daily strength to look through the wide-angle lens with His eyes. Tim had a full day with all the therapies including a full hour in the pool where the therapist was able to bend the left knee more than any other session!! Tim has told everyone he is so excited to go home! We thank each one of you for walking with us through this part of the journey and ask for your continued prayers as we turn to a new 'chapter'. We will try to stay updated on Caringbridge, but maybe on a weekly basis—I'm hoping on Sunday night. Goodnight]

Martha, Tim's aunt, commented about his grip. "One of the things I remember most about Tim's time at Craig was sitting beside him letting him hold onto my hand and talking to him while he was still in the coma. I had to be careful because as long as I kept my hand really still he would hold it loosely, but the minute I moved it, he would tighten his grip so much I could hardly stand it. I could coax him into loosening his grip by begging him not to hold on so tight and promising him I wasn't leaving. Whenever I think of how tightly Tim held onto my hand, I am reminded of how tightly God hangs onto His children no matter what happens in this life. While I was always thankful when Tim would finally loosen his grip a bit, I am thankful God doesn't!"

Tim made great strides during his time at Craig. You could already tell that "No, you will not be able to do that" was not going to be a part of Tim's vocabulary. He showed them what a determined fighter he is. There was no doubt in anyone's mind who knows the Malms that they all will continue to fight as they go home to Albin.

Thoughts from physical therapist Jason Kamm: "I have some patients who help me understand what really matters in life. Tim Malm is one such person. Tim shows me and those around him the definition of positivity. His rodeo accident was a life changing event that caused his body great trauma. It is a struggle for Tim to get out of bed in the morning, stand up from a chair, or even brush his teeth. Yet, these things do not discourage him; they motivate him. The physical struggles that Tim faces each day would break many people but not Tim. He faces those struggles and does so with a terrific attitude. Each day when I see Tim for his therapy, he always greets me with a smile and an update on the number of Facebook friends that he has. No matter what he is asked to do or how challenging an activity may be for him during therapy, he faces it head on and with a positive attitude. Not once is Tim in a bad mood or depressed, rather, he smiles and says "Let's do it!" He teaches me the value of positivity and the importance of attitude when confronting the challenges that life has in store for all of us. Time would not be able to have his amazing attitude without his firm faith in God. I have seen him abandon his wants and desires and place his life and illness in God's hands. Tim allows God to work in his life and in the lives of others by speaking at cowboy church services and by his amazing witness to the faith. He brings positivity, determination, hard work, and reliance on God to everyone that he meets. I think of Tim when I hear the famous quotation from Saint Francis of Assisi, "Preach the gospel at all times, and if necessary, use words. "Tim's faith in God is powerful and real. It helps him in his daily struggles and sustains him. Tim's faith teaches me the value and necessity of keeping God in the center of my life."

I truly wished I could have included all the postings from the internet. While writing the book, I went back to day one and read them all again. I told Dixie and her family to go back and read them all with Tim so he would know how many people were praying for him and concerned about him. Like I said earlier, they all had similar threads. They all talked about how "Tim's Story" was impacting their daily life and how their faith had grown from watching the Malm's faith. I encourage the readers of this book to go back to those postings on Facebook and Caringbridge as well.

On October 1, Tim was released to go back to his home in Albin to continue his recovery there. He would have many people involved in this process which would help Dixie and Howard during this time. His family and community in Albin would also play a huge role in his recovery. Even though the daily posting of prayer support and words of encouragement on Caringbridge would slow down, the Malm's knew the thoughts and prayers of thousands of people followed them home. They continued to cherish all the thoughts and prayers posted there from time to time.

2009

Malms 2009

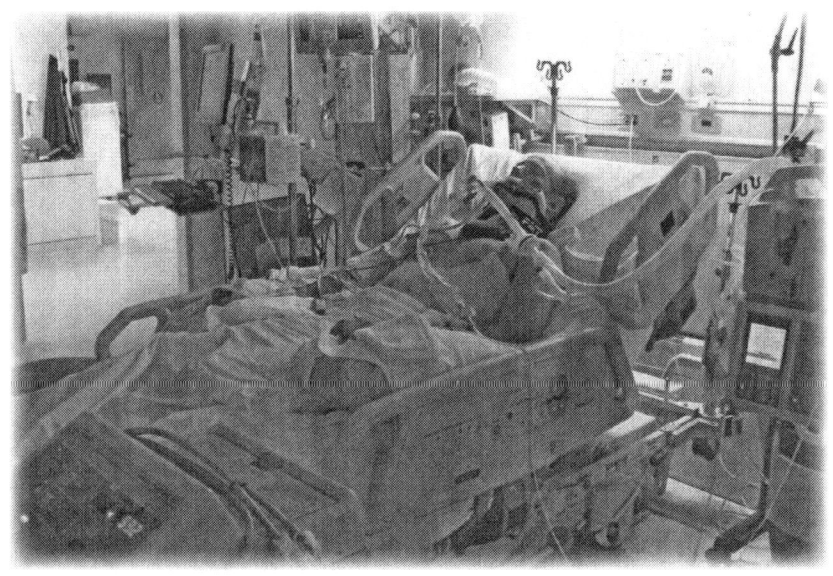

Cheyenne ICU June 2010

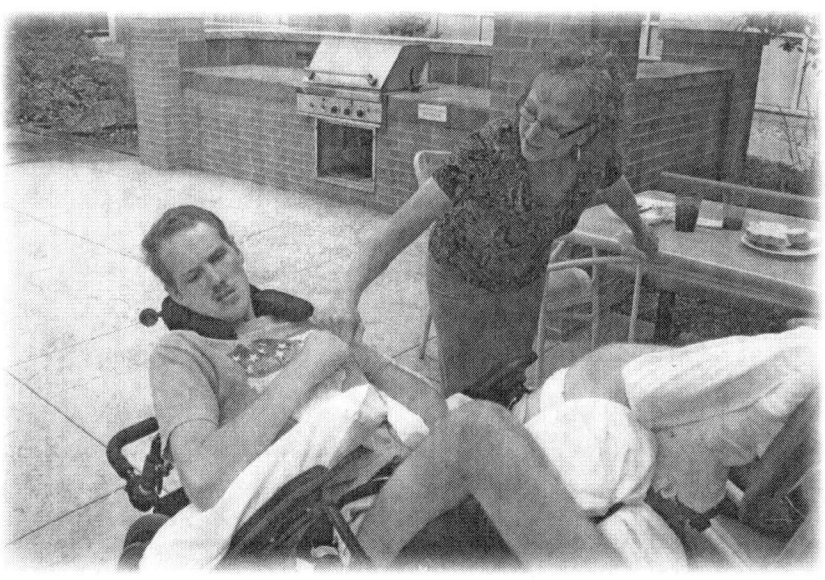

Summer 2010 Shena and Tim at Craig in Denver

Tim 2009

Tim with sisters Jessica, Beth, and Cassady on Christmas 2011

Tim's blue truck with Bethany

Malm family 2012

Chapter Five

Home in Albin (2010)

Carl and Nancy Brown, friends of the Malms wrote: "This accident will give Tim more opportunities to witness for the gospel than winning the world ten times. Tim has and will continue to affect all of us who have had the privilege to know and appreciate him."

Friday, October 1, 2010—The BIG day going home! Unbelievable—but we are ready for this next 'chapter'—Tim has told everyone that he is excited to go home! Lots of hugs and tears, lots of goals for when we come back in January for an evaluation. Tim did well all morning while we loaded Bill's suburban and our navigator. Finally after signing the last paper, we left Craig Rehab Hospital about 1:45. Tim told Howard after he finished his lunch "let's get the heck out of Dodge!" Many hugs and many tears later, we finally were discharged. We saw our first fly today and I never thought about us missing the summer with the flies! We told several that even manure will smell great—so hopefully we will be out to the ranch with the cattle tomorrow! Pray for Tim's emotional processes—he has asked more about the accident and even asked Howard today as we were leaving when he might rope again? For me, some things are best when only the Lord knows!—but it's great to have goals for motivation! He was weighed before we left and gained another two pounds, so he's gained back ten of the forty he's lost—we also told him one, maybe two milkshakes a day would be his limit here so we gain weight as we gain strength. Speaking of that, we did stop for a milkshake on the way home. Funny story about the 'bad' chocolate milk—Howard had taken all the "Malm" products out of the family fridge at Craig and put in our little ice chest for the trip home. Whenever we couldn't understand Tim, we would have him spell the word. After taking a drink from the carton, he spelled "e-x-p-i-r-e-d". He had me taste it (I don't like chocolate milk anyway) and I spit it out my window—couldn't believe Tim had swallowed it! Tim later asked if I had the accident on video? Saying yes, he then asked Howard if they could watch it of which they did (I never watched it-it will always be in my mind) . . . Tim didn't say much. Got home around 6:00; Tim traveled fine. It's so hard to believe we are home . . . when you found yourself calling the hospital and/or the housing apartment home for the last four months! I hope all ya'll give thanks tonight for the home that you have and continue to hold Tim in your prayers. We are scheduled to go back in January to Craig—with many goals to strive for between now and then! We pray that the Great Physician was honored and many were brought closer to Him while we were there. This is all about Him—praise Your Holy Name! So good to be home even though there's lots and lots to catch up on and rearrange for this different 'season' of our life. I'm excited to see how You will use these surroundings and environment for Tim's progress. Howard and I slept out in the living room with Tim on a twin bed we put out beside the couch. Like in the words of my daddy and Shena—"It'll be alright." Psalms 5:11 "But let all who take refuge in You be glad; let them ever sing for joy. Spread your protection over them, that those who love Your name may rejoice in You!" How we thanked the Lord for His protection today and we take refuge in Him as we begin 'chapter 2' at home here in Albin, Wyoming, (or as we say-Albin, America)!

Sunday, October 3—3 John 1:4 "I have no greater joy than this, to hear of my children walking in the truth." Some words from *Find Your Wings* by Mark Harris speaks of this:

> "It's only for a moment you are mine to hold
> The plans that Heaven has for you will all too soon unfold

Candra Marlett

> So many different prayers I'll pray for all that you might do
> But most of all I'll want to know you're walking in the truth"

Now talk about only in God's timing. Looking back at my 2009 calendar, I sang this three times. Recalling the words from the song, there were many memories (rodeos, State Champion Calf Roper, National Reserve Champion Calf Roper, College rodeos, etc.) and talking of the plans will all too soon unfold . . . but the strength of the whole journey has been in knowing that Tim knows the Lord and has a personal relationship with Him and that he is 'walking' in the truth. Our prayer from the beginning is that many, especially Tim's friends will have begun their walk or will begin their walk soon, plus let Tim know when they see him.

Tim came home with all his mental ability; it was his physical ability that needed the most therapy. We prayed for his personality and humor to be restored and God totally brought that back. How we so enjoy seeing his smile and hearing his laugh. Tim so enjoys attending our church every Sunday. It's a sight seeing he and Howard wheeling up our only paved street (Hwy 216 is our main street) especially in the snow. Tim has had much patience with his parents these past two days . . . has slept fairly well and is ready to begin therapies to so he can get back to work! We took him to see his horses then to our outside working chutes to watch the family work some calves, hear the calves, smell the familiar smells, and he did well. He had two steaks at noon! We ask you continue to pray for all the planning with the therapists this week along with all the adjustments of home. It is really good to be home! Thank you again for your encouragement and prayers. Until next Sunday.

Week of October 4-10, 2010—Our first week home filled with all the 'newness' of trying to get some routine in a home and family that has never known routine! We will be working with a Wyoming home health care service of which they will be building a ramp off our front porch within the next few days/weeks, so now we have help lifting him off the porch or we may try some of our four-wheeler long ramps that we have! We met our in-home therapists from a company in Cheyenne and Howard was here for their evaluation. A couple of in-state brain-injury program coordinators have visited with their programs for Tim and us while we are in rehab here at home—seem confusing with all the information so we pray for guidance with all this! Tim used the word "useless"—hard to hear him say that, but in reality, that is a picture of Tim that he has always had if he is not totally independent and taking on whatever task it is. We pray You will show him Your usefulness with him on this 'journey' for You, Your Kingdom, our family, his friends, etc. We pray against negative thoughts or depression in this house or in Tim's room, mind, ears, or eyes! We thank You for Your strength for us. Howard had to legally get guardianship of Timothy—a situation you never think about but because of his age he will need to sign papers and all that business 'stuff'. When they asked us some of those hard life questions concerning health care (level of life)/nursing care facility/DNR & death (organ, brain activity) it was super hard because we had never thought about those. We have to ask our kids some of those questions sometime and get it written down in the case they aren't able to make those decisions. We washed Tim (kinda a 'spit bath' during the week, but we took him to our community center to use the showers up there since we don't have a bathroom that will work with his shower chair yet. He did great in and out of the vehicle and shower—thank You! Tim had an excellent Phy & Occ therapy session on Friday!! The two guys who work with him really pushed Tim and he was able to bend that left knee the most we had seen! He was able to stand more on his left leg and his upper body balance is improving!! Left arm is bending more and more!! Speech Therapy is supposed to start this week—we'll see how that goes!!

We celebrated Grandpa's birthday which we thank You again for the relationship that he and Tim have—more special than most. It has reminded me a lot of Daddy's life and his influence not only with me, but my kids. Makes me so thankful for the strength You have given Mom, especially with this 'journey' we are now on. The verse Psalm 89:1—"I will sing of the Lord's great love forever; with my mouth I will make your faithfulness known through all generations" came to mind. I sing a lot while working cattle because it's loud enough no one hears you! As I watched Tim sitting and 'waiting on the Lord' as He heals and restores him, I continually praise Him for His faithfulness. Tim was able to go to church today!! So good to be back with our church family and in our community-as the saying goes, 'there's no place like home!' Howard pushed Tim down to Main Street and then to our church. We had about four men carry Tim in his chair up the stairs (he doesn't fit in our little elevator with the leg extension on his chair) He shook hands with everyone and knew everyone's name—it was an emotional day for everyone. We love and are so thankful for our home church, their prayers, encouragement, and support. What a week! Tim is sleeping well and we have not had any pain medications all week!! We continue to ask for prayer over that left side for it's movement, Tim's continued patience and humor with us, and for him to stand this month on his own!!! Big prayer—Big God!! I'm so thankful for the friendship and father/son bond they have with each other—I truly hope this journey has brought several of you father (parents) and son (children) closer to each other and to our Heavenly Father. Also, please pray for this weekend—Tim has stated that he wants to go to the college rodeo at Cheyenne! Have a great week and God Bless ya'll.

Week of October 11-17, 2010—Our speech therapist started this week—Lord, how I pray for You to bring back Tim's real voice. We will have to look and listen to some family movies so I can remember how it sounds. I can't believe I can't remember how he used to sound—I can remember his laugh. The staff at Craig told us that Tim would probably sleep a lot! He never slept or took very many naps when he was little, so why should it be any different? He finally took a nap and we layed down with him—first time we all took a nap since we have been home! Proverbs 16:9 "A man's heart plans his ways, but the Lord directs his steps." This verse hit me because we, along with Tim, have to make plans (sometimes 'plans of attack') for the day or activity because they sometimes change within the hour! We did fulfill one of Tim's plans to get on a four-wheeler this week—Howard behind him with Andy driving and yes, they went real slow and just made a big circle where we work cattle. I'm sure Craig would not want to know that! Cipale's brought over real Italian lasagna—Tim really enjoyed it! Tim improving every day and how we continue to ask for more movement with his left side, overall strength, strong eye movement & alignment! How we praise You for his mental state, laughter, smile, dimples!!! We prayed for all that—You are amazing and so faithful! Coach Cullen came for about an hour visit—such a special friendship and Tim really enjoyed him coming all this way! The highlight of the week was hearing Tim tell everyone, "I walked" when asked what he did in therapy! With both therapists on his sides, Howard behind him holding hips correctly, and me standing on a bench high enough to hold Tim's head up—WE walked! Tim was able to shift his weight to his left leg long enough to swing his right leg forward and put weight to the right leg and the therapist on that side would move his left leg forward for the next step. He walked three or four steps forward and backward for each time he stood up. It was our first rodeo outing as we went to the LCCC College Rodeo in Cheyenne! There were so many people and college kids who talked, hugged, cried, laughed, etc, with all of us throughout the morning slack. It was a very good, but extremely hard to be in that arena when I'd seen him rope there so many times—especially the great run he had last year at this rodeo! It was great to see so many of you and for all the encouragement you have been and are to us!! The part of the verse about plans and direction of steps—well, Tim sure is praying and hoping those plans and steps come together and he is there next year!?! Only in God's plans and timing, but it's great to dream and have goals! Some of our Colorado friends (Tallents and a cousin) came home after the rodeo and had a fun time! It was so good to see the patches the NJC rodeo team wore on their jackets with a cross, Tim's name, and his verse-Phil 4:13 on their vests! PRESS ON!!! Had a great service in our home church—our church surprised us with giving us a 'love check'!—brought tears to us both! Tyner's came out with Jen's famous Chocolate Cake-Tim loved it! They had the Tim Malm Roping Benefit poster framed and gave it to Tim—what friends! Thank You for another week—we have felt the prayers and have seen Your healing hand.

Week of October 18-23, 2010—Tim and the girls wished us "Happy Anniversary". The Petersons brought over a 'catered' anniversary dinner and ate with us. It is our 24th anniversary, but it really hadn't even crossed my mind with the reality of being home with Tim, the girls, the visitors, the therapists. So thankful they and all the prayers of the many praying for us keep me going. Just turned our family calendar to October from June! Time has taken on a whole new concept and also a greater dependence on His timing. Howard did another great job having Tim all day! Shouldn't worry, he had all day with Tim at 4 yrs old and on, I could hardly keep him at home 'cause he needed to be out working with Dad! Thank You again for allowing me to be married to my 'bestest friend' and for choosing him for me! Funny story again with Tim's spelling . . . I thought he was getting sick and he was trying to spell V-O-M-I (I thought vomit?) but finally he spelled the full word, 'vominos', and said it was Spanish for 'hurry up'! I told him I have hard enough time with him spelling in English, not even trying for Spanish! We were trying for an earlier lunch to get down to Creekside to work some more cattle and he thought I needed to hurry a little! Praying for continued health and strength for us—especially Howard 'cause he does so much of the Tim's transfers to and from bed, chair, etc. Lots of other prayers for insurance situations, healthy immune system against colds, girls with school, etc. Had very good sessions with our therapists, doing whatever 'homework' (exercises & activities) they have left for us to do. Practicing on making sounds (ch, sh, r,) make you realize how little we take for granted what and how we learned so long ago. Went to our community center's little pool and did some water therapy—little cooler than the 95 degrees of Craig's pool but he could stand it and he did well! Howard took Tim's roping steers to the sale at Torrington, so with no school today, Cass and I stayed with Tim. When we were trying to get him transferred from his chair to the bed in the living room, Tim and I fell onto the loveseat and I crawled out from under him while all he did was laugh! Cass helped us and we finally made it to the bed—with an even greater appreciation for Howard and his strength! We are so blessed with friends who come by and give Tim a massage, friends who bring over veggies they have frozen/canned from their garden along with bread and jellies! Lynette brought by Pizza Hut food! (Still warm even from Torrington!) Our friends, Dwayne and Chaurisse brought over pizza and we watched some football (while she massaged Tim's feet) after a great day in church with family and friends. Good friends, good times, and a good week! You are a good God!

Week of October 24-31, 2010—Psalm 33:20-21 "We wait for the Lord. He is our help and our shield. In Him our hearts find joy. In His holy name we trust." Today in our home church here in Albin our sermon dealt with sufferings, trials, hard times, etc. and one of the songs that we sang was *Still* (Hillsong) and the chorus' lyrics—

> "When the oceans rise and thunders roar
> I will soar with You above the storm
> Father You are King over the flood
> I will be still and know You are God"

As we said many times through this journey—the waiting with God, on God, for God, etc has truly been life. This song encourages us to walk in the trust with all the 'storms'. Tim had a good week—we are so encouraged that each day we see or hear another daily miracle(s). He is talking clearer and louder. While he was taking steps during therapy on Wednesday, the therapists noticed that he had started to really do a good job of shifting his weight off the left leg to the right so the left leg was easier to pull/move forward and backward to make his steps on that side. We see less and less 'pain' in Tim's elbow and a little more movement with left fingers! Had a good pool session and really worked hard on stretching and moving left arm . . . we continue to pray against any HO, if any, in that elbow area and work-out the stiffness, clear the passage ways from the brain to the body for the 'messages' to get there when sent. That's part of the frustration for Tim is when he mentally tells his arm, fingers, leg, whatever to physically do something—and then he doesn't see it do what he has told it to do! Tim was able to 'talk' on the phone to several friends even though we had to 'interpret' some phrases for them to understand right now. It would be easier if Tim wouldn't use phrases that some of the friends don't even know what they mean! I think a lot of his phrasing comes from being around his grandparents, older ropers, roping buddies, and maybe his "Southern" family/cousins! Tim got to go pet and 'talk' to his horse, DJ! It was hard and it seems like DJ knows something is wrong and tries to nudge Tim to 'get up and go'. We pushed around in his chair watching Howard check tanks, fence, and other ranchwork. Tim said how much he misses all the work that he loved so much How we pray he will be 'back in the saddle' around here soon! SOON—again, a word that has taken on a whole new concept! Went to Creekside and worked cattle all day—Tim did extremely well sitting in his chair and in the vehicle for that amount of time. Gordon and Fanny came over after the Halloween Carnival to visit and like almost every night, Grandpa prays just with Tim, head-to-head, in their own way & time! Sunday church service was closed with our church family circled around and singing "Bless Be the Tie". People said they enjoyed seeing Tim sing and then hear him give a healthy "amen!" at the close! A friend brought the words of this old hymn that some of you have heard on the radio with a new 'beat'—*My Savior Lives* by Ross Parsley. I think that it is the name of it. Look at the words . . .

> "I am not skilled to understand What God hath willed, what
>   God hath planned;
> I only know at His right hand is One who is my Savior!"

Oh, how it speaks of our journey. As I am writing this I can hear him and Howard talk about how all this is in God's big plan and we just have to wait and watch Him work all things for good (Rom 8:28), His good, and Tim's good. What, when, and how that 'good' is . . . in God's hands. We are so thankful to see His hand every day in all different areas of Tim's progress. His speech is becoming clearer and it is such a blessing to hear him laugh! We are anxiously waiting for his strength to increase as much and as fast as his weight—we are going to try to do a weight check this week and we all have our guesses as to what that number will be! He has greatly improved with his neck/head tilt, turn, and holding up—PTL! While holding his left ankle from turning over to the outside, Howard, Tim, and I can "walk" together about three safe steps!!! (about as far as Tim trusts us!) Again, we are so blessed and we thank God for each of you for all the food, visits, calls, cards, etc, that continually encourages us—what a God, what friends & family, what a community! Please continue to pray for Tim to get stronger, gain more movement, adapt to medicine changes, and keep progressing in God's timing. Busy week and we look forward to watching You work next week as we trust and believe!

Week of November 1-7, 2010—Been home one month from Craig! We thank You for daily miracles, continued strength, needed rest, and his attitude! Tim got to vote this week and did just fine in his 'cubicle' with the help of our election officers (family & friends!) Interesting watching Tim doing a speech exercise with moving Smarties around on his tongue from front to back! It's harder to try doing these things when we have to think about them! Worked some more cattle and Tim was out with us for about seven hours and did great. Sure miss my Daddy—this week, Thursday, would have been his 76th birthday! When I get tired, it gives me a boost to hear in my head his last words he always said on the phone with me . . . "Take care of my babies". I'm trying, Daddy! Tim had great therapy sessions and was excited to have movement in his left leg moving it off and on his bed! Seeing more and more movement in that left arm—You know how badly we need to have full-function there and how much it would help in other areas (mainly balance)! Tim did great in church—great to see him sing! We heard a sermon on Proverbs 3:5-6 and Jeremiah 29:11—Your Ways, Your Plans! Had good family friends from Torrington (Kay & Wade) come by on Sunday afternoon with a beautiful shirt. Tim loved it and will enjoy wearing it for roping because it has extra-long arms! I would like to share with ya'll some thoughts from a letter written to Tim from someone very dear . . .

> "Tim, while praying for you the Sunday morning I spent home sick, the story of David's life when he was a boy was brought to mind. He had to spend many long, lonely, and boring days sitting out on the hillside tending sheep. We do know that one of the ways he used all that time alone was to develop his physical skills. I haven't found you a 'harp' yet—but I hope and pray this sling shot serves as a physical challenge for you to conquer and shoot with great accuracy! But, more importantly, God worked on David's heart and I want this sling shot to remind you that God is not "'wasting" these days while you're in your chair. The greatest work I believe God wants to do during this time—as you wait and watch Him heal your physical body—is to give you an even

greater heart for Him. I gathered five stones to help remind you to mentally shoot the "giants" with this sling shot that are in your life right now—as He did with David, God will help you defeat these giants!" Thank You for a good start with this week of our second month home. We are excited to see You work and show us Your hand of healing with Tim."

Week of November 8-14, 2010—Tim is getting stronger every day, especially on the right side. He can almost pull himself completely up to a sitting position! We had snow this week—another area of Tim's 'pre-accident life', snowmobiling, that he will greatly miss with the girls, Lee, and Alan! Starting to take the Didronel out of his 'medicine box'. For someone who just has had aspirin, Ibuprofen, Tylenol, TussinDM, and Vicks in the medicine cabinet—this pill box assortment is a little bit overwhelming. Tim has a few a.m. and a few p.m. pills so thankful and especially that he can swallow them with water! Tried moving the living room arrangement around with the extra bed' Tim sleeps good, but lightly, and from about 11 to 5! Howard and I try to take turns getting up and/or sleeping up here with him, but how thankful we are for the monitor! The girls take turns sleeping beside him on the weekends because they need their sleep during the week with school and go to bed earlier than 11:00! Tim is spitting better when brushing his teeth—funny the things that you notice now, like wanting your son to be a good spitter! Lord, we continue to thank You and ask to keep Tim's focus on You! He talked about being so helpless, like a baby having to relearn and learn all over again. Lord, it'd be amazing for Tim to walk in church on Sunday or maybe in November? We pray miracles for both Tim and Shena! Had good therapy sessions and the "Sisters Speech Team" (Jess and Cass) helps Tim with speech homework, Beth helps with his talking on the phone, and visitors are understanding him more and more! Physical and occupational therapy have gone well—excited seeing Tim lift his left leg some—maybe we will stand by Thanksgiving? We thank You again Lord for Tim's humor, laugh, and smile! He's about had it with these external catheters, but thankful for them! We are thankful we all can laugh! The WRA (Wyoming Rodeo Association)

Finals will be held next week in Torrington and Tim ended up 5th for the season! I think it starts in March/April and goes all summer, and they have the finals now? He said, "I should be there roping?" We just keep working and waiting . . . You are faithful and we trust You totally, not understanding, but accepting as we wait in Your time! Coach Cullen and his family tried for 2 and 1/2 hours to get here to go with us for our church Thanksgiving Day service/dinner, but the roads were so icy and snowy they had to turn around at Stoneham! Black ice—sounded like Oklahoma ice! Cast ALL your cares on Him . . . 1 Peter 5:7—You have 'em Lord. 1 Thess 5:17 "Give thanks IN all things, for this is God's will for you in Christ Jesus." I've heard many sermons, read devotionals, and I've capitalized the important word to focus on—IN. He promises to be with us in all situations. Gratitude is a choice and here the action is to give thanks—for that is God's will. Some of you may have questioned that this circumstance of Tim's is or is not in God' will . . . the will here is to give thanks IN the circumstance, not for it. Today, our church had its Thanksgiving Service and Potluck. During praise time, several spoke and those who spoke of Tim were so precious and encouraging. Tim raised his hand to speak . . . "I'm thankful to be alive, thank you for praying and keep praying!" He was very excited to have his jeans on—we will work on his belt, buckle, and boots soon! He had very good therapy sessions both days—able to sit in an armless chair, bend left knee up and half-way down, then I could push it on down to the floor, spit better when brushing teeth, bend left arm more, learning how to whisper, and his attitude continues to be very positive. His patience with us gives us encouragement and laughter!! I've heard about and will be finding the book by Kerry and Chris Shook, *Love at Last Sight*. It talks about having relationships develop and get better and better every time you talk or see someone because you never know if it may be the last sight—More on the book after I read it (many of you are laughing right now when you read that I am reading a book!) We hope each and every one of you are planning a great Thanksgiving and you make a gratitude list! We love you!

Week of November 15-21, 2010—Busy week! Had snow off and on several days. Howard has a little head cold so I'm sleeping beside Tim.

Britt, Michael, and Josh all came by for visits on Monday. Howard brought another load of calves home from Creekside. Howard and Tim did well on Tuesday with the therapy sessions while I was in Pine for my MK Open House. Seeing more bend in Tim's left knee! Yea Lord! Tim had to practice picking up M & M's and Pizza Rolls in OT—Tim likes that kid of therapy. Philemon (verses 4-7) with emphasis on verse 4 . . . "I always thank my God as I remember you in my prayers . . ." This verse is a picture every night as we pray with Tim. To hear him pray and thank God for everything He has done and for his progress, his thankfulness for the day's activities or visitors, and his requests for not only himself, but others is a joy! He always asks God for 'another small miracle tomorrow' and sometimes specifically states what he is asking God for or to do. This morning we had the tv on and he and Jessica heard the preacher talk about Timothy (in the Bible) and his mother, Eunice. Jessica said he was talking about you, Tim. Tim said, "No, my mom's name is Dixie, not Eunice!" We have had another great week, especially with Thanksgiving and having Bethany home! He did walk three steps with the help of Beth, Howard, and me at our family Thanksgiving. Tonight, we walked about ten steps to his bedroom (with help) and he did great! For my birthday (in about two weeks) he wants to totally walk by himself—I told him that would be a great gift!! Please pray that his left ankle continues to strengthen to hold him so he is able to shift his weight and balance himself to walk!! We hope to be back in the pool this week. We will be watching and taping the NFR Finals starting Dec. 2—and we pray that it will be used by God as a stimulant as Tim watches and recalls his roping experiences, passion, etc. We are so thankful for all of you and your prayer support—it is such an encouragement to Tim. The girls read and reread all the cards we saved and Tim really enjoyed them. He can read large print fairly well and we continue to ask you to uphold his sight and alignment to strengthen and heal—both optic nerves are good and vision in both eyes is good—just waiting on God's restoring and timing with all the nerves, dilation, and alignment. Pray and Believe!

Week of November 22-28, 2010—Therapy sessions went well, but especially in PT/OT when it took all of us to get Tim in his saddle which now stands on the iron saddle rack that Coach Cullen, Mitch, and Joe made for Tim. We took pictures. Great to see him up there and at the same time, almost heart-wrenching! They will be using it for developing balance and trunk control. Did some cooking for T-Day on Wednesday and Tim said he wanted to 'walk' a few steps in front of everyone—that would be what he could 'bring' for the family dinner! We had Thanksgiving down at LaGrange in the community center there since there are too many of us to all fit in anybody's house. So much to be thankful for . . . for Tim being here with us, all our Malm family together, talking/skyping with so many of my Walton/Cooper family in Arkansas, living in America, etc, but above all, You, Lord, knowing You as Lord and Savior of my life, each one in our family, being Your children because of Jesus who died on the cross and rose on the third day, and is coming back someday for us! Went over to Tyner's for ribs, bean, and rice—had a great time! Got to meet Jenny's dad, Murray, from Florida—he has a group down there that prays for Tim! Richard had some roping runs of Tim's—it was very hard to watch them, but knew their hearts meant well and Tim seemed to enjoy seeing them. Tim wants to 'walk' by my birthday—that would be a great present! Had to take Beth back to DIA, but will see her next month! Drove to Craig Hospital and visited with Debby and Bobby, and also with Garrett and Cindy (R). Brought home pizza from Cheyenne. Talked to Shena today . . . trusting & believing! Miracles & Blessings from You—daily strength, prayers from all over everywhere, rest & refueled for each day, growing faith in the lessons You are teaching, watching You in the 'simple, little to the big miracles in Tim, safety and protection for our girls with all the miles they cover, another day for Shena, family, friends, life. Ps 4:1 "Answer me when I call to you, O my righteous God. Give me relief from my distress. Be merciful to me and hear my prayer. (NIV)" We are reading from the Psalms this month. We know God is hearing us, but Tim has asked if we think God is answering . . . When we recount all the miracles and how far and how fast he has come, he agrees that God is answering; he just wishes he could have bigger and faster answers! He has repeatedly thanked God for this time that he can rest and relax! It sure makes me stop and think of this journey as a long walk, especially when I'm use to running! Learning to rest and wait in and on the Lord is a continual life lesson for me! Our church had a special time of annointment and prayer for Tim today—Tim asked for it as we are beginning our next six-month journey! It's still unbelievable that it has been six months, and yet at times it seems like yesterday! Won't it be great when there will be no calendars or clocks in Heaven!! We continue to reread the Caringbridge messages to Tim—we finally finished all the cards! He truly thanks each and everyone for all the words of encouragement! We really enjoyed the pool this week and plan to have another day this week. He is moving his left hand/arm more and more—this will help with balance when he will be standing and walking with a walker, and we pray and believe that will be very soon! He has really enjoyed the NFR rodeo and has made quite a few comments. He really enjoys all the telephone calls (I'm sure he is calling some of you a little too often?), cards, visits, messages, etc. He received a call from Joni Eareckson Tada on Friday! He went to a basketball game to watch his little sister play on Saturday morning and then sat in the vehicle parked by our working chute in our big building and worked cattle for about three hours. While he still needs help walking, he is now lifting his left knee/thigh and heel—and then we hold his ankle and move his toes!! Praise the Lord!!! Continue to pray for his physical needs—left side to be restored and healed back to full working status and continual healing of the nerve endings (brain) as they reconnect and redirect. His emotional needs—to not get discouraged, but continue to persevere and Press On! We are thankful for every day of Life—Tim usually opens his prayers with thanking God another day! My birthday is a week away, so pray for Tim's ankle to be strong enough for him to take a few steps by himself hopefully, prayerfully, and miraculously by next Sunday, but if not, then His grace will carry us through to the next goal date! Have a Blessed week as we truly look and see the real meaning of Christmas!

> **Tim's sister Beth got to spend some time with Tim during Thanksgiving Break and posted this on her return to college. "Tim, I had an AMAZING time with you this past week. You are getting so much stronger and your voice is getting so much clearer! I**

loved seeing you walk during therapy, at Thanksgiving dinner and from your door to your bed! I also loved seeing you on your saddle. I had so much fun watching TV and movies, playing countless games of thumb wrestling and rock paper scissors, reading you your cards, calling people and just plain talking! You are my hero and have definitely showed me this past week to never give up on GOD and that miracles can happen. I LOVE YOU SOOO MUCH!!!! Can't wait to come home and hang out again with you over Christmas break!!"

Week of November 29-December 5, 2010—Tim "Walked" with Howard in front and me behind about ten steps to his bedroom! Now sleeping in his own bed and room! I pray that the beautiful calf roper quilt hanging on the wall, along with all the horse and roping pictures are encouraging to him. People are amazed at seeing the log bed with the calf roping metal piece in the wood headboard, along with the M-A-L-M log letters in the footboard! Hearing Tim pray brings a comfort and peace and closes my day off right—it is sometimes really hard to pray after him at times! We are starting to feel and see that 'double-edged sword' of sitting, hearing, and seeing Tim having to watch activities that he loved and so badly wants to do again—this week he watched as Howard and Gordon moved bales, cut strings, and ground hay! Can't believe December is here! At the first of each month, new goals are set and it seems there will be time to reach them. Then, it seems as if we just turn around and time has taken the month! We have learned and continue to learn that TIME has a lot of 'faces' . . . slow for Tim, but we tell him he is improving every day and we pray that You will give him the eyes and ears to see and hear himself every day! This month will mark six months since the accident—Tim said, "Six months of my life has flown by while time seems to stand still with me." We encourage him with Your Word in Jeremiah 29:11 . . . "For I know the plans for you . . ." Tim has always 'looked out' and has a sensitive side to him for his sisters. We had another pool time—it's a sight to see us bundle him up with our wind and get him in his chair to wheel into the pool area. We move as fast as we can getting out and into the shower before his lips turn blue! The water feels great, but even in the enclosed area, he gets really cold from the pool to the shower! Look forward to the day he can walk in there! Tonight started our week with watching the NFR (National Finals Rodeo) and of course, every performance of calf and team roping will be taped. Again, Tim watches it with 'heart tears' talking about being out there . . . goals and dreams in Your hands if that is where You want him and You restore him back with the gifts and talents You gave him. What a testimony You are developing in him to show Your glory and Your power!

Tim made a remark this week, "I should've just roped calves that day!" I told him we can't live with any "should've's"! Why the accident was allowed we will never know and I'm not sure we want to know, but we will grow through it with God's strength (Phil 4:13)! I thank You again that I was in the arena that day and that it happened here and not somewhere else. Looking back, I don't know how You gave me the strength and composure to get him back to breathing, but I think I could've have handled me at least trying rather than getting a phone call from someone telling me that nothing or no one even tried and we lost him. Thank You again, for being there right beside us and allowing us more time with Tim—Sovereign Lord Almighty! Great church service—at the end they asked Howard, me, and all our kids up to the front and pastor anointed Tim with oil on his forehead as all the overseers prayed. We know it's not a 'magical' time, but just a time You describe in Your Word for total focus on You and a prayer time for others as we bring Tim before You in a corporate time of prayer and worship . . . Thank You! Some 'elves' came over and put up Christmas lights up and down the ramp—kind of looks like a runway! Grandpa and Grandma came over and watched the NFR with us. Tim prayed not to be left like this and for faster and bigger healing! Mom and I share a 'fix-it' mentality to situations and both Shena's battle and Tim's journey we can't 'fix'—another lesson You are teaching us and drawing us toward total dependence on You. In Your hands and in Your time . . . Joni Erieckson Tada sent us a devotional book (*Diamonds in the Dust*) and our reading today was 'He Leads'. The verse, John 10:3-4. "He calls his sheep by name and leads them out. When he has brought out all his own, he goes ahead of them, and his sheep follow him because they know his voice." The devotional dealt with the times and thoughts of 'sheep' (people) expecting God to come help clean up a problem with a broom and dustpan, a bottle of glue, hammer & nails, or a rope. Reread the verse again—the shepherd leads and the sheep follow because they know his voice! He is not surprised by our trials—and we know Tim's accident didn't surprise God. He was, and is, truly there on all sides (Ps 139:5-6) and the prayer Joni closes with is so fitting . . .

"Thank you Lord for leading me. Thank you for charting all of my days, planning every moment so that it fits miraculously into a pattern of good for my life." Tim has been trying to look for the good with this injury and we try to encourage him with the many encouraging words that have been written and spoken. He has a grateful heart and thanks God for all He has done and is going to do. He prayed last night that if he couldn't walk by himself for my birthday, then maybe on Jesus' birthday-so Christmas is now our goal!! His vision is sometimes a little blurry—but we think that it is a good thing because the alignment is coming closer together and he doesn't seem to see double! Continue to pray for eyesight alignment, strength & balance, and left arm & knee/quad to progress daily. In all your Christmas attitudes, activities, and actions—we pray that others will see and hear the true Shepherd and follow Him—JESUS! Merry Christmas!

Week of December 6-12, 2010—Two months since coming home and Tim sat in an armless chair and held a sitting position for about ten seconds—that's improvement! Starting to work with computer and trying to control that mouse! Most people remember how big of hands Tim has and his fingers get in the way with that mouse! I'm sure he'll tackle that soon and get it done. Watched NFR almost every night and caught up on the DVR taping again the next mornings also! Friends and family brought back autographed pictures and a t-shirt from several PRCA Cowboys at the NFR—some of them knew Tim and wrote words of encouragement to him! What neat acts of kindness! Local friends, Ron and Julie (R), want to set up a scholarship at the community college (LCCC) in Cheyenne in honor of Tim. Ron and the scholarship lady from LCCC came by to meet with Tim and get his feedback on the particulars of it. It will be called the Tim Malm Cowboy Spirit Award and will go to a rodeo student. It will be presented at the fall college rodeo—of which Tim commented he wanted to be there and meant NOT in his wheelchair! Bethany was asked to share about Tim to the boys' BBall team at her college where she is one of the managers and the only girl! Tim's vision isn't double, just blurry at times, so thankful that the alignment of his eyes is improving! During our Bible reading at night, Tim can see the chapter book clear in his Bible, and sometimes can read out of a giant-print Bible! Watched the NFR finals-very different watching it this year with him.

We had our soup dinner & cantata (I sang, "Mary, Did You Know?") The song took on different meaning than the last time I sang it . . . Mary looking at her baby not knowing His future and seems like I'm looking at my 'baby' and not knowing his future. I do know WHO holds the future and we continue to walk daily with Him! Today would have been Mom & Dad's 56th Anniversary—holds special meaning for me being born on their anniversary. I really miss him, but Mom says that even as hard as Shena's battle was for him, she didn't think Daddy could have taken this journey of Tim's.

Today I had the opportunity to sing at a Christmas special in Pine Bluffs—it was so good to see so many people that have and continue to pray for Tim and to thank them. This song has been one of my favorites and I hope and pray that the words really cause people to look inside that trough in that manger all the way to the cross and beyond to be able to accept the gift of Christmas—the gift of salvation, eternal life. The pastor spoke about a mustard seed faith Christmas! Each of you have shared these past six months for us to have a mustard seed faith Christmas this year—we pray the Lord has strengthened you and we give Him all the honor and praise! Tim had another good week—we continue to see progress in so many areas and we are trying to 'wait on the Lord' (Ps 37) as He strengthens Tim toward that day of walking on his own with God's strength (Phil 4:13)!! Bethany flew home for Christmas vacation and Tim was very happy to see her! He has enjoyed getting out to go band steers (ranchwork) and the day I drove to Denver to get Beth, Tim was able to help himself and he and Howard got in the vehicle themselves (it usually takes all three of us)! Continue to pray for full restoration from head to toe with special emphasis on the left-side abilities and the eye alignment. Again, we wish all ya'll a MERRY CHRISTMAS!

Week of December 13-20, 2010—Last week before Christmas Break! Tim apologizes for not being able to 'walk' on my birthday. After therapy on Tuesday, we went out to work in the big building to band bulls. Tim used the car 'electric' blanket to keep warm enough. So thankful we can work indoors even with the big end doors open! He continues to ask You for healing so he can work with Grandpa and Dad. We had snow and cold weather—was five to six degrees on two mornings! NJC was on Break, so Tim got to talk with Coach Cullen. A steer roper called, talked it over with Tim and Howard, and he bought Toby from Tim, telling Tim he could buy him back if he ever wanted to . . . excited to have him sold. I know it wasn't the horse's fault or Tim's steer roping that caused the accident, but I don't know how Tim can even think about getting on him or ever steer roping again. High school friends came by while on their college break. Lee brought "Albin Café" hamburgers and had a good visit—it's so hard on him to be with Tim, but he does it anyway. Tim remarked how he misses all the things he and Lee did together—just like brothers. I tried to help Tim stand out of the recliner, but we ended up just sliding in down to the ground and waiting until someone stronger could help get him up—thank You that Tim could laugh about it, even if it was at me. Howard and Tim had a long day on Friday working cattle in the big building with the cold! Even working together, Howard and I are really tired—can't imagine Debby, spouses, or single parents being the caregivers alone! Thank You for Howard's physical strength and all what he does with insurance, paperwork, ordering supplies, etc. I can't imagine how people live with life's struggles without You! Psalm 56:13 "For You have delivered me from death and my feet from stumbling, that I may walk before God in the light of life." We are reading through the Psalms and Tim is memorizing this verse. We are setting our walking goal for this month! He is so close to getting the last toe (the big one) off the floor in order to kick his lower leg out for the step!! He is texting some—as many of you know! He also has called his own phone to tell himself he's doing a great job and keep working! We are enjoying these messages and it will help him listen to his voice as God heals and restores it back to his tone and intonation as it was before the accident. He has some assistance in pulling himself up and now can hold himself upright for a longer period by himself without any help. Continue to pray for all the strength, coordination, timing, etc that is coming back!! We also praise and thank God for all the protection against any germs that Tim has not caught-especially with all his visitors. He really enjoys all the visits and cards!

> **On December 23, 2010, Tim's aunt Shena lost her battle with colon cancer. She had a special relationship with Tim and had the opportunity to visit with him during his stay at Craig Rehab Center. She so wanted to be able to witness Tim's recovery, but God had a different plan. I'm sure one day she and Tim can talk about it together in Heaven.**

Week of December 19-26, 2010—God Almighty, Lord and Savior! Talked with Joe on Monday and we cried a bit together, then I 'talked' with Shena—of course, I could understand "Alright" and "I love you" (two times)! Told her I loved her and that I am still praying . . . I prayed for her to be radiant and the days to go well on Friday (Cooper Christmas) and Saturday (Layn Christmas)! With Tim's late hours and the girls' early hours, my days and nights are running a little short! Watched Tim's National HS Finals DVD—always hard, just makes us pray harder and trust You more for full restoration! Talked with Mom and Candra and talked about Shena, praying for her to not be in pain, and for Joe & the kids. On Wednesday, the girls and I went to a funeral of a steer wrestler that was married to Jessica's jr high bball coach. Saw and talked with several of Tim's friends who also attended. Sat there, so thankful how we had been spared a funeral with Tim, wondering if and when we would be having one for Shena. They held the phone up to Shena and I told her again that I loved her and that Christmas was coming and she would spend it here with us, or in Heaven with her Heavenly Father and her Daddy—I could understand "yeah". It was hard to hear her moan and groan with the pain and meds, but it was almost overwhelming to say "good-bye". After praying, I laid beside Tim for a while . . . praying quietly that my girls would have the relationship I have with my sisters, and with Tim. Thursday morning, Mom called at about 9:10 to tell me Shena was going to spend Christmas in Heaven—she had just died with a smile on her face, out of pain, with Mom, Joe and all her kids beside her at home. The same 'numbness' I had with Tim that night in ICU came over me again, but I thank You again for holding me together as I called family and friends who Mom wanted me to call. Our family went to the pool—it was good to get away for a little bit. Being related and really good friends with our funeral director, Philip, Mom called from her car as she was ahead of Philip driving the hearse with Shena as they were all headed to Walters. Plans were to have a memorial service on Sunday evening in Walters, viewing Monday afternoon in Kingfisher, funeral Tuesday morning in Kingfisher with burial at Walters following!

Thank You for all the time Mom was able to spend with Shena these past seven years, being raised in Walters, Cotton County, Oklahoma, in our church (First Baptist), our school, and our community—but above all, being raised in a Christian home with loving parents with a great picture of friendship & marriage, an extremely-close friendship & relationship between us girls, a wonderful childhood, a legacy left by our grandparents, fabulous friends, and many, many memories. As much as all that means to me, Lord, You reign above all—loving me unconditionally and dying for me on that cross for my sins so I will live with You eternally! Thank You for Shena's life and influence in my life. She will be greatly and deeply missed.

Howard, the kids, and I had our little Christmas—opened a few presents in between watching two Christmas movies. Mom had sent a framed picture of us four girls of the weekend we spent together in November. Thank You again for that time! Being in a Swedish community, early church, and family heritage, we celebrate "Julotta" 6:30 a.m. on Christmas morning in church. Had dinner and family time at Grandpa & Grandma's out at the ranch. Britt and Lexi Bath came over and brought up the WRA leather jacket for the season—it is really nice. I'm thinking it will be a little small right now for him and one of his sisters will wear it! I drove to Denver early Sunday morning to fly to OKC and be picked up by Sug and Joe on their way from Arkansas to Walters. Prayed for strength to sing at her Memorial service in Walters and You were so faithful with giving me strength and composure. Crazy—I broke my right little toe the night before helping Tim walk to his room so, it was a little tender to walk on! Sunday's service had about 350-400 people so they moved it into the sanctuary. Lots of family and friends, hugs and tears, laughter and memories! Monday night after the viewing, we all went to Shena & Joe's (will I ever be able to not call their home that?) to eat on all the food that was brought in, share memories of Shena, then of course—only in their house regardless of the circumstances, we had football on watching Curtis (L) playing for the Atlanta Falcons. He is from Kingfisher and a very close 'family member—I'm sure it was hard on him to not be here with Joe and the kids and having to play. Tuesday was a HARD day, but oh, how You were honored with the service and burial—about 2000 people signed her book with the memorial services and burial! We pray many decisions were made to follow YOU! So many good friends (some I hadn't seen since high school), some influential coaches I had, and cousins I hadn't seen . . . and so many asked about Tim and told me they were praying! Took about an hour a half for everyone to walk by Shena and us—she wanted for it to be like Dad's where she stays at the front of the church and everyone walks by there and then the family has their time, but leave her at the 'alter'. Being two hours away, we all had a quick bite of lunch and flew to Walters—some on I-44, and some through the country! The burial was filled with more friends, coaches, and classmates!

Tim called to tell me he sat up twice by himself!! Thank You for that huge hug of encouragement, Lord! I rode back to OKC and stayed with some cousins to catch my early flight back to Denver. Thank You for traveling safety with many miles. I sure know the difference between living on emotions and living on prayers—am praying for some 'renewed' rest! Our devotional, 'Taking Inventory" really had us looking back at the first six months and this journey of the last six months . . . even when we don't understand, we love You and trust You!

My "New Year's Prayers' are—to keep us healthy, healing & restoration for Tim, Bethany to do well at school and bless her with good friends, Cassady and Jessica to mature in Your way, and for You to glorified with this journey our whole family is on! Bethany made it safely to Tulsa and on to Branson, thank You! We thank You for all the blessings on this year and thank You ahead of time for all the 2011 blessings (grace, mercy, faithfulness, strength, love, sovereignty, trust) We love You! On Sunday, a classmate and now pastor of Howard's-Dan D. spoke and mentioned Howard, Tim, and I when talking about Persistent Prayer . . . Tim's prayer question to God is "How long is persistent?" Our new prayer goal of walking is Howard's birthday, March 17!

Chapter Six

Home in Albin (2011)

Week of January 3-9, 2011—For the first time since we've been home, Howard and I went out of the house together to our church's January Home Prayer Meetings—Fanny and Gordon stayed with Tim for the hour. It felt different? Coach Cullen surprised us with a visit; then a guy the same age as Tim who was in Craig Hospital with a brain injury (from a horse accident) came by on his way through. Everyone knows how Tim loved driving his 'Big Rig' and it's hard to imagine when he will gain his driving abilities back. Good to hear Tim pray and stay persistent . . . Tim has had very good therapy sessions! It's great to hear and for his therapists to say and see improvement in strength, sitting balance, bending control about every time they come! Keep on keeping on! Everywhere we go we are asked about Tim, so many people—so many praying for him! Tim is praying for healing to be quicker, he's trying so hard to work within Your timetable . . . to be "still' and wait on the Lord! As many would say . . . Tim be still? That's a miracle in itself for this young man who was always working, roping, etc. Tim finally took a little nap (about 20 min) today! Improving with speech therapy, but it's so hard hearing him in his monotone-type of voice. How we pray for that 'normal' voice that You gave him to be restored as we remember, that bright, common-sensed, stable young man who wants to go back to college at NJC and rope again. I constantly have to put any and all my questions, fears, worries in Your hands, thank You that I can do that. Forgive us when we let our eagerness and excitement turn into frustrations at times for Tim-we see improvement and want to push from there, in our time. Tim prays so hard for his left side and eye alignment. Chris (L) came over to the house and gave Tim a much-needed haircut! He held his head without the head rest!—he so enjoys her visits! Lord, how thankful we are for what You have done, are doing, and will do! We pray for continual physical strength for Howard and I, as well as emotional strength watching and helping Tim. This is a whole new 'season' of our lives and our family's life—especially for Tim. I think of so many of the caregivers we know who are in their 'seasons'. Tim prays as we do to be able to walk back into Craig whenever we go back—that's the 'mountain' we are asking to be moved (Mark 11:23) or give us the ability to climb over! Tim is doing some sit-ups and starting to ride the recumbent bike, even though it takes both Howard and I to hold his left foot on the pedal and me hold his left hand and head up! Had some more snow on Sunday and we bundle Tim up and Howard is the '4-wheel drive' with them wheeling down to church in the snow! I look forward to all of us really walking to church next winter! Tim didn't have to have us lift his left leg any today in church, yea! We are seeing more alignment with his eyes, yea! He took a nap on Sunday (like we all did)—that's two in a week!! Exodus 14: 15-16 This is the passage where God tells Moses to 'raise your staff and stretch out your hand' when they were crossing the Red Sea. This was in one of our devotionals this week (Joni's book, *Diamonds in the Dust*). Just an ordinary stick, but with God, when, where, how, and what He chooses to use—any 'thing' takes on new meaning and becomes extraordinary! She states in her book, "God can exchange the tragic meaning behind accidents and injuries for something new and positive." She points us to the Cross—a symbol of torture and pain now represents hope and salvation! Her wheelchair (tragedy and confinement) now gives her freedom and mobility. When Shena came to see Tim (ICU-in Cheyenne in June) she gave me a plaque that hangs in my home—Live for Today and Hope for Tomorrow. We pray, along with Tim, that as we continue to see and look for the positive with this accident and injury, that it has drawn people to personally know that hope through Jesus Christ so we may have those eternal tomorrows. With the cold spell it's been hard to get to the pool—we may need a scuba suit! Continue to pray for progress toward walking (Tim asks God to work quicker!), sitting up, and his positive attitude as he waits and watches God work with this 'ordinary' (and ornery) piece of clay—to God be the glory! Have a blessed week! Excited to watch You work this week!

Week of January 10-16, 2011—Happy January to all—hard to believe where the time goes. We passed the seventh month hurdle since the accident. This has been a hard week emotionally for other reasons, but also for Tim in some areas. Tim had good therapies—always something new and he uses meets the challenges! You've strengthened that left ankle and the knee is bending more and more—he could also 'walk' to his bedroom without his blue neck-thing! Tim made a comment tonight that was unusual for him: "I wished God had taken me if He is going to leave me like this." Hard to talk after that, but we did and then we prayed. We said we're going to get back as far as God takes us, and we're praying and expecting 100% full healing and restoration. Back to where he was wasn't 100% because God is always growing us—we just have to be willing and obedient to the Gardener! We are sure thankful and glad God allowed him to stay with us and we stand on Jeremiah 29:11, For He know the plans He has for You! Lord, Tim needs Your encouragement tonight. Praying that it will be soon that he can control the computer mouse, write with steadiness, text, etc. to keep him from just 'thinking' about the situation as we slowly travel this journey. We are noticing a softer tone with his voice! Tim texted Lynette on her birthday! Tim loves church potlucks and we had the first one since we've been home. He did fine getting downstairs with the men carrying him and of course, enjoyed the food and company! Tim thinks he wants to try sitting in a chair next week! I long for the day he stands for one song, then two, and then can really walk down the aisle and thank everyone himself for all the prayers and encouragement of his church family—he will give You all the praise! He has shown great trust and faith in God while growing through these grace moments. Ephesians 5:15 & 16 says for us "to be very careful, then, how you live—not as unwise but as wise, making the most of every opportunity, because the days are evil."

I often refer to Jeremiah 29:11 about God's knowing of His plans—but that not only refers to the future, but involves day to day because it is the present and every moment in the present that moves us a moment further into the future. Sometimes life gets us to rushing and running that we lose focus of the right now—Oswald Chambers has said, "Grace is for right now." We know hardships, trials, sufferings, accidents, injuries, and even death can be and is used by God and His Holy Spirit to renew us in His image. Phil 1:6 tells us we can have confidence in that "He who began a good work in you will carry it on to completion until the day of Christ." Tim is getting closer and closer to walking on his own and just like a runner getting closer to finishing a race, he wants to reach this goal and finish it NOW so he can move on to the next race! We have added more therapy time with us using a Thera-cycle (arms and legs) and though he's not able to use the left leg quite yet, he is using the right leg and both arms. His texting is getting better, writing legibly, and reading more at distances (closer and farther)! He thanks God every night for the his progress and for him to see it clearly—we see it in so many ways, but Tim needs to see it in big ways, even though we assess the day of his progress. Continue to pray for God to give Tim a vision of his progress and continued trust in God's healing and His timing. We thank you all for the encouragement-Tim reads or has us read any cards, texts, Caringbridge comments, etc. so we thank you again. Pray and Believe that Tim will walk by himself in January! Goodnight, Lord! On to another week of waiting and watching You!

Week of January 17-23, 2011—Tim played solitaire on his computer—helps with control of the mouse! Tim's prayers are conversations with You; it's so humbling to hear him pray. I moved Tim to his bed today and we didn't fall this time!! Tim worked on the Tower 200 with his arms-any weight working that left arm is good. Tim got on his saddle and worked with stacking cups in front of him and pulling himself back into sitting position after each cup! Who would have ever thought his saddle would be used for therapy like this? Talked with Beth (as we do almost every day) and she's doing better with homesickness—especially after she talks with Tim, he tells her "it's gonna be alright" (sounds like Shena!) Tim went out to the Ranch with Howard and I one day and got to pet two of his horses, DJ and Conoco. Grpa and Grma came over as they do almost every night—it's encouraging for Tim to have them! Tim was taken off his blood pressure medicine this week, will be so glad to be off of everything! Tim did sit in a church chair on Sunday!! Sermon centered around 'Answered Prayer'—thank You for the many You answer daily and we trust and believe in the BIG ones we are praying! Ps 73:23 "Yet I am always with you; You hold me by my right hand." This verse stuck with me this week because Tim has stood up and held on to Howard with his right hand a couple of times—only about fifteen to twenty seconds but his balance and strength continue to show progress!! Ps 83:1 "O God, do not keep silent; be not quiet, O God, be not still." Tim continues, along with us, to pray and he thanks God for and asks Him to continue with his progress!

We want to 'hear' Him everyday so we have to listen throughout the day in all the ways He 'speaks' words, music, encouragement, creation, friends, family, therapists, etc. He is working really hard and praying just as hard to walk a few steps by himself by the end of January—so continue to pray with us that God will bless him with that goal! We will take pictures and start trying to post them on here! He has started a weight workout with his arms and the Thera-cycle (we're hoping this starts burning calories!-the men at church have noticed his 'chair' is heavier when they carry him up and down the stairs to get in our church! I'm sure the man on the mat that his friends carried him up to the roof and let him down didn't weigh or was as tall as Tim is!) His vision is getting stronger and clearer-PTL!! We are hearing intonation with his voice, so continue to pray for progress to continue. Tim prays that God will show him progress where he can see it in big ways—we pray for persistent prayer and timely progress (God's timing because it is perfect!) Thank ya'll for your persistent prayer and encouragement! (Tim also can work a wireless mouse with his computer, so the day he can type may be just around the corner!) Have a Blessed Week!

Week of January 24-30, 2011—Tim called me on my phone to tell me he won at solitaire! Tim is now starting to sit on the side of his bed and keeping his balance pretty good. Tim lifted both legs up and on the bed on in the living room this week, YEA! Worked some calves and Howard was able to take Tim by themselves while I was gone to Cass' ballgames and Cheyenne. Saturday night was a treat with the Martin's—they brought chili & cornbread! Good friends, good food, good times! One of the devotionals this week was "Don't Worry" Tim's worry is not walking and not roping again—I hurt when he hurts. On Sunday, the sermon was in Habbakkuk, about sufferings and hardships! It was meant for us and I think it encouraged Tim. SUSTAIN, like I wrote in the update about You, Your Word, Your promises to sustain us!! Night, Lord

Week of January 31-February 6, 2011—Tim stood pretty good in this walker with the hand extensions and took a right step, but the left side kinda tones up, but we know it will come around sometime with time. Therapists still came out and they were pleased with Tim's improvement—the speech therapist could hear intonation!, OT with arms and hands, and PT with balance, strength, and walking with the walking with three of us around him. Our former pastor came by for a visit—it was good to see him. We were so excited on Thursday that Tim rolled over on his left side, could move his head smoother from the right and to the left, PTL! We all got Tim down on his stomach using the big wedges hopefully to get some weight bearing on that left shoulder, arm, and hand. A contractor friend, Mike, and Chase (friend who works with Andy down at LaGrange) have gutted the upstairs bathroom and will start the total remodel so we will have a bathroom that Tim can have his shower chair roll in to the shower! Thank you for the kindness and generosity! It will be a little chaotic for the girls getting ready in the little bathroom downstairs, but we will make do and it will be fine. Tim wants to title the book Candra is talking about, *In His Time*.

Our week's devotions focused on You, not the if's, allow, permits, causes, etc. Prayin' & Believin'! Our first week of February in our devotional book dealt with faith, dreams, empowerment and suffering-we had several good discussions along with the questions. Exodus 4:11 "The Lord said to him. "Who gave man his mouth? Who makes him deaf or mute? Who gives him sight or makes him blind? Is it not I, the Lord?" Here it was asked if God causes or allows, plans or permits, when it comes to so many situations in life. The point was made that the verb (cause, allow, permit, etc) is not so much the important thing as the noun: GOD. 1 Chronicles 29:11 "Yours, O Lord, is the greatness and the power and the glory and the majesty and the splendor, for everything in heaven and earth is Yours. Yours, O Lord, is the kingdom; You are exalted as head over all." What struck me here are the words-greatness, power, glory, majesty, splendor! Knowing and trusting that this situation and Tim is in His hands—'everything is in His hands' sure allows us rest at night and grace and strength for each day. We have had very good days this week and it has been extra encouraging to see and hear Tim speak of his progress! We have seen increasing strength from lifting legs onto and off beds, speaking, rolling over onto his stomach, getting on his hands and knees ('all fours') on the floor, and watching his left engage to take a step! He has drug his left leg/foot a few inches by himself so we are close!! We are excited to see what miracles God has in store for him this week! I think the biggest improvement is seeing him adjust his head and neck to center which holds his eyes in alignment! PTL!! We thank you all for your continued prayer support—it truly is our 'Daily Bread'. Pray that we might crawl or step this week! Keep Praying and Believing!

Week of February 7-13, 2011—Hard to hear Tim as he talks about how he wonders if he did something to make You mad, did something wrong, etc . . . please show him Your love and that this accident was allowed for only Your knowledge knows!? How he prays to rope again. It's so peaceful to close everything up with "I'll leave it in Your hands"—I pray that brings You honor to hear that trust and submission. The therapists tried an E-stim (electronic stimulation) machine that will help continue muscles being stimulated to work. We saw Tim drag his left foot this week! To have physical movement and/or improvement that Tim can see is great encouragement from You—thank You! "Little" jobs like when some bulls got into Tim's horse pasture and Howard had to go sort and fix fence just stabs Tim—he wants to so badly get back to doing that! Watched "Facing the Giants"—one of the kids' favorites! You know we've had and have 'giants' this year—but You are our leader and healer! Everyone clapped, giving You praise, in church when Tim had Howard tell everybody during praise & prayer times about giving him the strength to drag his foot! Tim's prayers for his friends, healing, roping, etc. is so sincere! We're still reading through Psalms—sure makes you stay in a thankful and grateful state. We are sure enjoying and growing through the devotional book, Diamonds in the Dust, which Joni Eareckson Tada gave us. Acts 17:27: "God did this so that men would seek him and perhaps reach out for him, though he is not far from each one of us. For in Him we live and have our being'" This verse with the devotional dealt with security (who we are) and significance (what we do). Christ is our source of peace, joy, strength. etc. and He is in us—that's our security! Our significance is felt when we place our trust in Him. Deut 10:12 "And now, O Israel, what does the Lord ask of you but to fear the Lord your God, to walk in all His ways. to love Him, and to serve the Lord your God with all your heart and with all your soul." What and how much does He ask? Everything!! When we get discouraged or weak, God promises to empower us to do all that He asks—even if it is everything! These two devotional thoughts with the verses have been encouraging to all of us this week. He wanted to give it as praise in church this morning and everyone clapped with praise to the Lord! We are excited with the daily miracles and are extra grateful for God showing Tim this one! We wish each of you a "Happy Valentine's Day!" and thank you for all your love!

Week of February 14-20, 2011—Valentine's Day! After Tim and Howard went out to load heifers on trucks to some neighbors who had bought them ('neighbors' who live about thirty-five miles out west!), Tim wanted to "walk" up and down the ramp—He did great with Howard in front and me behind him! PTL! Ran some more tax book stuff down to Ken's so Tim went with Howard and he walked down the ramp again! It's been quite the place for therapy with all the bathroom sounds from saws, hammers, and such! Tim wanted to show Jason, our PT therapist, his "walking" on the ramp!

Tim's math skills amaze us all! Howard gives him lengthy problems containing multiply/divide/square, etc. and he does them in his head as usually only he and Howard get the answer, before any of us girls! One night it was about 11:00 and they were doing some problems and

Cassady could hear them—"No more math at 11:00!" He calls himself the "human calculator". Bethany called and was having a hard time with Satan putting fears about Tim in her thoughts and we told her to just give them to God—He's in control! Had a pool day this week and afterwards we pulled by the elementary school and several adults came out to see Tim—one was the neighbor who had partnered on the roping steers with Tim, and one of the others was one of the EMT's that hadn't seen Tim since the accident!

Tim worked on his computer and set up his Facebook page—before the accident Tim did not have one nor had time for one! School got out early on Friday so Kaden came over here until therapists came—Tim was down on all fours then with all us, he and we could get to a standing position!!! Tim really felt like You were going to do something big and special??? Excited to see You work! Watched the last game of the season, lots of people visited with Tim—we had hope he could have 'walked' in this year, but maybe next year? Praise claps for You when Howard told in church that Tim took two steps in the pool this week!! A Great Week—looking forward and excited for this week as we trust and believe in You & Your healing touch!

Psalm 128:1 "Blessed are all who fear the Lord, who walk in His ways." Psalm 130:5 "I will wait for the Lord, my soul waits, and in His word I put my hope." The order of choosing, accepting, and submitting to Him (fear the Lord) and then walking in His ways is clearly seen here. Walking through life without knowing and trusting in the Author of Life is the incorrect order—kind of reminds me of how important crawling is to walking. Our second verse we read during our reading this week encourages us to wait on Him and where our trust and hope is in.

We continue to walk with assistance up and down the ramp and he drags his left foot and leg—huge progress!! The therapists work on a variety of exercises including getting him down on the floor again, but this time he went from the floor to his knees (with everyone helping) and then pulled up using his leg strength! I'm sure the next time he'll have less help because once they show him something he usually works on it before they come back! Continue to pray for balance, coordination, strength in the function of his left arm, hand, foot and leg the way God created them to work! His voice is getting better and better, but continue to pray that God brings his former voice back soon! He went to his sister's ballgames on Saturday (almost gone 7 hrs from home and did well sitting in his chair and vehicle) He really enjoyed seeing and talking with so many people!! Thank you all for the time you took to encourage him with your words, handshakes, and hugs! Have a Blessed week!

Week of February 21-27, 2011—Tim started off this week with holding up his left arm/hand with his right hand all the way to his face!—it's a start! He also got his i-phone and the font is smaller than his old one, so we pray his eyesight will improve for it! They have told us that there was no damage to the optic nerves so we continue to pray you'll give us back those beautiful blue eyes that had such good eyesight. Praying for a good eye doctor that You would have for us so Tim can be doing exercises beyond what we have him do. Therapies went well—worked on the Theracycle, and Tim got his left hand to move around some on the pedals (scratched up my table a bit, but it's fixable!) Midweek prayer time centered around Tim telling God about his confusion with some of the verses like . . . faith the size of a mustard seed, ask and believe . . . ask and receive . . . where two or three are gathered . . .

Had a pool day on Wednesday and Tim "walked" up & down the stair instead of using that cold chair! Tim also had some saddle time and balance work on the big yellow ball this week. Little improvements every day, with the highlight of the day seeing Tim sit up in bed by himself with only Howard holding a hand at his back! Took away another pill this week, yea! Hoping to take away another medicine next week. Thank You again for the words You give—hope others see You through all this! No steps in February . . . maybe March? We'll continue to PRAY & BELIEVE! 1 Kings 18:37 "Answer me, O Lord, answer me, so the people will know that You, O Lord, are God, and that You are turning their hearts back again." We have and are seeing those answers that we know so many of you have been praying along with us to God. We so enjoy the bulletins, newsletters, and devotionals from the many church/Bible study groups and individuals's hard to put in words when you truly feel the prayers of God's people.

Candra Marlett

Week of February 28-March 6, 2011—We all went out to work heifers. Tim kept warm and sat well in his chair, just hurts him not to be able to help—all during his high school years he was able to work on the ranch almost every day before going to bball practice (Nov-Mar) and work on his homeschool CD curriculum at "Tim's School of Fun". So thankful he could do that with Howard, Grpa, and the family! I went through Tim's truck and trailer this week and wow, was that hard . . . Had a good cry with just You, seeing Tim's boots, jeans, National jackets, etc. in the sleeper of his truck . . . His trailer with all his clothes, boots, Bible, etc.—Grma and Aunt Margaret had cleaned, weatherproofed, and mouse-proofed it after Tim's accident and it had been parked inside the big building for protection, but mainly that Tim wouldn't see it when he came out to the Ranch. Working cattle at the other end of the building doesn't allow him to see it, but this is the first time I made myself go in.

Had a guest speaker in church who talked on Philippians! What timing You have when we just finished reading that book in our reading last night! Thank You for the moisture from the snow! We pray for possible steps this week with the walker, continues improvement with his eye alignment, voice to return to pre-accident tone, function of left arm/hand—our list is long, but You're a good and gracious Father who wants good things for His Children, so because of because we are Your Children, we come to You! Thank You for another week and looking forward to this week of miracles! He continues to ask God to 'answer' quicker with his progress. We ask you to pray for the suffering-character-hope attitude (Romans 5:2-4) to continue as we all watch and 'wait on the Lord' with Tim's healing and restoration. Continue to pray for strength, coordination, balance as we are ever so close to taking those unassisted steps, for vision and voice quality to continue to improve, and for the full function of his left arm! Tim set up his own Facebook and learning all about his updated phone as many of you know—the computer time has been great for him—he so enjoys reading the texts, wall posts, emails, cards! He likes to talk on the phone as many of you also know—thank you for your time with your acts of encouragement and prayer support. Next Sunday will complete our ninth month on this journey—so we ask you to pray for renewed energy, focus, and strength especially for Tim, but also for us, as we walk with Him day by day!

Week of March 7-13, 2011—Tim rode 1.7 miles and did great on the recumbent bike! Hearing more intonation with Tim praying at night especially—PTL! I think praying is his best speech therapy! He prayed that he would not be left like this and we pray that You'll keep Satan from putting those thoughts and fears in Tim's thoughts, his heart, his room or this house! We did take him off the Zanaflex and pray that his body adjusts so we don't see any increase in spasms. Praying that You stimulate, regrow, reconnect those nerve endings that You created to work the way You intended. Wait-Work-& Watch! Had a pool day and we continue to see the benefits of the water with Tim! Therapies for the week went well—seeing more and more control with his left foot coming through, the ankle is still weak and there's not much flexibility with it. We're praying for some steps by Howard's birthday! I'm really tired, I know Howard is also—would love a whole night sleeping by him, but I know this is just a 'season' and in Your time Tim will be up walking and total control over his sleeping (more than 5 hours!) and his body! We prayed that someday soon he could 'walk' up and down the stairs at church—whatever and whenever You give the healing, balance, coordination, etc. Excited for next week, thank You for the good week we've had.

Acts 17:26 "From one man He made every nation of men, that they should inhabit the whole earth; and He determined the times set for them and the exact places where they should live." Psalm 118:8 "It is better to trust in the Lord than to put confidence in man" This was our memory verse this week and it draws into the first one in showing that God is in total control and has planned and determined everything about each one of us. The time you were born, where you grew up with the family activities in your specific area, the friends and friendships along the way, the experiences you've been through to exactly where, what you are going through, and who you are today. That shows the awesomeness of our God! To know, believe, love and trust in that God that knows everything about me keeps me on my knees knowing we can walk together on this journey of life. Some of you may already know this information about Psalm 118:8, but again it shows God's planning and design. I heard it in a sermon. Psalm 118:8 is the exact middle (chapter and verse) of the Bible; there are 594 chapters before and 594 chapters after totaling 1188! The shortest chapter, Psalm 117 is before it with the longest chapter, Psalm 119 after it. To have this as our 'center' verse of where our trust should be in our life! Tim continues to have progress every week and his therapists are so pleased to see this steadiness. We hope to go practice on our stairs at church this week—Tim really wants to 'walk' into church and his new goal date is for Howard's birthday which is this week! He really swings his left foot and leg through and can place the foot down on the floor so we are really close to putting the weight down on it to take those steps!! The bike is great for him and he now pedals with both legs and feet equally and up to two miles—more this week! We are hearing stronger voice quality. Even with the time change, he starts his day about 5:00 a.m.! Be thankful he doesn't call or text any of you at that time! Rarely a nap, and it's usually around 11:00 before it is quiet around here, but it is a blessing to hear him read, pray, and talk! God gives rest and we are trusting Him for this season of our life. Thank you again for holding all of us up in prayer as you have and continue to BELIEVE

Week of March 14-20, 2011—Monday night's prayer just broke my heart, so I was glad to see them go out to the ranch. Because of the fear of being left like this, he said it might have been better to just have 'gone on home'. God, we've told him that You could have taken him, but You didn't and that You know and have plans for him here and we are so grateful. I'm so thankful that You do encourage him through Your word, friends, and family and that he usually just has a thought like this once in a awhile and usually gets back on track in his prayer for his thanks and requests. We pray and have prayed for so long for Tom and Gayle fighting his battle with Lou Gehrig's disease. Our hearts break and for Tim to ask You to heal Tom first as You are healing him brings tears to our eyes. We took Tim to 'test' a few recliners—he is wearing out the one we have! Need a bigger one for our big guy! Thursday was Howard's birthday and just like our anniversary, we worked cattle! We don't do gifts, but I did find the card I bought a little while back! He came back in time for us to have therapy and it took all of us (and the big yellow ball), but we got him down on the floor! I had control of the left hand, and had to curve it over a big can for his hand to relax! The Torrington College Rodeo is next weekend and he wants to go, but not in his wheelchair, so it's in Your 'court' as to a miracle! The first spring rodeo was in Gillette this weekend and it's killing him reading and talking with Coach and others. He did really well at Torrington last year and I know that weighs in on it also. Jack calls, and the female friends encourage him with their calls, but he sure would like to hear from some of his buddies—I told him they were busy and they probably don't know what to say, do they talk about rodeos, roping, etc. or will it hurt Tim to hear all that? We pray that as we sleep in Your Hands at night that we will awake to see him miraculously healed, walking, and talking the way You created, grew, and matured him before the accident. Another friend of Howard's called and didn't know anything about Tim—we stayed at their house on the way to Nationals '08. He and Howard had a long talk!

Highlight of the week was when Lee came over and went with Howard and Tim to go shoot pistols! People look at us a little questioning when Tim tells them about his shooting! He does really well and brings home the target boards to show me if I haven't gone with them. All the grout dried and Tim took the first shower in the new bathroom! First time Tim stood with Howard holding him as they rode in the little elevator at church! We carry the chair up and wheel him in to sanctuary—someday he will walk up & down those stairs and not need the wheelchair! Healing for Your glory! Romans 6:13 "Do not offer parts of your body to sin, as instruments of wickedness, but rather offer yourselves to God, as those who have been brought from death to life; and offer the parts of your body to Him as instruments" God's timing always amazes me—When I asked Tim what book he wanted to read next he said Romans and after we read and prayed, here I am typing this verse. It was during one of our nightly prayer times that Tim told the Lord that he sure didn't understand the timing of or the allowance of this injury, but that he was trusting Him for the healing and the 'good' (Rom 8:28). How God chooses and uses experiences and people is in His hands, His power, and His purpose! The closing prayer of this devotional is a tough prayer to really put your heart in and mean—Lord, I want to be someone that You might delight in using for Your glory. When You desire to accomplish a certain task, I want You to think of me. That's why I offer myself unreservedly to You. Please take me, cleanse me, fill me, and use me. (*Diamonds in the Dust*, Joni Eareckson Tada) The Lord is teaching, refining, cleansing, etc. us all in different ways! Tim has improved this week—especially with his left fingers! The therapists had him down on all fours and one of them helped hold the hand out flat so Tim could do three push-ups! Continue to pray for his vision to improve (Tim normally shoots left-eyed, but his right eye is a bit stronger for right now) He is reading smaller print every week! Tim is also planning to attend the college rodeo this weekend so pray for emotional strength not only for him, but many of his friends. Also, please read Habakkuk 3:17-19 . . . no this or that—YET—rejoice in God, salvation, strength, feet, and walk!!! Thank you again and again for your prayers and encouragement and BELIEVING!

Week of March 21-27, 2011—Tim started the week off with riding four miles on the bike! We are having to do less and less of 'holding' left foot, left hand, and head! Tim got three calls telling us about the cover on the Pro Rodeo Sport News magazine with Cimarron (Boardman) winning the San Angelo Rodeo on Red Bull! Cimarron told in the story's interview about Tim owning the horse and that he was riding him right now and so on. Tim was really happy for Cimarron. Therapies have gone well with working on the bench for balance and upper body strength and standing in the walker with people on the sides, not everybody all around! Tim enjoys visitors, even if he's just meeting them for the first time, but especially when close friends take the time to drive over or up here. It had been a long time since Tim had seen Mitch or Joe, but it was a good visit and supper with them. The 'high and the low' of the week came together when we went to the Torrington Rodeo—lots of hugs, tears, handshakes, laughs, and many friends. I was concerned so much for Tim that I hadn't emotionally prepared myself! Talk about emotionally drained after the day! Lord, You know his heart and how he's hurting to be healed by YOU! Thank You for the moisture with the snow! Went to Rodeo Church (Torrington) then watched the finals.

Down to one pill a day, God, You are so good! I think we are seeing better sleep and fewer spasms—PTL!! Goodnight, Lord, we love You! Psalm 27:8 "My heart says of You, "Seek His face!" Your face, Lord, will I seek."

A story is told about passengers on a ship becoming alarmed as a storm on the sea came up and waves of water were coming on board. One of the passengers sneaked upstairs into where the ship's captain was strapped to the wheel while he was steering the ship. He smiled at the passenger in a reassuring way and the passenger went back to the others and told them that he had seen the captain and with the captain's smile, the message was 'all is well' (kind of reminds me of the song, *It Is Well*). We've had a different road this summer, but many of you have prayed and kept your eyes looking down that 'road' for Tim to come back-physically! We have seen, heard, and felt that "All is Well" from Him through many of you with words, cards, hugs, prayers, gifts, etc. Thank you again for all the extra time spent with Tim and us this weekend. It was both good to watch the roping, but extremely hard—it continues to be a passion for him and he prays God will let him rope again. We thank you again and again for your prayer support and encouragement. To God be the Glory!

Week of March 28-April 3, 2011—Have had some great therapy sessions with Tim showing more balance sitting on the bench without back or arm support, "walking" with the walker (still with us beside him), three steps with the left foot without any help lifting it!!! and had a saddle session with improvement there! Up to five miles on the bike this week. It breaks my heart, yet I am so glad he has 'special' times with Howard when they talk at night—I go down stairs to our bedroom and while I'm writing, praying, cleaning through things, I listen to them talk and it blesses me and also makes my heart cry. He prays for You not to leave him in that chair, and to allow him to walk down the aisle of our church praising and showing our church family how You have healed, and to thank them for all the time they have spent in prayer for him and our family! Tim praying to "walk" by May 1st—which is the weekend of the Laramie College Rodeo. We believe anything is possible with You! His desire and passion for roping burns even more now—hard to believe it could ever be stronger than it was.

I think I'm more tired than I let myself think or let others see. I pray that my girls grow with me during this time and thank You for them—we are so blessed! (Even though You and I know their 'halos' are bent sometimes!) Had great moisture from the four inches we had on Sunday morning. Always a sight to see Howard and Tim wheeling to church in the wheelchair (Howard is the 4-wheel drive!) Sunday's are hard with waking with the expectation of maybe this is the Sunday he "walks' in to church and then closing the day and week without the "big miracle' as Tim calls it. Lord, we thank You for bringing us through another day and week, asking for a good night's sleep for the next day and week ahead as we trust You, believe, and work hard climbing this 'mountain' in Your name and with Your strength! Ecclesiastes 3:12 "He has made everything beautiful in its TIME. He has also set eternity in the hearts of men; yet they cannot fathom what God has done from beginning to end." Psalm 57:2 "I cry out to God Most High, to God who fulfills His purpose for me."

Trying to live in and wait on the Lord in His TIME to make things beautiful and to fulfill His purposes is not only a daily struggle, but oh, what a blessing it is also! Knowing that we can trust, believe, and walk with Him as His children, and also be confident that He finishes what He starts! Tim continues to pray asking God to not only totally heal him, but to restore him to be able to rope again—Tim feels God is going to because He hasn't taken his passion for roping away and He started and worked with Tim just like Tim has started and worked with his horses! Our devotionals this week dealt with changes in our lives as the seasons change. We praise Him for the seasons and giving patience to wait for the changes in our lives. As He's working with each of us, we gratefully thank Him for giving grace in the tough times to praise Him! Tim had really good therapies the saddle working on upper body balance, but his highlight as many of you read on his Facebook was to pull/lift his left leg and foot all the way through for three steps without anyone touching his leg! PTL! He is starting to shave by himself, so we hope to soon be standing at the bathroom sink shaving, brushing, and combing his hair! Continue to pray that God really shows His healing power with Tim's left hand/fingers and upper arm functions-he's able to lift his hand and forearm, arm wrestle, and improving with opening his fingers more and more!! PRAY & BELIEVE!!!

Week of April 4-10, 2011—Therapy had Tim working on the big wedges on the floor and he could hold himself in a pushup position (bent knee)! Left leg pulling through more and more! Tim hit the six mile mark this week and had great improvement on the wall weight thing we have (Tower 200) and even saw some movement with his left fingers—good to see! Tim "walked" in to the bathroom and gave the new toilet a try—another huge hurdle to work on. Lord, please restore, refuel, etc. me—the tiredness sometimes 'leaks' out with my family. I pray that my attitude actions, tone, volume, everything about me comes across to show love, a balance between tough love and unconditional love, 'momma' love, 'wife' love, patience, support, encouragement, etc. to have meaning in and for their lives. Tim would really like to say a few words at Laramie. He asked us if he should ask Coach Luper. We told him if he felt like God wanted him to do that, He would work it all out. Great worship service today as Tim "stood" with our assistance and held on to a chair in front of him with his right hand during the songs—several people saw him then would tell the person next to them and they would look! Six months from when we came home from Craig and the men would carry him up the stairs in his wheelchair to being able to 'stand' a bit with us! Showed me how fast time goes, but also how slow it has been—especially to Tim. 'Slow' anything was not ever in Tim's vocabulary or thoughts—except in the roping (tying the calf) thought of 'gotta go slow to be fast' with his hands and tying string! I think Tim took nap number nine since we've been home on Sunday afternoon, so we all took a nap also! Praying for Your direction and words for Tim (for Laramie), stamina, balance, eye alignment, voice, cold clears up, and functionality of that left arm/hand—BIG list, but You're a Big GOD! Goodnight!

Romans 8:38-39 "For I am convinced that neither death or life, neither angels nor demons, neither the present nor the future, nor any powers, neither height nor depth, nor anything else in all creation, will able to separate us from the love of God that is in Christ Jesus our Lord." What a verse! To say it all and truly believe it, takes your breath away. Because of the Cross we can totally trust in Him when we accept Him and His gift of salvation and then be able to stand behind this verse! Love hung on that Cross and love arose from the dead three days later—and we will never be separated from that love. Talking with some friends this week, we talked about that total trust to let Him have our circumstances. So many times I've trusted Him to guide me in situations to know how to handle the situation—but there are times in our lives when we have to totally give Him the circumstance and in love, 'wait on Him'. Ran across this the other day . . . 'In the blink of an eye, life can change. Don't worry—God never blinks'! In a way I can see that as trust. We have put our trust in Him and continue to fully trust Him daily and nightly for and in this circumstance. We don't know the 'why's' or the plans of this journey—but we do 'know whom we have believed' (great song and verse!). Tim has had another week of improvement! His therapists mention several statements about his left fingers/hand opening up more and more, strength, balance, clarity, etc improving every time they come! Praise the Lord—he is off all medications and feels really good, and this cold he has had is breaking up! Looking forward to Spring and getting out! PRAY & BELIEVE!

Week of April 11-17, 2011—Tim rode two times on Thursday for a total of nine miles, plus they brought the E-stim machine and used it on Tim's arms and legs! Tim went to Cheyenne for a chiro apt—had six ribs and two neck vertebrae 'out'! Thank You, Lord, for Tim's positive attitude, smile, laugh, and hard work! Today marks five years ago when Dad went to the hospital and You took him 'Home' seventeen days later—so hard to believe still, but know he and Shena are together with You. Watching for miracles this week! Isaiah 9:7 "For to us a child is born, to us a son is given, and the government will be on his shoulders. And he will be called Wonderful Counselor, Mighty God, Everlasting Father, Prince of Peace." Whether your fear is of the here and now or fear of the future—this Prince of Peace is the only One that can not only GIVE, but BE that peace for all times! Even though we place our lives in His Hands, that placement does not guarantee protection from suffering-but He promises to always be there! That Hand to hold on to (and squeeze at times!) and trust that He is standing right beside us brings peace beyond understanding. We have experienced that many different times and I can't tell you how many people told us of the peace God gave them through Tim's attitude. What encouragement!

We pray that this week with Good Friday and Easter that each of you will "look inside and ask the question, What did He die for? In this day and time, walking daily with the Prince of Peace is what allows us to walk down our journeys of life. Tim has had a progressive week! A new electrical stimulus machine the therapists are using has Tim's left side muscles working overtime! (I still think our cattle hot-shots would work as well) After being stretched and popped back into place, he felt really good and we think that it will help greatly with balance and strength! He was able to stand during the music portion of the service this morning and with better balance than last week. He was able to get out and shoot some, hitting eight for eleven of his targets! We ask you to specifically pray for these next two weeks for balance and coordination-Tim wants to take steps without our assistance by May 1st! He continually sets goals and prays nightly that God will heal him "quicker", but continually places his trust in His timetable! Have a Blessed Resurrection Day!

Week of April 18-24, 2011—Tim had a four minute standing time on Monday! Yea! After therapy on Tuesday, we jumped in our vehicle and drove to Pine for a chiro apt and I can't believe we forgot Tim's wheelchair! They had us pull to the back where it was flat ground and we rolled Tim in on an office chair! We laughed as we drove home (I'm sure that will knock us down from 'Caregivers of the Year'). Continue to thank You as we see improvement and 'little' miracles—we are trying really hard to "Be still and know You are God" and WAIT on You and Your timing!

    Wednesday brought him riding eight miles on the bike—and at a higher level of resistance than any of us can ride! He typed and worked on his Laramie speech—slow with just his right hand, but he's persistent. Thursday's therapy was a sight with Tim's cowboy boots and his shorts! We tried them because his left ankle sometimes wants to roll. Easter weekend allowed the girls to be home on Friday. Saturday, we got Tim in the dually pickup and the girls rode DJ and Bandit in the arena while I walked Conoco around, talking with You. Tim and I had talked while the girls and Dad were in the barn about not knowing if we were ready to go in the arena? He went with Grpa and Dad to unload things off the dually. He petted, rubbed, and 'talked' with his horses like they were old friends . . . brought tears to my eyes! We sat in the navigator while they put up the horses, and Tim said "I miss them so much, I can't tell them what happened, they don't understand why I'm sitting in this chair and not riding them, why we're not roping . . ."

We came home and finished Tim's parallel bars (Howard made them with steel pipes!) and he used them a little with our help. We skyped the Arkansas clan and it was fun seeing and talking with everyone! Easter Sunday today!! Tim got on four-wheeler with Howard and Andy on the side—they rode around a little and then we took pictures around it with everyone! Had the annual 'Martha' scavenger hunt all over the Ranch. Kaden sure misses Tim on his team! Lord, how we thank You again and again for the Cross and what You had Your Son do to die for us and then You raised Him up so we could become Your Children. I will never understand that love, but have accepted You and I thank You for my salvation and my family's.

Tell Daddy and Shena, "Happy Easter, Hallelujah" Love you, Lord. Good Morning! We pray you will take the opportunity to worship with family and friends praising and thanking God for who He is and what He did on that Cross! But don't stop there—he's not hanging on that Cross, one crucifixion was enough! He arose and He is coming back for those who are His followers! One of our devotionals focuses on Phil 3:20 "I want to know Christ and the power of his resurrection and the fellowship of sharing in His sufferings." Coming from the South, we like to tag on "fellowship" anytime believers have food around! Not that that's bad—I just think we often times have stretched that to give the picture of an event, rather than an attitude or bonding whether it be between family, friends, but most importantly with God the Father, Son, and Holy Spirit. This verse seemed odd to me to have both fellowship and suffering together? Seem like opposites. Can our deepest fellowship with Him be found in the midst of suffering? Again, my picture of fellowship is comfort, happy, food, etc., not tears, pain, confusion. Because of His sufferings on that Cross, Jesus knows our suffering personally and we can rest in that fellowship as we walk closer and hang on tighter to His Hand!

"No one ever cared for me like Jesus,
There's no other friend so kind as He;
No one else could take the sin and darkness from me—
Oh how much He cared for me!"

What a great hymn! Tim has had a good week. He is over his cold so his breath control with speaking is stronger—as many of you know with his phone calls! He averages about seven miles a day on his bike, along with many therapy exercises, e-stim machine, weights, etc. So thankful Tim is strong enough to 'walk with assistance' and get in our vehicle so well! We wheeled Tim into the arena and he petted and talked with his horses like old friends. On the way back to the barn, Tim commented how hard, but how good it was to be in there, see, smell, and feel his horses. It's hard for me to see Tim emotionally hurt through this journey, but I have never understood how God watched His Son on that Cross! Just like I've told so many about the sovereignty of God and dying for me—He didn't ask me to understand it—just accept it! We continue to ask for the balance, coordination, left hand/arm function, continued positive attitude, and complete trust and joy in the Lord as we watch Him heal and restore Tim. Blessings to You!

Week of April 25-May 1, 2011—Tim went out to fish ponds with Howard to clean aerators and then they did some target shooting—had improvement with Tim's left index finger! The E-stim machine really makes Tim tired so he took nap number thirteen on Tuesday after doing several things in therapy and the machine! Yea!! Tim called the miracle of walking, the "Grand Miracle" and is praying for the weekend in Laramie! (I doubt if he remembers or even knows the first street in coming into Laramie is Grand street) After working with Tim's left fingers and hand while Howard was out loading some bulls, I went down to Jessica's track meet at Pine Bluffs. Tim had another saddle day and it took one less person to help him on it! Weekend turned off cold, even had a little snow! God's timing amazes me and with it, I asked for and needed an extra dose of emotional strength over the weekend. Five years ago on Thursday, I flew home to see Daddy and eventually said "good bye" and ushered him into Heaven singing songs with Mom and my sisters around his bed!

What a morning Sunday was—I went early to get ten dozen doughnuts for Rodeo Church. They told us they usually have around 60-70 and there was about 150-175! With the confusion of announcing and the fliers printed with the 10:00 or 10:30 start time, some came in late and missed Tim's "sermon' so I'm to send about ten families DVD's of Tim. LOTS of tears, I don't know how Tim talked with being that close to them seeing and hearing the tears and sobs. They stood up with him as this was the first time Tim 'stood' that long and then they gave him a standing ovation at the end . . . Lord, we give that to You. This journey is all about You! I sang "That's What Faith Can Do" while everyone held hands—thank You for getting me through that! Besides the emotional weekend, service, and rodeo, Tim had some added emotional time with some of his friends that really weighed on him, but he said he was 'giving it to You and moving on'. Stayed for the awards ceremony which was TOUGH on the heart! Thank You for the weekend!

Lamentations 3:37-38 "Who can speak and have it happen if the Lord has not decreed it? Is it not from the mouth of the Most High that both calamities and good things come?" Another verse that asks you to accept His sovereignty over all time and things along with and during life's calamities that God has known about, has allowed, has planned, etc. It was stated in our rodeo church today that God knew all about Tim's accident just as He knew Tim would be there today speaking's another reassurance of Him knowing that nothing catches God by surprise. He all-knowing! To FULLY trust in Him, in that situation, in His timing, in/with all areas of your life because of the Cross is what Tim spoke on today in rodeo church. He typed up his thoughts as he felt God had laid on his heart and with assistance from us and with everyone standing with Tim, he read his words as God strengthened and spoke through him. It was encouraging to Tim and there were so many tears from many, many friends. We had a great crowd and along with the other speakers, God touched friendships and lives! PTL! I will try to print his testimony in a few days. Tim had prayed to walk into the rodeo church at Laramie this weekend at the last rodeo of the college season, but we are still waiting on God's timing. Tim has progressed with moving his left leg/foot fully through almost every step—PTL for God's healing of muscle memory and nerve restoration. Notice the 'ing' of healing-it's ongoing, and we look forward to the day we can add the 'ed' to healed! But until that day, we continue to ask and receive enough grace, love, and strength for each day! Please continue to lift up Tim's left hand/arm to become fully functional this week and praise God for all the many blessings He gives us daily. We especially thank you for your continued prayers and encouragement. We want to also thank everyone at Laramie for a great two days with your support to Tim and our family with your hugs, words, and the time you took to touch or talk with him. He pleads to God to let him rope again so we set that goal to be there next year! When we said that, we said "that would be UNBELIEVABLE but we have an UNBELIEVABLE GOD! Have a great week!

Week of May 2-8, 2011—Tim started the week off by moving his 'goal date' to walk by Bandit's birthday (you know you're close to your horses when you plan things around their birthday!) With Grpa & Grma delivering bulls out in western Wyoming, Tim went out to the Ranch with Howard to sort bulls, again a hard time watching ranch work he loved doing and so badly wants to get back to doing! Wednesday was the five-year mark of Daddy's Celebration Service—lots of memories! I so thank You for my Christian Daddy—tell him how much I loved him and that I'm trying to "take care of his babies"! Tim had more new exercises in therapy sessions this week—had to get on his bed, get straight, roll on his sides & belly by himself! Had some floor time on the big wedge doing his push-ups with our extra help with his left hand and leg, but he did great, and we see improvement! Friday held a good time with Tim on the 4-wheeler riding, checking & fixing fence—and he balanced himself while Howard would get off to staple, stretch, or whatever to the fence! He's still a little heavy on the throttle, so he doesn't get to run it alone! Saw improvement on his parallel bars (I think it's the parents' awkwardness that is a sight to see!) This nicer weather has Howard and Tim out shooting some—they really enjoy that together! Church was eye-opening with the picture of the replica of Noah's Ark that was built in the Netherlands—still it was half as long and only a third wide of God's specific measurements! With that You showed me through all Your 'specifics', You know and created all of Tim's specifics, and we pray those specific spots (nerves, muscles, joints, fingers, eyes, voice, brain messages, etc) to be healed, renewed, and restored.

Sure enjoy my surprise writing journal Bethany made (with the help of the other three) covered with younger pictures of them on both front and back covers! Thank You again for allowing me to be the "Mom" of Timothy, Bethany, Cassady, and Jessica—my angels with the 'bent halos'! John 12:36 "Put your trust in the light while you have it, so that you may become sons of light." Our church has some beautiful stained glass windows that because of the specific placement of the pieces of glass, they depict a beautiful picture—one of ours is Jesus praying. This journey with Tim is much like shattered, broken glass—shattered dreams, broken heart. Just like the time and careful placement of those pieces and/or the beauty from stained glass or pieces of broken glass, their beauty is seen because of the light that comes through them. With trust in God's timing, healing, and restoring, Tim's life story may have a brighter light than what it may have had before the accident—only God knows His purpose and plans for Tim.

(*Shine, Jesus, Shine*—another great chorus/song) What a blessing it is and continues to be to hear Tim totally put his trust in God's timing and promises even though he asks Him to move quicker and to show him the little 'things' while he is waiting for the big 'things'. Tim continues to work hard as he trusts Him. Tim has had a good week! We, along with therapists and others, notice daily 'things' with his rehab. PTL!! His left hand has shown some improvement, so please continue to pray for full function. He was able to ride with just Howard beside him on the four-wheeler as they checked fence one day. He had good upper body balance as he would sit and wait when Howard needed to get off to mend some fence. We used the parallel bars in the yard to walk (with us). We see improvement there! He sat in a chair while shooting at some target boards this week and was very accurate. He was able to do some push-ups on the wedge with his arms while on his bed.

He made a comment last night that 'Wow, eleven months"—It's hard to believe we are just a month away from the accident's one-yr date. The timing of not walking by himself is the main struggle Tim has to daily give over to God and trust Him—Tim always closes his night with praying that tomorrow may be the day that God lets him walk out of his room on his own! It's such a blessing and encouragement to watch and hear him set goals and reset goals! He is an usher in a wedding in about one month—it would be great to see him stand on his own and what else God has restored in May! We continue to thank you for all the prayers, love, and encouragement from you as you continue on this journey with us! Happy Mother's Day! I thank God for my Mom—one of her many characteristics is her emotional strength because of her faith in God—watching her through many life situations has and is such an encouraging example for me. So very thankful for my 'other' Mom (Howard's Mom)—such a prayer warrior and encouragement, love you! Keep Prayin' & Believin'!

Week of May 9-15, 2011—Tim "walked" up our two stairs from the backdoor into our kitchen tonight, YEA! After speech on Tuesday, I prayed quietly to myself for not only Tim's voice to return to 'normal', but that I recognize it! Also, praying the Tim not only has his balance returned, but that he recognizes where 'mid-line, balanced" is, and can adjust! Found a song going some through books my friend, Nancy, gave to me. It's a John W Peterson one titled, *I Will Trust When I Cannot See*.

(Chorus) "I will trust when I cannot see—When I'm faced with adversity And believe Your will is always best for me—I will trust when I cannot see."

Friday was Bandit's bday Tim didn't have his "walk" miracle so now he prays to walk when Beth gets home! Tonight Tim wanted to sleep by himself on Saturday—It's been since Oct 1, so a little over seven months that Howard, I, or one of the girls has slept beside him for some part of the night! It's not strange to me remembering how he would sleep beside Bethany when she was in the crib, or when they all four would sleep in the living room! He had a good night, so he said he would try it again on Sunday! Tim rode seven miles Sunday evening! Thank You,

Lord, for the friendship and marriage Howard and I have with You. It's good to be in our bed all night together. Pray for May Miracles!!!

Tim's writings that he spoke at the Rodeo Church (UW College Rodeo—May1st) were printed in the *Rodeo News* magazine issue that came out this week so I will send it this week for our update. He typed this on his computer and then we enlarged/printed it so he could read it when he spoke.

God Said To Be Joyful by Tim Malm

First off I would like to say thank you for praying for me, and please continue because I plan on being back here next year. I felt lead to say this morning just make sure you're fully trusting GOD because you never know what the next few minutes of your life may hold. Now I'm not saying that an accident will happen to you if you're not trusting GOD but I am saying make sure you are trusting Him. I thought I was trusting Him before my accident and He showed me lots of little things that I wasn't giving Him. He has given me new meaning to fully trusting Him. I truly believe that God has a purpose for this accident. I don't know what the purpose is but I'm just going to live in His timing and trust Him and see where He takes me. That doesn't mean it's not breaking my heart to not be here competing. I'm just saying to live every minute and make sure you're taking advantage of every opportunity because everything happens for a reason and for God's purpose. The verse that's kept me going through all of this is Philippians 4:13, "I can do all things through Christ who strengthens me." Now I am here to prove this because if it wasn't for His strength I wouldn't be here. Good is coming through this because I've had an impact and met people through this that I never would have had contact with. I've learned through this there is a difference between being happy and being joyful. God said to be joyful. I'm not happy with this situation but I'm learning to be joyful. And I count it pure joy that this happened to me because I must have been doing something right to make Satan take notice. I can just see it now—Satan arguing over whether I would curse God. Satan has lost and I want to honor God. Just remember God will never give you more than you can handle. John 10:10 says, "The thief comes only to steal. and kill, and destroy. I came that they might have life, and might have it abundantly." Who all here loves their parents?—well God loves you a million times more and wants a personal relationship with you, it's that easy. God loves you so much, He sent His Son to die for you. he arose from that grave and is coming back again someday for His followers who have trusted Him. I'll be with Him and want you to be with us. I want to again thank you for everything. Keep Praying and Believing!

Tim had another week of improvements. His therapists noticed great improvement with upper body balance while on his saddle and more use of the left hand and arm. He has used our other door entry with its two stair steps into the kitchen along with our assistance. Continue to pray specifically for the left hand and upper arm and left ankle to be strengthened to hold Tim when he takes those steps. Bethany will be coming home this weekend so please keep her in your prayers for that long drive! PRAY & BELIEVE!!

Week of May 16-22, 2011—I was encouraged to speak at and give an update of Tim at a Women's Bible Study group in Pine Bluffs. They have been praying and staying up with Tim with all the weekly Caringbridge updates, it was good to meet some of the many people praying for Tim and for our family! Tim got to 'swing' his rope this week! Hit the 'confusion' verses he calls them (faith/mustard seed, two—three gathered in My name, Ask-Believe-Receive, nothing impossible, etc.) when we prayed. I'm so thankful he is so open with You and with us about what he's thinking! Lord, we persevere and trust You. She drove on in on Saturday and we took pictures beside the big sign we'd made and taped to the house, "Welcome Home Beth" We made her wait for Tim to "walk" down the ramp to hug her! He so badly wanted to walk for her by himself—another goal date—Father's Day! Wouldn't that be the greatest present for Howard to see his son walk!?! Tim roped the calf dummy while I held on to him from behind—stood fairly good! I'm strong, but I'm not a very tall 'horse' for Tim who now stands about 6'2" or 6'3"!! He prays so hard to rope again—watches NFR calf roping tapes in his bed every night! Long week, but You have blessed in so many ways—we pray for a good night's sleep for all!

Ephesians 2:10 "For we are His workmanship, created in Christ Jesus for good works, which God prepared beforehand, that we should walk in them." Tim is daily evidence as he displays his trust in His Savior and Lord to heal and restore. It was good to watch him work in his saddle and swing his rope! He was able to sit in his chair and rope the bale and dummy! It was a year ago today that Tim was one of Bethany's escorts for her graduation, and two weeks away from it being a year since Tim's accident—what a year! We've trusted every step of the way when we could not see, and we will continue to trust Him to walk where He leads and we cannot see! We will continue to ask, keep the faith, and agree with all of you, in Jesus' name, for complete healing and restoration! We get to go see the neurosurgeon doctor that had Tim for the first time since we left Cheyenne ICU—he has been keeping up with Tim in other ways, but it will be good for him to see and hear Tim! To God be the Glory! Please continue to pray for left hand/arm function, balance, and steps—the wedding is in two and a half weeks, plus he would like to walk into church in two weeks!!! PRAY & BELIEVE!!!

Week of May 23-29, 2011—The therapists observed us loading and unloading Tim in our navigator! We "passed" enough to get home from Craig, but it's not a typical wheelchair-patient load! I thank You and ask You to continue to give to us all—Tim does better and better with stepping up, while Howard lifts/stabilizes, and I hold Tim's right arm/hand as the 'bar' to push on. He hasn't hit the back of his head yet! Thank goodness the seat goes all the way back to have enough leg/feet room! Went to Dr. Beer's and after waiting an hour in the office, got to see him about ten minutes for a "how ya doing?" apt! He's still impressed with all of Tim's progress! Bethany and I went to Cheyenne on Wed. and finally found Tim a pink long-sleeved shirt for Lori & Brett's wedding—he's supposed to hand out the programs. Lord, we thank You for all the moisture this week, ending of a great school year, and now, I have a sophomore in college and high school, and an eighth grader! Looking forward to this next week with our whole family!

> ". . . We pray for Your mighty hand to ease our suffering
> All the while, You hear each spoken need . . .
> And what if trials of this life
> The rain, the storms, the hardest nights
> Are Your mercies in disguise?"

This is a song by Laura Story which has really encouraged us and goes along with Zechariah 4:6 "Not by might nor by power, but by My Spirit,' says the Lord Almighty." The verse centered around a devotional on the irony of God where it uses the dictionary's definition of irony ad "a combination of circumstances that is the opposite of what might be expected." We can sure see how all 'blessings' can and does show the irony of God with His sovereignty, timing, healing, restoring, love, peace, comfort, mercy, and forgiveness. The prayer for the day—Mighty and Powerful Lord, I praise You for the marvelous way You accomplish Your purposes. Blessings encourage us as we wait, watch, and work as God accomplishes His purposes in our lives. Choosing to see, hear, feel, and receive His blessings is a choice and we receive them with a grateful heart. We are almost at the one-year date of Tim's accident and time has both flown by and stood still at the same time! We have been and continue to be overwhelmed with blessings of answered prayers, friendships, hugs, encouragement, gifts, tears, spiritual growth, etc., but above all—the faithfulness of our God.

Tim continues to show improvement in different areas; stronger left arm support doing push-ups on his bed, taking off/putting on his own t-shirt, left hand opening out straighter, left arm/hand movement in and out from his side, and the highlight of his week was to sit in a fold-out bag chair beside the chute and prod cattle while they worked at the ranch all day Friday! We continue to ask God daily and nightly for His miraculous hand of healing and wait expectantly—He continues to provide the grace, strength, and perseverance for the day! Even though we ask God to move this mountain—He does expect us to keep digging! We ask for prayers this week for renewed and refreshed hearts and feet as we walk this journey with Tim, especially with the one-year date coming up! Be Blessed and Be a Blessing!

Week of May 30, June 5, 2011—What a week! I thank You again for taking care of us with all the different directions we were going! Tim had some great therapy sessions with "bed" exercises—getting on and off, balance sitting on the side, "walking" a little better with Howard, me or the therapist and beside the parallel bars, and got to rope on the dummy some! WOW-One year on Sunday! Pat (McL) was our speaker today—he did a fabulous job! At the end, I spoke a little (was very hard with lots of people crying!) and then the whole church got in a circle around the church walls while I sang, *What Faith Can Do* (I had to turn my back to them).

We thanked our church family for their prayer support and encouragement. One of the main thoughts we wanted to stress was this faith journey is for Tim, but it's not about Tim—It's all about You, Lord! We pray for all to see Your power, Your majesty, Your healing, Your love, and Your faithfulness! We thank You for carrying Howard and I, Tim, our girls, and our families through this year. One of the goals Tim had set was to be walking today, but we are standing in Your timetable and will continue to work and wait, trusting You! The 24-hour prayer event starts tonight at midnight! Lord, it's hard to put in words what this last year has been . . . when the numbness finally wore off, we had no words or feelings, but to actually live on the prayers of Your people, our family, friends, and so many that we will never meet or know, and to feel You hold us with Your faithfulness, love, strength, and grace. You gave us 'manna' just enough for the day, and we accept without understanding—Your promises and plans whenever or however. I wish there were words other than 'Thank You', but I can't think of any. We thank You for what You have done, are doing, and will do this next year. It's okay to have 'blind' faith when you walk with the only One who can see you inside and out, and can see the future. Thank You for Your hand, and we won't let go. Lord and Savior, Father, Son, and Holy Spirit, Healer, Sustainer, Creator, and Eternal God Almighty—we love You! Thank you for the response we have had on Facebook, Caringbridge, and in our church to all of you who have signed up for a half-hour prayer time for the 24 Hour Praying for Tim event from midnight tonight to midnight tomorrow (June 6th). For anyone missing out with this info, look at the Wed. June 1st journal entry for the info and join us. It has gone nationwide from coast to coast and it is going to be exciting and as I said in church this morning—this is for Tim, but it is all about GOD! We wanted to mark the date and one of Tim's aunts and his sisters worked on this and we thought this could be the best way for us to celebrate, thank, and ask God for the year and the next year! We would welcome any comments, verses, songs, etc—whatever God lays on your heart as you spend your time with Him. Yes, the list of prayer requests deal with a lot of physical requests, but above all, we want this faith journey to bring people to a relationship with Jesus Christ and/or deepen relationships between Him and His followers because of the Cross. Like a coach encouraging his weary players to stay in the game—Persevere! We thank all of you and the many, many people who are on our 'team' with us—only in Heaven will you know what you and your praying have meant and means to us. Some of you may have watched the video clip of Tim on Facebook . . . he stood with assistance (Howard behind him with me bent down beside his left ankle) and roped the calf bale dummy! We roped again today and he only needs me standing behind him so Howard can watch him rope—four catches in a row! He was able to ride on the 4-wheeler (blister on his left thumb from holding the handle) while helping tag baby calves. He has raised his left arm a little more this week—PTL! We are going to have an MRI on Wednesday to have an updated one since we left Craig in October. Balance is improving—especially with standing! A year ago on the Sunday night of June 6, 2010 our lives were changed in so many ways, but only because we have a changeless God will we be able to someday say . . . for the better. PRAY & BELIEVE!

Week of June 6-12, 2011—Very uplifting and encouraging to read throughout the day from those who have prayed during the 24-hour prayer event! Drove Cassady (picked up Karissa) to Torrington for her dental cleaning then on to Mitchell to pick up all the meat from

Robinson's—it's great knowing even your meat processing business are believers and praying for us! Tim roped really well today and I might add his 'horses' (Howard and I) did well also! Howard and I fasted throughout the day and I really enjoyed reading His Word and praying outside during some quiet time—thank You for that! I hope You felt honored and glorified as many prayers were prayed throughout the 24 hours. Reminds me of where the prayers were like incense—a pleasing aroma to You! What a blessing to have Galen (H), Bob (A), Ken (M), and Frances (pastor from Uganda) come by and have a mini-prayer service with and over Tim. They assured us that they would be praying for Tim in Uganda! Tim had an MRI on Wednesday and while we were in Walmart, Dr. Beer's office called to let us know everything looked stable—PTL!! Church was really good and Tim stood for some of the singing—little bit by little bit, a little more every week! Tim roped 10/10 on the dummy tonight! Lord, we pray for safety as we will leave early in the morning for the College National Finals Rodeo at Casper. Will be up there Monday and Tuesday with our family's first mini-get away! We pray for all the 'newness' of traveling together with Tim and his wheelchair! Matthew 17:20 He replied, "Because you have so little faith. I tell you the truth, if you have faith as small as a mustard seed, you can say to this mountain, 'Move from here to there' and it will move. Nothing will be impossible for you." We sure have prayed this and we think we have watermelon-size faith compared to the mustard seed—and we have prayed and shouted "Move"! But, we always thank Him for the day and ask for the strength, grace, and 'manna' when we wake in the morning if He is going to have us WALK over this mountain! The saying goes "Trust God to move your mountains—but He expects us to keep on digging!"

I've sung the song (*When Answers Aren't Enough* by Scott Wesley Brown) many times and want to share some of the words with you.

> ". . . Instead of asking why did it happen
> Think of where it can lead you from here
> And as your pain is slowly easin' you can find greater reason
> To live your life triumphant through the tears
> When answers aren't enough—there is Jesus"

Week of June 13-19, 2011—Isaiah 30:20 "Although the Lord gives you the bread of adversity and the water of affliction, your teachers will be hidden no more; with your own eyes you will see them." This devotional caught my attention . . . it's not one of my memorized verses! It discussed deeper that the 'bread and water' are times of refining, sifting, pruning, and polishing for us for His reasons and with God's Word as the 'teacher' we can see His purposes. But as Tim has said so many times . . . the Lord rarely gives a time on when He will show His purpose, His healing, His answers . . . and that's where faith and trust keeps us going. So thankful that we can rest every night and daily walk hand-in-hand with the 'Bread of Life' and 'Living Water'. We rely on that daily 'manna' with the prayers and encouragement of all of you and thank you again for your time with Him praying for Tim and his whole family.

Long, long day! I think the emotions played a huge part! We were up at early and left at 3:38 . . . reminded me of the many times we would leave early like that when we headed out for the high school rodeos. Tim and Howard would go to the Ranch and get Tim's horses, then back in for us to 'pack up'. We always prayed as we pulled out for travel protection, arena protection, keep all the kids safe, and not hit any animals on the road! Everyone would usually be asleep and it would just be Howard and I awake as I watched for cattle, deer, etc. I enjoyed driving when everybody would be asleep—had some really good prayer/quiet times! Today is 'different' . . . Howard drove the Navigator with Tim and Cassady while I drove Beth's car with Bethany and Jessica because we all can't fit in the same vehicle with Tim's wheelchair. Howard said Tim was awake the whole way! Time, time, time—a year ago we were in ICU with Tim in Cheyenne~ two years ago Tim and Dalton (after the Douglas HS Rodeo) had left us to take the horse trailer home while they 'bummed' a night with Mitch (McA) so they could watch the CNFR calf roping slack at Casper! It was hard for me to stay focused on the day with all the flashbacks of memories! The NIRA (National Intercollegiate Rodeo Association) President, Mr. Walters, talked with Tim and we thanked him for the tickets. Tim told him he was planning on being back in Casper next year—in the 'box', not in this chair! After the slack, we went to our motel and everybody slept! Met with Coach Cullen at Applebee's! The day was filled with hugs, tears, handshakes, etc. from many, many people from not only Wyoming, but many he knew from other states from roping at Nationals (3 years) and other places he'd roped. We met many of the parents of kids from Texas, Alabama, New Mexico, Oklahoma, Can't hardly remember where all from!

On Tuesday, the evening performance was good and then everyone wanted to stay for the Cowboy Church they have afterwards—which started about 9:30 with pizza, then Cory Ross (Cory Ross Ministries) came and talked with Tim before the service started. He had come through Cheyenne last year on his way up to (CNFR) Casper and saw Tim in ICU, prayed with us over Tim in his ICU room! Tim spoke during Praise and Prayer time—did great, quoted Phil 4:13—many tears under the tent, but Tim stayed strong through it all! We left Caper about midnight with Howard driving the navigator and again, he said Tim was awake the whole way! We got home about 3:00 a.m.-almost forty-eight hours from when we left on Monday morning! THANK YOU for all the protection!

The rest of the week, we 'listened' over the Internet to the rodeo and watched the results. Tim had a good therapy session on Thursday—even though still tired from Casper, he worked hard! We were told how other kids talked at the following church services about how much Tim and his faith had affected their lives! Thank You for that encouragement—gives Tim a glimmer of showing some purpose, some good from this accident and how You work all things for good . . . (Rms 8:28)Coach Cullen, TJ, and the girls came by on their way back from Casper for a visit before heading on home. Again, we thank You for guiding Tim to NJC with his coach and his friends there. Father's Day—not any solo steps, but Tim "walked" a little further to and from the elevator at church. Lord, Lord, Lord—how we thank You for a wonderful, even though very emotional, productive week, and look forward working and waiting for Your healing Hand—physically, emotionally, mentally, in all ways! Continue to pray for full function of his left hand/arm (we are seeing some improvement every day), balance, coordination, muscle memory/strength, and praise God for his positive attitude and motivation. We will hit the one-year date of when we went to Craig (June 21st) this week and we are going back to Craig (June 27th). Pray for all that that will entail for us—especially Tim since he doesn't remember a whole lot about Craig. Keep Prayin' and Believin'! Have a Blessed week!

Week of June 20-26, 2011—What a week of devotionals for us! (Life is Hard)—1 Thess 3:2-3 "We sent Timothy, who is our brother and God's fellow worker in spreading the gospel of Christ, to strengthen and encourage you in your faith, so that no one would be unsettled by these trials. You know quite well that we were destined for them." The statement that trials are not for our pleasure, but for our profit encouraged me to know there is purpose and only God knows so I can leave that in His hands.—Gal 6:9 "Let us not become weary in doing good, for at the proper time we will reap a harvest if we do not give up." This is one of my perseverance verses I say when I need that 'second wind' to keep going. The prayer at the end of this devotional sums up some of our days; Lord, when my heart gets tired and my soul gets weary, strengthen me with your grace. Tim has had a very good week even though it started with a dental appointment on Monday, but he did well with that. Therapies went well with more intentional movement with the left hand/arm. He is lifting his left knee and extending his left foot for his steps and gaining balance with almost every step and using less and less of our assistance. His highlight of this week was to stand up on the outside of the parallel bar with his left hand grasping the bar (I helped hold the elbow above the hand) then with no one standing behind him, one therapist on his right side, one therapist on the ground by his left ankle—he was able to rope a bucket!!!

We lost the speech therapist we have had, and we will miss her, so no speech therapy today or probably for a couple of weeks. Saw more improvement and movement in Tim's left hand and arm—how we pray for full-function! Tim back on his bike routine and roping the calf dummy almost every day! Tim starting to work on cursive writing—he never did have very good handwriting, so maybe there's hope this time around!? He also worked outside on the bars with Bethany, while I held the full-length mirror so he could see to make adjustments to his standing. They went to the Ranch and sorted heifers. Richard ("Gil

Bates") and Jen came over for a visit. We hauled heifers home from Carpenter—with Howard driving the truck while Fanny, Earl, and I stayed with Tim at the corrals. The second load we drove the navigator behind the truck, and then Grpa and Grma stayed with Tim at our house while Howard and I ran the truck back down to get the last load and bring home. Tim enjoyed it, but he misses it so much.

Praying for You to heal in time to work this summer, standing, walking, talking "normal"—didn't think how good "normal" could be! We thank You for all the safety with the cattle, loading, and the roads. We packed up for our week of returning to Craig for an evaluation time—a little apprehension about the week, wondering how Tim will respond to all of it? . . . . In Your hands. We are packing to leave for Craig tomorrow for re-evals Mon-Thurs., so we ask for all ya'll to be praying for all that will entail—especially with Tim seeing, hearing, and doing all he did at Craig! It will interesting to see if any of that memory of that time will come back—I'm not sure if I care if it does or not, so we will leave that in God's hand. I'm praying that not only will he see how far God's healing and power has brought him, but will also be motivating and encouraging. This is definitely a time when the Holy Spirit has to intervene and pray for us, because of not knowing what to really pray for. We do know that our gratitude and thankfulness will never be fully expressed to our Lord and to all of you, thank you again and again. Cassady found this anonymous quote and we leave it with you for our 'moments' in the next few days at Craig.

"Happy Moments, Praise God! Difficult Moments, Seek God! Quiet Moments, Worship God! Painful Moments, Trust God! Every Moment, Thank God!"

Week of June 27-July 3, 2011—Left about 6:00 a.m. for the week at Craig. Like I've told many people, Craig is a great place, but you need to be prepared for their 'world' . . . they had talked with me before we left in October and wanted to talk with us after our evals. The inefficiency of time is the biggest complaint I have, because I see ways it could be better. The first day is repeating a lot of assessment info that could all be found out via phone, email, dvd, etc., so Monday was just a waste of time except we try to find some 'silver lining' in situations like this . . .

After just the short meetings with OT, PT, Speech, the doctor, Tim was discouraged with talk of maybe being a candidate for this "Z" cut surgery in the Achilles to allow more flexibility in walking and it would help him to not hyperextend his knee when putting pressure on the left to take a right step. The highlight of the day was having a 'cookout' over at Jenny and Jim's with the Tallents and McAdows! Good fun and friends! Laughter is the best medicine! Tim "roped" a stool for everyone in the gym before we had our last 'team meeting' before we left which was very short. June has flown by and to close it with the last four days at 'snail's pace' was both good and (I won't say bad) but it sure could have been spent better! We did get to spend time with good friends and we thank You for protection with all the Denver traffic, and time with our girls. Tim did great under the circumstances, and we completed the evaluation time at Craig (wished for more of the positive times and less of the wasted times). Thank You again for what Craig has meant in our lives. The girls and I went over early (caught a few garage sales!) to pick up Beth from her shuttle—had some good laughs at Sonic! Big day for Tim at church—he "walked" (with Howard on left side and Tim holding the banister, me behind him) up the stairs at church!!! Spent the afternoon up at Booth's for their 4th of July Celebration cookout—enjoyed it and Tim did well with being outside and visited with several people! Thank You, Lord, for a long, emotional week and for bringing Bethany home safely. We pray for this week of getting back in the routine of living in a very flexible and changing schedule!

Week of July 4-10, 2011—Tim spent his 4th with roping the dummy. He would have 'been on the road' going to a lot of rodeos if this accident hadn't happened, but this is the 'where' and the 'time' that the Lord has Tim in. Tim is praying to be able to 'walk' on Albin Day!?! This week "we" had our garage sale! Even one of the therapists bought something! Getting ready for Albin Day tomorrow! Saturday was a FULL day with Grandpa and Grandma being Grand Marshals, along with Tim—all in a RED convertible (one of Tim's favorite colors)! Took pictures with all the grandkids around the car, along with the Albin Day Queens, Katelin and Bailey! After singing the National Anthem, handing out water bottles on both sides of the street, we came home after the parade to rest a bit and get out of the heat! Went to the Night Show where a "Minute to Win It" was played by several of the community. It was great, even though our 'game show host'—Ron Rabou, fell through the stage, but luckily wasn't hurt! Jillian (McL), with Bethany's help did a beautiful job with the slide show and also had a special one, "Tim's Journey" with pictures to the song *What Faith Can Do*. With the lights turned out, you could hear the sniffles and when the lights were turned back on, there were lots of tears! It was the first time our community and the many visitors had seen pictures of Tim in the hospital 'hooked up' with all the tubes and machine, in therapy time at Craig and at home, roping pictures, and family pictures—even a first for Timothy! We hadn't realized he had not seen the hospital pictures. First time I had seen even a few tears on his face, but he handled it great! Thanks, again for that emotional strength You give him to handle situations, usually with his smile and laughter—no one sees the broken heart inside. Today was Mom's birthday—she and Tim celebrate their July birthdays in our family. Tim now prays for 'steps' by his birthday—#21! He keeps saying how he should be 'out on the road (rodeos) and getting ready to go back to school'. He was in terrific shape and strong when the accident happened, he feels like "time's a-wastin'—he doesn't ask "why" with the accident, he just wants to get things rolling and to hear God say, "Tim, pick up your mat and WALK!"

God, You gave us an amazing weekend with our community—we ask You to bless them and our surrounding communities that have been so supportive, encouraging, and caring! Isaiah 50:10 "Let him who walks in the dark, who has no light, trust in the name of the Lord and rely on his God." One of our many 'trust' verses and it gives a picture of this journey when we leave it in His Hands every night and face the next morning Psalm 63:6 "On my bed I remember You; I think of you through the watches of the night." I so enjoy our time with Tim at night with our reading in His Word, our devotional time, and our prayer time. It sets up your focus even stronger for when you can enjoy the quiet, silent time while lying in bed. Tim often tells us in the morning dreams and thoughts he had through the night and/or plans he would make for the day and what he would say on Facebook in the morning while trusting and praying alone through the night. We are excited for this week so please pray for Tim's balance to continue to improve with his Achilles' tendon lengthening to allow his left foot to flatten and not hyperextend his left knee—we are seeing improvement in this area! Prayers also for Tim—his birthday is Saturday, July 16th, and he will be 21! He doesn't remember last year's bday at Craig, so we will remember this one! Have a blessed week and PRAY & BELIEVE!!!

Week of July 11-17, 2011—Ephesians 1:3 "Praise be to the God and Father of our Lord Jesus Christ, who has BLESSED us in the heavenly realms with every spiritual blessing in Christ." Today our sermon was over chapters 1-3 with this verse as the focus. At the end of the worship time, all three girls (Bethany, Cassady, and Jessica) and I sang the song, *Blessings* (by Laura Story). I printed the words a few weeks ago. God's timing amazes me for us to sing that this morning when only He knew who the speaker would be and what he would speak on! I told our church family how looking back in my journal on July 16, 2010 (Tim's 20th birthday) it was the first day we were allowed to take Tim out of his room for one hour for his birthday party in a family room in another building! I also looked at my entry on July 17, 2010 and spoke of two things: the first being that Howard and I were excited that we could get Tim's right hand and arm to lower past his arm rest—now everyone knows how strong and full-functioning his right side is!! Secondly, we were told that Tim would probably come home with the feeding tube and machine so we would need to know how to operate them—well, God doesn't deal with 'probabilities'! Tim came home eating a full diet without the tube and has done great with all his eating! Blessings!!!

Therapies went well this week and we had over an inch of rain—of which I pray for this moisture to get to OK and TX and other dry areas! We had a great afternoon for Tim's birthday and he will remember this one! Thanks to all for all the cards, emails, posts, hugs, gifts, etc. but above all because like we said in church—Keep Prayin' and Believin' cause we're going to see more BLESSINGS! Pray for this week as it holds a full day (Wed) of Cheyenne Frontier Days (roping slack) all morning through afternoon—this was the year Tim had planned to rope at Cheyenne. It will be great to see many friends! Thursday, we have a Dr. appointment in Denver and if decided on, Tim will have an

Achilles surgery to "Z" cut which will allow his left foot to flatten and left knee not to hyperextend. Just when Tim is beginning to "walk" with assistance better and better—if he has this surgery it will be off that foot about four weeks in some form of a boot. Just pray that either the Lord does a miracle before Thursday and stretches that ligament/tendon and surgery will not be needed or that all goes well for this 'leg' of this journey! The special gift of the power point presentation I talked about last week has been put on Facebook (Tim Malm).

Keep praying for Tim's left hand and arm—we saw more movement this week with lifting from the elbow! PTL! Tim roped several times this week. He's frustrated with mentally knowing what he needs to do or change with his roping, but his muscles, arms, hands, fingers, etc. won't do what he tells it to do! Girls working on steers whenever possible—another thing that Tim did was get the steers 'started' for Fair with the girls! I'm not sure that would be at the top of his 'to do' list once he gets up and going, but it was time together for them. Tim is lifting his left leg without having to use his right hand/arm to lift it! Lifting left arm a little more! On Friday, Cass, Jess, & I went to Cheyenne for groceries so we'd be ready for Tim's Birthday Bash on Saturday. What a fun and busy day on Saturday—the girls set up the little park beside the church with tables, chairs, tablecloths, & paper goods. Surprised to have Tammy and Charlie (D) come all the way down from Douglas! Great to visit with them before everyone else came. We had about eighty people come eat Okie beans, potato salad, several salads brought by others, and homemade ice cream (Butterfinger, Vanilla, and Chery's Banana Nut). Jillian (McL) made a huge cake with the calf roper design she'd used on Tim's cake down at Craig last year! A "good time was had by all" as were the words in the newspaper that my good neighbor, Norma Jean would have used—she is missed greatly! Tim had several birthday calls. A good day . . . only a day of walking or roping could have topped it. Church went well. Tim did a good job "walking up and down the stairs"—still with the right foot stepping on the next step with the left following, but it's coming! Thank You for another year with Tim, and holding our family together day by day! Looking forward to Your work this week. We pray for renewed and re-energized minds, bodies, and hearts!

Week of July 18-24, 2011—Tim's surprise came today—a golf cart and trailer. He drove it around with Howard riding with him and did pretty good. Will definitely not leave the keys in it! Have prayed to see those blue eyes of Tim and on Tuesday we saw them really big when the little twin bed we have in the living room that the therapist do his stretches on broke and fell! Quite funny to see his upper body on the mattress all the way down on the floor with the lower body still at the regular height! Also worked on the saddle for upper body balance and we see improvement! Wednesday was a great day filled with emotion! Tommy (H) had given us a parking pass behind the roping chute stand at Cheyenne. Tim had several friends come up after they had roped and he had visitors all morning. They announce Tim and told a little about his story and he was encouraged by the big applause, even though down deep, he would have liked for it to have been for him roping there! This was supposed to have been Tim's first year to rope at the 'Daddy of 'em All' Cheyenne Frontier Days! Who would have thought that five years ago in '06, when Tim was a freshman calf roper in his first year of high school rodeo and he roped right there in that arena, and also the following year—that he would be there, not on his horse, but in a wheelchair! He enjoyed meeting Roy Cooper, Fred Whitfield, JoJo Lemond, Brent Lewis, and others who came up in the stands to meet him. So glad to see his friend, Jeff Chapman when we went back the second day of slack on Thursday! We try to be efficient with our time and travel . . . we left Cheyenne with Tim and had the appointment with the doctor about the 'Z' cut surgery and the doctor had tentatively scheduled surgery if she decided that Tim needed it or not. We decided yes, so we stayed the night and had surgery on Friday morning. We had all prayed in the pre-op room, and I was glad they let Howard go into the surgery room until Tim was asleep before coming out and sitting with me. Rhea brought over all colors of markers for his cast and it was sure good to have her there. It was about 4-ish when Tim 'woke up', and of course, he was "starving". They would only let him have crackers and apple juice! He finally talked them into giving him a slice of cheesecake! His cast was red & black! After we had to make a Spoonbenders stop in Loveland, we made it back to Albin about 9:15!

Had a great devotional tonight and we thank You for all the peace, safety, protection, surgery, & recovery! Pray this surgery is a 'tool' You have guided us to have and will benefit Tim with his walking! Tim doing well dealing with the pain on Saturday and today—we have to rub the left toes and up in his knee/thigh area at times. Howard stayed home with Tim and they didn't go to church, so I went with the girls. Tim's 'Southern' friends, Monica and Tyler came by for a visit while they are in Wyoming! We look forward to 'walking' with the cast and without it soon! Thank You, Lord! James 1:12-13 "Blessed is the man who perseveres under trial, because when he has stood the test, he will receive the crown of life that God has promised to those who love Him. When tempted, no one should say, 'God is tempting me.' For God cannot be tempted by evil, nor does He tempt anyone." Again, God's timing in knowing we would read this devotional at this time amazes and encourages us! To know and keep the difference between trials and temptations is crucial in our daily walk. Trials—tests God allows and puts in our path to prove our faith and produce perseverance, and as we are told, that we can also choose to have joy with them. God does not place temptations in our path. It's when we allow ourselves to take our focus off of Him and leave the path because we either failed the test or resisted His grace to persevere/obey—that's where temptation entices us to complain, choose a 'my' path, etc. So knowing this, we ask our Lord to help us daily to choose to face trials with joy and guard us from temptations. Tim has done extremely well coping with this first week of having this cast on his leg. Very little complaining even though he has withstood what he tells people of his 'bearable pain'. He quit any pain prescriptions last Tuesday morning and has just taken some ibuprofen and Tylenol—hasn't had any since yesterday morning. We've asked God to relieve him of any unbearable pain and He has—PTL!! He as "walked" on it some and we continue to see improvement even with the weight of the cast! He is marking off the days when he gets the cast off!! We are praying for concentrated effort and use of the left hand and arm these next couple of weeks—restoring to full function is our plea! We are seeing more use of it and just want more and quicker! He hasn't been able to sleep much more than about three hours on average at a time with this cast and all the little throbbings, itchings, etc. that come with a cast, but we will all get through this "season" together as we enjoy laughter through half-opened eyes! The girls have been a huge help and we have this week as our last full week before our county Fair all next week and then Bethany will be (pushed) off to college. It's becoming an emotional time for her and Tim so we enjoy the days left of our summer that went way too fast in many ways, but way too long for Tim on this journey. We enjoyed being in church and listening to the finals of the Cheyenne Frontier Days—of which Tim would love to be able to rope there next year. Wouldn't that be amazing—we leave that in the hands of our amazing God. PRAY and BELIEVE!

Week of July 25-31, 2011—Meds helping a bit, but also makes Tim sleepy . . . he took naps in the morning and afternoon off and on all week. He quit the prescription on Tuesday and now just taking Ibuprofen! Was a long week with Tim not sleeping through the night, and Howard and I waking throughout the night, taking turns rubbing Tim's legs or toes, talking with him, lying beside him, etc. We have found using vibrators on his cast, even down inside of it a little really helps, so I have fallen asleep and dropped the things several times! He does well with how many times we get him up to stand and have 'walked' a little here and there around the kitchen and into his bedroom—seems to be staying forward over the heel and not hyperextending the knee! YEA, Lord! Grpa & Grma came over several times—so thankful for all the 'checkers' times and the visits, means a lot to Tim. Church was good, the girls brought their little friends (the "C" crew!) to church. I slept while Tim and Howard listened to the CFD Finals on the computer! Again, the June and July have flown by, especially with the girls gone so much with child care, lifeguarding classes, getting steers ready, harvest with Jessen's and Anderson's, and just the summer! How we thank You for the many miles of safety, provisions in so many areas, travel/doctor/surgery on Tim's left heel/Achilles', Craig Eval,—You are so faithful, trusting, forgiving (especially when we let out tiredness sometimes affect our attitudes and mouths), and we thank You. Looking forward to getting Tim moving on the foot/leg and watching You heal!

Week of August 1-7, 2011—Tim wrote 'Happy Birthday" to Kaden today on FB! Went to Torrington early on Monday with Beth for a dental apt. The therapist came out and he and Howard got on each side while I was behind Tim holding the cast and he 'walked' fairly good! I'm not sure if the added activity with the stretches and 'walking' had an impact or not, but Tim didn't have a very good night, so Howard and I were several times and for longer periods of time with Tim and the leg. I finally taped the vibrators on to the cast and we both got some sleep! (I'm not sure if that is recommended medical practice or not, but we all got some sleep!) The OT therapist came out, and worked on Tim's left arm/hand . . . Tim frustrated it's not improving as fast as he wants! We are seeing his fist come forward better and faster with the exercises! Andy came and helped Howard and the girls wash and clip steers for Fair next week. Martha and I went in for Jessie Berry's wedding—was very nice. Tears filled my eyes to see the dances and prayed that Tim will be able to dance with me at his wedding . . . plenty of time and thankful we don't have any of those plans to be decided upon at this time!

Church went well and Tim was able to sit the whole time with a regular chair with the cast propped up! Girls went over to unpack trailer for Fair this week. We played a game and it was fun. Lord, how we pray for vehicle, animal, and personal safety for the Fair this week. Thank You for this opportunity this week. Praying for less and less pain and more recovery with Tim and the left leg/foot. Thank You! Ps 57:2 "I cry out to God Most High, who fulfills His purpose for me." Jer 29:11 "For I know the plans I have for you . . . ." Prov 25:2 "It is the glory of God to conceal a matter." This week of devotions and verses have dealt with His purpose, plans, and even "fairness". These purposes, plans, and concealments, are being fulfilled in His time and in His way because He is God—faithful, loving, just, trustworthy, gracious, and strong. We still stand on the promise that He will not allow trials to be more than we can handle because and only through His grace. Society will tell you that God is not "fair"—and that's right in their eyes because He isn't "fair"—He is just and a loving Father whose ways, plans, purposes, timing, etc. are far beyond us. We praise and thank God for Tim's continued thankfulness and trust that he expresses during this time in his life. Like us, he doesn't understand, but we accept and trust Him 'through and in' this circumstance. Tim is at one-third of the way through the six-week timetable with this cast on! He has had some restful nights and some restless nights, so we ride the healing rollercoaster while we sneak in little naps whenever possible to catch up from those restless nights. He is looking forward to going to our county Fair this week—all three sisters have steers so we will be going to Cheyenne three or four times this week. He has "walked" with a person on each side instead of one always being in front so we are seeing improvement in his balance, but continue to pray for balance and coordination. It frustrates him when everything physically came so easy for him before the accident. He wants to try to stand on the cast and rope the calf dummy this week! We ask for driving protection/safety to and from Cheyenne, more and more left hand/arm movement/function, and the throbbing from the cast to subside for restful nights. Thank you again and again for your encouragement and prayers!

August 8-14, 2011—Got up early on Monday and fixed breakfast burritos for all the 'Fair-goers'. Tim did well in his chair with us moving him around in the barn on all that sand! He feels 'helpless' when it comes to activities like this . . . he was such a huge help with all the cattle, and so enjoyed all the visiting with everyone at Fair. We talked with several who were there for weigh-in, and even more throughout the week at the different shows. Really enjoyed our last time to be out at the Tyner's (at their Cheyenne house)—Vince, friends from Florida had come up and fixed his 'ribs & fixin's'—Tim really enjoyed them. They will move into their Laramie home on Friday, wished we could have been more help to them. The girls came out and then all of them went back to spend 'Fair week' in Cheyenne. Tim really slept well all through the night on Monday! Tim went shooting with Howard on Tuesday. Since we leave early on the mornings we go to Cheyenne, I drive so Howard and Tim can rest; it gives me some 'quiet time' to pray for the day. Before presenting the trophy for the winners, Donessa Gaspar spoke a little about Tim—very kind and thoughtful words! Tim is adjusting to the difference in weight and balance well with the cast—'walked' better today and stood really well! It brings excitement with how You'll amaze us when this cast comes off!

Thursday's devotion—(1 Thess5:16) Be Joyful! Pray Continually! Give Thanks IN all things! Thank You again for this lesson! Tim has started doing squats beside his bed and in doing very well with even balance! We are halfway through the 6-week cast time! The 4-H Sale on Saturday was opened up with Tim standing up beside the fence and saying a few words of thanks and then he led everyone in the Pledge of Allegiance. Church was good, Tim 'walked' with us again up & down the stairs, and I kept together pretty good as long as I wouldn't let myself think about Bethany leaving this week headed back to Branson. Praying for the 'moves' this week with her and Tim's left arm/hand/fingers! Ps 84:7 "They go from strength to strength till each appears before God in Zion" 1 Thess 5:16-18 "Be joyful always; pray continually; give thanks in all circumstances, for this is God's will for you in Christ Jesus." The strength talked about is lived out with praying in, out, over, and through all of the day's situations, praising and thanking Him in a continual attitude of thanksgiving. He gives us that renewed strength so we can go from strength to strength. That strength comes also because of prayer—we continue to thank God for all of you who have prayed and continue to pray for us! I've said it before, but do take encouragement that He says IN, not for all things. His will for our lives is summed up as Be Joyful—Pray Continually—Give Thanks! No, we don't always feel thankful, nor does it say to be thankful . . . but He says to give thanks! Learn the difference because it will change your life and attitude! Pray also for Tim—he really misses school and with Bethany and his friends headed back it really makes it difficult. He continues to trust and wait for God in His time to take him back to school and the arena. Have a Thankful Week!

Week of August 15-21, 2011—Tim 'worked' in the saddle doing exercises to improve balance on Tuesday. We had a little "Bon Voyage to College" party for Bethany and had some friends over for food and hugs! Wednesday had me back in the "Mom's Cab Service" again with taking Jessica to volleyball practice at Burns—hard to believe how fast the summer went! While the girls went down to Jessen's, Howard and

I worked outside with Tim on the parallel bars (he stood beside them for 15-20 seconds at a time, holding the bar with both hands, did some excellent squats, did some sit-ups on the ab lounger, and other exercises. Bethany had her last devotional and prayer time with us on Wednesday night before leaving on Thursday morning. We took pictures outside (the sunglasses hid the tears well!) and she left about 8:30—I watched her until I can't see her car anymore and pray!!! Tim working really hard with that left arm—he can now take it off his headboard and 'stop' it about halfway down to his side! A few months ago, he could barely even let go of the log headboard or even stop it; it would just hit the bed! Thankful for what we have, but excited to see more! Tim did some more shooting on Saturday while the girls rode out with Jessen's for the Nusbaum's Back-To-School party. Sunday was extra special with not only our church service, but later on we attended the Hispanic Church with our friends for their cookout. Tim was able to thank them for their prayers and financial gifts, and Migel translated for him. There's no food like what Patricia and Migel can cook—we really enjoyed friends, food, and fellowship with our brothers and sisters in Christ! Tim and Jessica drove the golf cart home.

Thank You for the many, many blessings of the week! Bethany's safely at Branson (homesick yes, but in Your arms), miles of safety, good time with girls organizing their room and for school, therapy sessions, shooting time with Howard, rest, and trust in You for each breath—each day—each night—each 'step' of this journey! Thank You! God's timing and His knowing/planning of where we are when He chooses to speak to us through reading His Word, devotionals, songs, conversations, etc. amazes me. This week He has chosen many of those times and situations. Eph 1:18-20 (hope, riches, power), 1 Chron 16:8, 10-11 (thanks, glory, rejoice, look, seek), Phil 3:8 (know), 1 Thess 5:11 (encourage, build up), Matt 11:28-30 (come, rest, take), Col 4:5 (make)—all verbs with action! In order to have the strength to walk with Him and live out these action verbs, we daily have to move in His Spirit, pray unceasingly, and look to Him for grace and strength, all wrapped in His love. It has been a tiring week, but an exciting week also. Tim was 'back in the saddle' with therapies, and on Wednesday pulled himself up with both hands on the parallel bars and stood by himself for about twenty seconds. He also did several ab crunches, squats, and started pushing a grocery cart around the yard with our help and him holding the bar while stepping really well. He will have grass stains on the bottom of his cast when we go back to the doctor (Sept 7th) for her to cut the cast off and look at the foot. As some of you already read on his Facebook today—he walked with our assistance up and down the stairs of church and then when Howard had 'parked' him on our ramp while he and I took things in, Howard called me to come look! Tim had pulled himself up and out of his chair and was standing by himself!—it's hard to not be upset at him and also proud of him at the same time, but we do give thanks to the Lord for working with Tim in doing that, another daily miracle and hug of encouragement! Again, God's timing and His plans/purposes we have to stand on and trust even though this last spring Tim prayed to be able to go back to school and be riding and roping by now. We are all learning perseverance and patience through trust and to make the most of every opportunity (Col 4:5).

Week of August 22-28, 2011—Busy day started on Monday with physical therapy, then rushing over to Burns for the Back-to School Fair. Tim worked on the wall weight system for some of the OT session and we see improvement there. Tim trying 'walking' some with the grocery cart—doesn't work all that well on the grass or the first road, and we just have a little sidewalk, so we took it up the community center for Thursday's session, plus threw a football, shot some basketball, and used a racket to hit a ball. Eye-hand coordination fair, throwing was great, but without the one of the left hand, it was hard for him to control the bball—hard to watch when he was such a good freethrow shooter! He still has good form and follow-through, and can almost get it over the rim—we're just about three feet away from the basket, but we'll get there! Howard took a load of cattle in the truck to Torrington on Friday—how we pray that all Tim's driving abilities and road sense all comes back. Still remember hearing Mitch tell the story of how Tim kept from hitting 'sitting' traffic (due to construction) upon coming over a hill unmarked, how Tim drove his semi with the horse trailer into the ditch and kept everything upright, including the horses! A year before that on the same stretch of road with the construction, a cowboy from Lamar was killed hauling steers in a trailer! Mom came up this week and it is so good to have her here! Thank You for all the safety we all put on the roads this week!

I sang, *I Will Rise* in church (a little tough remembering that was one of Shena's song (slide show) played at her services). Praying for a GREAT school year, safety on the roads they drive and ride on, maturity walking with You, protection for what their ears hear and their eyes see, and good memories! John 1:16 "From the fullness of His grace we have all received one blessing after another." Grace amazes me . . . guess that's why it's called 'Amazing Grace', but like His love, mercy, forgiveness, blessings, etc. is continual. Our devotional entitled, A Breathtaking View of Grace, speaks of it as grace upon grace. Grace saves, sustains, showers both rain and sun, withholds judgment on nations, allows us to serve Him, worship Him, and walk with and in Him daily! The breathtaking part has had many moments along this journey with Tim . . . from seeing him on the ground not breathing (even though it was just for a few moments until 'we'—God and me—got him breathing again to seeing and hearing all the daily miracles, and then as we wait expectantly for the day when he walks by himself!) Many people have asked me about having the strength to do what I did at that moment and all I can say is 'only by the grace of God'. Many, many times we have stated that we have made it through and lived daily on your prayers and encouragement—I believe that is displayed through His grace and we all have seen blessings after another!

Thank you again and again. Tim's calendar is almost completely crossed out in red as he is counting and marking the days to when he gets his cast off! We have good therapy sessions and continue to see improvement—I am just holding the cast steady (it has no walking heel so it is not level) when Howard holds him while walking, so we are all excited to get the cast off and start the next phase of this rehab and walk soon!!! Continue to pray for his left hand/arm—we saw some more strength and improvement this week. Another prayer request is Tim's occupational therapist that has been here since we came home is having his last session this Tuesday—he is taking a new job in Colorado. We will miss him and it will take them awhile to find a replacement so Tim is stuck with us for a bit! Plans are being made for Tim to take an online class from his college so that will begin very soon! He misses college (even his teachers) and his friends at school—so he really enjoys the time they take to call and talk. The college rodeo fall season is starting back and that takes its toll on Tim—emotionally. He so badly wants to be on his horses and roping—we leave that in His time and His plans. Have a blessed week.

Week of August 29-September 4, 2011—We are seeing more movement with Tim's left arm—we pray for MORE!!! Great day in church—Tim "walked" in from the entry door, across foyer, then up the stairs! Ken and Linda brought out KFC chicken and we add some fixin's and had a great lunch and afternoon! Thank You, Lord, for allowing Mom here to help me with so many projects—the little bathroom is looking so nice, Bethany's room/curtains, Howard's office curtains, food projects, making memories . . . having fun! We praise You for the improvement with Tim and ask for continued patience working within Your timetable when the 'sands of time' seem to not be moving . . . remember how we use to shake those sand timers to make it go faster when it was the other person/team's turn! We all, especially Tim, wishes God would shake this 'timer' to go faster! John 15:7 "If you remain in Me and My words remain in you, ask whatever you wish, and it will be given you." 1 John 5:14-15 "If we ask anything according to His will, He hears us. And if we know that He hears us—whatever we ask—we know that we have what we asked of Him." Notice the "if's", the verbs, and the relationship. Such a strong promise to stand on and it brings great strength and peace especially during rough times. The verse also brings struggles when prayer is offered for days, months, and years and what you think you asked for isn't answered the way you thought you prayed. This verse shows perseverance to 'remain in Him' with your relationship and daily walking in His will then the answers lie with Him, His sovereignty, His grace, and His timing. One of the closing remarks in our devotional by Joni Eareckson Tada is that sometimes God says no, or at least, not yet. That's trust Him because He always answers prayers—in His way and in His time.

Tim has had a very good week with therapy sessions outside and on the saddle (of which the saddle and stand will have to be moved outside so Tim can swing his rope while in the saddle). His left leg is improving with starting to swing it over the saddle!! He is pulling himself up to a standing position stronger and with more balance! He has more and more movement with his left hand/arm—continue to pray for full function to return and be restored. Another praise is we have started "walking" with Dad and Mom on the sides and Tim "walked" from the church door, through the foyer, up the stairs, and same route afterwards! Balance was better—as we also had help standing behind him (up the stairs) and help in front of him (down the stairs) if/when we would need it. We will be heading to Sterling, CO (NJC) tomorrow—and Tim will show his younger two sisters and grandmother (from OK) where he went and prayerfully will return to college. We head to Denver on Wed. and they will take a look at Tim's leg/foot and then on Thur. he will have a foot brace appointment in Cheyenne to help with rehab on the Achilles/foot. He is very ready to get the cast off! He was able to do some shooting and also go to the barn to work bulls—he really misses working with family and cattle. In His time! Have a great week!

Week of September 5-11, 2011—No school for the girls! Mom rode with us as we all went to Sterling on Monday, to take one of Tim's horses, Kat, to an equine horse class the NJC students take and 'break' and/or train horses. Went to Pizza Hut with Coach Cullen and some of the rodeo kids. FBC Pastor John (Debby) Roberts came by and shared a 'coke' with us while we were there. He was Tim's pastor while Tim went to school there. They have been faithful prayer warriors for us! Tim visited with three more friends back at the college before we left for home. Tim talked and prayed how hard it was to see Coach, his friends, the stalls, horses, arena, college, dorms, etc. and asked for a second chance to go back! Went back on Wednesday for his foot/heel apt in Denver—drove through hard rain! I dropped Howard and Tim off at the door and went to go park and was gone thirteen minutes and was walking to the door when they called and said they were coming down the elevator! So I quickly went and got the navigator to come pick them up! Everything looked good for the doctor. We had to stop and get a Tim a Spoonbenders since we don't have one in Cheyenne! We mixed some of the different paints and came up with the color of blue that was on the steps, so Mom painted the doors while we were gone, plus did some other projects on the 'to do' list! Howard, Tim, and I went to Cheyenne on Thursday to Dr. Kuhn—he is working with the doctor in Denver with Tim's foot. We had to have him molded for the walking cast he will use when he gets the real cast taken off. Rushed home, picked up Mom and went to Jess' game down at Pine Bluffs! Mom left on Friday with all the fresh corn from Chery in the back of her SUV!

Saturday was a FULL day, I should say overwhelming!!! The pulpit candidate and family came in for the weekend and all the activities/meetings and arrive about noon. ! Had a big day with the candidate preaching, the potluck, and the Q&A time afterwards. I sang, "In God We Still Trust"—wow, was that fitting for not only Tim, but our whole family right now! Thank You again for Your timing with that! Lord, You gave the strength for this week! We pray for that continual and faithful strength (mentally, physically, and emotionally) and encouragement for Tim. It's amazing to hear Tim pray that You heal Cassady right now with this unknown pain, that he's strong enough to focus on her a few days! We pray for an amazing week of therapy sessions! Romans 12:12 "Be joyful in hope, patient in affliction, faithful in prayer." 2 Corinthians 12:9-10 ". . . My grace is sufficient for you, for My power is made perfect in weakness . . . . For when I am weak, then I am strong." Another great week of devotionals and reading His Word. How and why the Lord spoke statements in the order that He did has always amazed me. In the first verse mentioned above, He put joyful IN hope and the other two "in's"—emphasizing action or during that specific time (hope, affliction, prayer). He also tells us in statement or command form, not like an option or an opportunity, which gives us another time of obedience. That hope is not only our assurance, but in the 'tomorrows'—our future with Him. We take it also as 'daily medicine' for each tomorrow. The second verse of this update helped us through our week. I wanted to share the closing prayer for this devotional: *God, we give You our limitations and Your Spirit is set free to accomplish far more through us than we ever imagined. We bless You for our weaknesses.* This was the first weekend of the fall college rodeo season which has its effect on Tim also, but we thank all the friends who text, email, facebook, and/or call telling about their day and their rodeos. Please continue to pray for full function of Tim's left hand/arm—we continue to see improvement and believe that God will heal and restore in His time! Have a great week!

Week of September 12-18, 2011—Tim roped the calf dummy—stood well and roped SEVERAL times, and while sitting down in his chair! His 'horse' is tired!!! His PT therapist was his 'horse' one day! I went shooting with Howard and Tim—and yes, both of them can still beat me! I'm just happy all mine stayed on the target board! Continue to pray for function of those left fingers and hand! You know how badly we need them and how they could help in so many areas! Sunday was again one of Your 'timing' days with giving the best sermon for us—The Faith Struggle of Abram/Abraham! Our church voted and it was not Your timing or calling with this candidate and his family—we pray blessings for them and that You would call them to a rural setting and give them a great church! Tim "walked" up with very little help from Howard! Tim used the right rail (wore a glove so he wouldn't get any splinters) and Howard was on his left side for support. Lord, Lord, Lord, we thank You for the improvement with Tim's balance and coordination, sustaining Cassady, protecting Jessica and Bethany, and giving Howard physical strength to work with Tim, & rain! Psalm 40:5 "Many, O Lord my God, are the wonders You have done. The things You planned for us no one can recount to you; were I to speak and tell of them, they would be too many to declare."

Many of you know that I journal and to read back through the pages since Tim's accident and on this 'chapter' in our lives recount the many 'wonders' that He has done—and those are just the ones I wrote down for the day! We're so thankful for the written ones, but also for the untold number of unwritten and untold ones that were from Him. He sure would like the Lord to work some more on his voice with some intonation—most everybody understands him, he'd just like to have his old voice back! Pray his vision (alignment) continues to strengthen. We did some shooting this week and he does well with that (better than me!). Thank you for your encouragement—even today's sermon talking about Abram (Abraham) and the faith struggle he went through, learning to depend/trust in God for His plans and in His time! Have a Great Week!

Week of September 19-25, 2011—Therapy sessions showing improvement with balance on the saddle, coordination with roping, and other exercises. Yea!! Tim had a touch of a cold, but took two of his 'bombs' and will whip this one! Wednesday had us in Cheyenne for Howard to have x-rays of his hip, pelvic area, and knee. Showed what we've been told, that he badly needs a hip replacement! The ten years we'd hope for which began about five or six years ago is not holding out! Everyone sees him walk and asks if he did something or does he hurt? It really didn't hurt and he didn't know he was limping half of the time—but with helping in Craig with Tim and now at home, it has begun to give him pain. Lord, You know how we have prayed and will continue to pray that You restore Tim to walking on his own so Howard can have that done! We also had Tim's fitting of that walking brace. Physical therapy had him roping and then walking some with the new brace. They went shooting afterwards. Saturday was a highlight for the week! Worked calves down at Creekside and Tim was able (with Howard riding) to drive his golf cart gathering and pushing them afterwards! (Thank You it doesn't go as fast as a four-wheeler!) He was also able to have his chair close enough and high enough to work the chute handles for about two hours! Tim 'talked and texted' several friends—they are at the Sheridan Rodeo this weekend!

Church was good—always exciting to see and hear from Dick & Gloria! Everyone took a long Sunday nap! Lord, what a great week! We ask You again for good nights of rest and renewed energy for the days of this coming week. We pray for emotional encouragement for Tim with the college rodeo season going on. We pray & believe for full healing and restoration of Tim. We love You, Lord. Exodus 4:10 "Moses said to the Lord, 'O Lord, I have never been eloquent, neither in the past nor since You have spoken to your servant. I am slow of speech and tongue.'" This devotional has stayed on my mind this week. We are so thankful that God brought back Tim's memory, thought-processing. vocabulary, speech (even though it's still monotone—it's improving), his smile, humor, and laughter! I even thank Him for his orneriness! We all experience 'crazy moments' when we have allowed life to get crazy with schedules, busyness, lack of enough sleep, sibling 'discussions', etc. and we need to realize it's those moments that should drive us to our knees toward total reliance, dependence, and focus to God. The devotional dealt with talking WITH God, instead of talking TO God. Prayer is cultivating a relationship with the Lord and it is a Privilege because of the Cross that we can talk WITH Him! Talking also involves listening because it is a conversation—take time to 'listen' through the many ways He 'talks'! Even when we are give-out, dog-tired at the end of the day—what a refreshing and relaxing time as we spend time with Tim (and the girls when it's not too late) reading His Word, our devotional, and praying. To hear Tim converse WITH God is a blessing! We continue to walk daily in His grace, His strength, and His love as we believe in total healing and restoration in His time! He did get his new Achilles brace and is working at wearing it an hour on and an hour off! He has roped outside on the dummy and went shooting also. Therapies show improvements every time! We would like concentrated prayer for Tim's left hand/arm—even our therapist said for Tim to gain that would make immense improvement in other areas also! Tim continues to stay positive and trusting God for His timing and plans and we thank God for that everyday! We pray that many who read this will daily take time this week to 'Talk WITH God' and enjoy God's creation with the fall colors! PRAY & BELIEVE!!

Week of September 28-October 2, 2011—Tim held his head up and centered fairly well while he drove the golf cart—they made a short video while I was gone to Cheyenne. They started corn chopping on Tuesday so Howard just came home long enough to work with Tim during therapy (walked up and down the ramp and roped some after his stretches and inside exercises). Howard went back out afterwards and didn't come home 'til about 9:00! I rubbed on Tim's leg and toes, and we rolled him into his room to possibly help with the aching of his leg with that much activity. Not being out there with the corn chopping really bothered Tim—maybe next year! Reminded me when he was in elementary when he'd rush home and get to the ranch so he could drive the packing tractor and then later on when he'd drive the semi!

(He was ten when he 'honked' the horn in the semi when he drove by our house!)

On Tuesday I had an Open House down at Pine so Tim sat in Grma's car for about three hours watching the trucks and tractors bring in and pack the corn in the silo. Besides driving the tractor, there are so many things that would help Tim if he only had more function with his left hand (crawling, holding things, using the walker, rails, ramps, etc all towards walking!—How we pray for that! Speech therapy improving (working in his 'sermon' for Cheyenne LCCC Rodeo) and he did a lot of work on the big yellow ball with leaning and recovering his balance, it tired him out! Physically tired doesn't help and it plays on his emotions when he hears his friends about the Lamar College Rodeo this weekend! He puts on a strong front and tries to encourage them; you can see the hurt. Tim really can't believe it's been two years since he was there . . . we continue to wait and trust! The framed picture on the wall that Siri (S) took and the college had made for Tim's Benefit Auction (which the whole Malm and Cooper families bought) is of Tim at the Lamar Rodeo! He and Mitch did well there!

Friday was a great 'pick up' day when his friend Cole (G) came for the day! He had won the steer roping at Pendleton and brought back Tim a cap and a t-shirt, but just the time he spent with Tim was really good! He drove Cole around in the golf cart then Cole told us how Tim had tried to teach him how to drive his semi while at college—I can see them laughing and driving! Had one of Tim's ICU nurses, Jen (A) come out with her kids and visit with Tim. They are moving to Florida so it will be sad to see them go! She has kept up with us and been such an encouragement, both in the hospital and while we have been home. So thankful You brought her into our life! Saturday marked the one year date that we came home from Craig—the journey has been long, but how we thank You for the daily strength, grace, mercy, peace, and perseverance You have given, and ask for it as we start the next 'stretch of this road' on this journey. Sunday was a great day with cowboy poet/Christian Cowboy Ministries) Fred Ellis speaking and then a potluck afterwards! Looking forward to our next week watching You improve and bring more healing to Tim's left hand/arm, balance and strength to stand, coordination to walk, and 'mending' of his heart! Thank You for Your faithfulness and love.

Phil 1:2 "Grace and peace to you from God our Father and the Lord Jesus Christ." GRACE and PEACE—two words that could sum up our journey as we marked one year being back home from Craig Hospital this week! We came home on Oct 1, 2010 and God's GRACE and PEACE in huge daily doses and hugs have kept us, sustained us, and keeps us going. The devotional talked about the many overwhelming circumstances in life that just squeezes us and even takes our breath away that it drops us to our knees realizing that prayer is our only refuge . . . a place we can cry out to Him our hurts, fears, pleas, etc and then renew that trust and breathe again in His GRACE and PEACE. We so thank the many of you that still read this and the ones who write, but all ya'll who have continued to uphold Tim and our family in your prayers! So many people tell us that we are prayed for daily and we definitely know that and live on that! What a year since last October! We sure have a new appreciation of words like time, soon, and close as we talked about them the other night. If you remember we wrote so many times of how close we were to taking those steps or walking soon, and yet time has taken us on a mixed conception rollercoaster of the slowness and fastness of minutes, days, and months. But, oh how grateful and thankful we are and have been to have continued healing and improvement up that mountain of restoration.

Looking back in retrospect, Tim has prayed several times with that openness of his broken heart, but it is so rewarding to hear and see God renew his trust in Him and encourage him with the daily strength to be faithful to Him as he 'walks' with Him toward walking soon! We have been working small bunches of calves and Tim has been able to sit in his chair beside the hydraulic chute and run all the handles, plus drive his golf cart by himself and using it to move cattle! We continue to see more strength and use in the left hand, but as we asked this morning in church, that everyone pray specifically for Tim's left hand that God might show His power and healing for full-function of that hand. Tim has lost some of the excess weight that he gained and building strength back in that left leg. Hope ya'll are having a beautiful Fall! Until next week . . .

Week of October 3-9, 2011—Psalm 144:3 "O Lord, what is man that You care for him, the Son of Man that You think of him?" He cares for each one of us regardless of our weaknesses, hang-ups, baggage, or worries—as it says in 1Peter 5:7 (Let Him have ALL your worries and cares, for He (cares) is always thinking about you and watching everything that concerns you). Because of this care (love) it makes us want to follow and obey. I've used the Gal 6:9 verse several times in this journal—"Let us not become weary in doing good, for at the proper time we will reap a harvest if we do not give up." This journey is a picture (real life for us!) of a long obedience highway of life. Many of you have experienced those long, straight, boring stretches of highways (Wyoming has many!) and it takes discipline every mile. You have to find ways to keep your mind and body alert and keep your focus. Tim tells the Lord frequently that he is tired, bored, and sick of this journey, and wants to get to moving on his own. We have to rely daily, and sometimes minute by minute, on being in His Word, drawing on His strength and grace to make it another 'mile' on this journey. Continue to pray for our daily focus on Him as we thank ya'll for yours as we all travel together on this road of life. Please forgive me with not updating last night—some thought the world might have come to the end when they didn't see it this morning! Had a late night with some school projects and our devotional/prayer time then after a shower, I just melted into bed forgetting all about it until this morning. We are still working small bunches of cattle (calves) and I think we are halfway done!?! Tim runs the hydraulic chute running the calves into the head chute. He "walked" with side-by-side assistance and up/down/ stairs the best he has done since the Achilles operation. Balance continues to improve (keep praying) as he was able to sit on a bench with his therapist barely behind him barely helping while he roped! Tim drove our vehicle from the chute/corrals through the pasture to the highway a couple of times. With our early snow on Saturday, Tim has started to pray to be able to drive the snowmobile this winter!—only in God's time and I give Him all my worries and cares! Please pray for Tim this weekend as he will be speaking in the Rodeo Church at the Cheyenne college rodeo. Again, he is looking forward to seeing so many friends, but it is emotionally hard for him watching and not being in the arena . . . again in God's time. Have a warm and blessed week!

Week of October 10-16—We unloaded the ROM (Range of Motion) machine that it took about four men to unload! It'll be tough, but I think it will be very good. Thank You for letting Bettyanne find it and for the medical/financial means You provided for her and this study she will be doing on Tim! Tim worked hard (as usual) in therapy doing squats on the step, boards, and standing. In speech, they worked on his 'sermon' for LCCC Rodeo Church in Cheyenne this weekend! Thank You for the strength You gave for the day of fasting—praying for Tim's left hand and arm, it's restoration and function. The week stayed busy with working calves, MK Fall Open House in Pine, and the Sat/Sun times in Cheyenne—What a Week! Overwhelming is the word again! Cassady packed for FFA Nationals and went in to Cheyenne with us and met Elaine & Rylee so she would be ready to leave—to have my kids scattered in about three different states weighs a little on me, but You gave me a peace about them and they are all in safe hands. It was good to see, hug, laugh, etc with so many family and friends, and to go eat with Coach Cullen at Texas Roadhouse. It was neat to meet the manager who Tim thanked him for all he did with the food for the family while he was in ICU. Tim did great in rodeo church; they had a Kubota four-wheeler thing that Howard and Tim had driven into the arena. I sang, *In God We Still Trust* and Lord, it is our statement of this journey, but also for the country. I want to print Tim's message he gave at the Cheyenne college rodeo today. We are emotionally spent, but so filled with encouragement, love, and the gift of friendship—thank you all for "filling us up". Rodeo church has averaged around 70-100, but they estimated around 300 there today and we thank God again the attendance of many friends! The strength of the people standing up as Tim "walked" with Howard to where he spoke was special—thank you. It was beyond words to see and know the ones who asked Jesus into their lives today and hear from others how their "walk" has been strengthened from being on this journey with us. The words to a song I recited today is "Life is hard . . . but God is good".

During the rodeo, the presentation of the Tim Malm Cowboy Spirit Award brought tears to many as the whole arena stood in honor of Tim—that was a huge heart-breaker and a heart-builder. Tim and Howard had driven out right after the last calf was roped. Unplanned and just out of his friendship with Tim, Riley Pruett had won the calf roping and before he walked over to receive his belt buckle, he took his rope off his horse, walked over, and gave it to Tim! I was across the arena from them and could hear people say, "Riley just gave Tim his rope!" It was also one of the 'goose-bump moments' to feel that awesome quietness and then to hear the soft rumble as people began to stand while they were reading about Tim and the award scholarship established in his name by Ron and Julie Rabou. (Hope they can be there next year with us). Thank you Riley for the friendship act when after winning the calf roping and receiving your buckle, you gave Tim your rope! God, we pray You were honored—because the focus is meant for You, this is all about You! Thank You, Lord for the enormous week we had and made it through because of YOU!

Tim's message . . .

Hello and Good Morning! God has really laid something on my heart to say today. For most of you, I haven't seen since Laramie last year. Wow! What a difference a year makes . . . from roping here two years ago to last year not having my left leg bend and having my parents translate everything to today. God is good all the time and all the time God is good. Some of you might be asking what "good" is . . . Physically, I'm super close to taking steps on my own, standing with only someone behind me while roping the dummy, close to handling some personal care, standing in the shower, driving my golf cart and car, working the hydraulic chute working calves, and other things,. Mentally, I will be taking macroeconomics, an online class from NJC in a couple of days. Spiritually, I'm learning patience with, trust in, and complete dependence on Him. The question about the blind man in John 9:3 about why he was blind and whose sin caused it has me wanting to tell you to not ask that question with me cause this accident was allowed to bring glory to God and show His power. I also believe it was allowed to happen to get the attention for some to walk closer with him and for some to come to know Him as Lord and Savior. It sure got my attention! I am walking closer to Him as I wait on Him in His timing to show the "big gift" of walking, and the "great, big, gift" of roping again! There have been times that I have been discouraged and I'm sure you have been also with how far along I am, but I am right where God wants me to be at this time. I ask you to keep praying and believing. I keep trusting in the verse, Jeremiah 29:11, "For I know the plans I have for you, says the Lord, Plans to prosper you and not harm you, plans to give you hope and a future." Everyday I trust in Him, His plans, that hope, and that future. My prayer for you is that each of you come to know Him and have that trust or renew your trust relationship with Him as we pray today. I ask you all to bow your heads and close your eyes . . . Now with every head bowed and eyes closed, pray this prayer with me to ask Jesus in to be your Lord and Savior . . . Dear Lord Jesus, I'm sorry for my sins . . . I believe You died on the cross for me . . . Thank You for the cross . . . I need You and want You to be Lord and Savior of my life. I ask You to come into my life and be Lord over all . . . In your Son's precious name. If you prayed that prayer today, I'd like to see you raise your hand as a sign of your decision to trust Him and so I can pray for you . . . Amen! I want to thank you for this opportunity and with the Lord's help and strength, I'm gonna work twice as hard and give my all to be back here year! Thank you!

Week of October 17-23, 2011—Monday turned off cold (35degrees) so we worked calves in winter clothes—Tim did well and kept warm enough with his snowmobile suit on! Tuesday was our 25th Anniversary and how thankful I am for the friendship and marriage You have blessed me with Howard! We completely trust You as we walk together on this journey. Went to Cheyenne on Wednesday for Tim's appts with Dr. Kuhn and do strength tests with the PT, Teresa, there for Bettyann's medical study on Tim and the ROM machine. ! Even with the colder weather, Tim still ropes on the calf dummy outside! Had good therapies always with some improvement—just slower and frustrating for Tim and where he want to be! They weaned some calves on Saturday and Tim was able to hold on to the chute handle and stand for about three minutes—we thank You for little miracle like that—it encourages Tim. Tim prays to have some solo steps before Bethany comes home for Thanksgiving! God, You know his heart and how it aches to be up and out—especially with fall/winter coming! We wait as we try to "Be still and know You are God".

Psalm 1:3 "He is like a tree planted by streams of water, which yields its fruit in its season and whose leaf does not wither. Whatever he does prospers." The autumn colors are just gorgeous, and I love the colors God chose to use. He also chose to use trees to teach us—as we grow and walk with Him daily. There must be a consistent balance of growing taller and deeper—the branches reflect the roots! The prayer in our devotional sums it up: May our roots grow deep in Your Word, Lord, and may our branches grow high. When winds of adversity come, I then will remain strong. Tim has had another good, steady week, even though he wants steadiness to move faster and bigger! We ask for continued prayer for Tim's left hand/arm—we are seeing improvement every day, but we ask for FULL FUNCTION from our healer, faithful, and gracious Father! Have an awesome autumn and take a few extra moments to thank Him for His colors, His trees, and His lessons! Until next week . . .

Week of October 24-30, 2011—Tim and Howard had an adventure that I'm glad I wasn't around—they sometimes do things when I'm not around and then tell me later! Tim wanted to get in Carl's (RED!) combine for a round of corn harvest. They have a skid-steer with a really big wood pallet which Howard and the wheelchair both fit on. Carl lifted them up to almost even with the combine platform and then weight shifted—they fell off, from about six feet in the air! Howard's foot ended up in one of the wheels, and luckily (God's protection) Tim landed upright in the chair then fell out! Thank You for 'taking care of those who sometimes don't take care of themselves!" It reminded me of stories told of Howard and Carl's childhood! Tim remarked that it was probably the RED (International), and not the GREEN (John Deere) that was the problem! They all laughed about it and I'm sure we will be making a chiro trip! Tuesday went to Jess' game in Burns (played well) and then it took us about forty-five minutes to get home with it snowing all the way home! Tim worked on his online class he is taking from NJC. Macroeconomics! We make the font bigger so he can 'read along' while Howard (or me) reads in the book! This is definitely not for me! Howard got kicked in the hand when unloading the calves he'd brought home in the truck from Creekside—made it safely with the snow and slush!

"Cabin Fever" set in a bit with emotional tiredness reacting with some remarks, so I have to give them to You, because people mean well, just sometimes our 'tongue' interferes! SO thankful for a loving and forgiving family! On Thursday, we went back to Sterling . . . Tim's horse, Kat, got 'kicked out' of Equine class and we needed to bring him home! Tim visited with some of his professors (Mr. Pollart, Mr. Anderson, Mr. Briggs), Coach Cullen, and some friends—both good, but yet emotionally draining. Therapy had Tim on the balance ball and then on the floor! Helping hold his left hand flat, he was able to do a few push-ups! Yea, Lord! Worked in strong winds on Saturday and Tim was able to stand for the last five after working in his chair—I held him so the wind wouldn't blow him over! Our eyes were really red from all the dirt and wind! Andy, Stacy, & family, Lynette & Kent, and the Anderson's all visited throughout the afternoon and evening at different times—it encourages Tim. Thank You for their time!

John 16:33 "In Me, you may have peace. In this world, you will have troubles. But take heart! I have overcome the world." Today's devotional had us remember Eric Lidell (Chariots of Fire—English runner) who did not run one of his races in the Olympics because it was on Sunday. He did win his other race a few days later, but he will be remembered for his decision and choice on the Sunday race. The prayer for the day—Lord, let me see the finish line of eternity and run the race on Your terms. Let me play out the race of life as if the tape were against my chest. You have won the victory and I praise You for it. It is such an encouragement to hear Tim pray and totally put his trust in God—to live in and live with that peace that only God has given and gives to him daily. To watch him wait with trust as God heals and restores as he works so hard at everything is unbelievable—a picture of balance (work) and commitment (peace) to God. The people who know Tim knows he is a perfectionist and a very hard worker so the physical effort is not the question—it's the timing of God's healing and restoration, and that's where the faith and peace keep him going day to day waiting to 'walk in His strength'. Tim feels his vision is improving—I do, too! PTL! Tim is improving in speech, writing, balance, coordination, and also with more use of the left hand/arm so please keep praying for full-function and full restoration! Excited to see God's hand at work this week! Pray for BALANCE—those 'steps' will be coming soon with more balance and function of the left hand/arm! Have a Blessed Week!

Week of October 31-November 6, 2011—Monday morning we heard of a neighbor friend a few years older than Tim, fell off a ladder working on a barn at their place. Tim and I were home and immediately prayed and it was awesome to hear Tim pray—especially that he wouldn't have a serious head/brain injury! Howard, Tim, and I went to Carpenter to put out salt for the heifers down there. Had some trick-or-treaters for Halloween! Tim is practicing standing up against a wall and we had therapy up at the Center "walking" on the lines trying to regain balance, coordination, and strength. Friday was Daddy's birthday—still hard to believe it's been almost 6 years since he went Home! Miss him every day! Great Church worship and Tim stood against the wall in the foyer and several people commented and gave a shout of encouragement to him! Lord, we started another month and it has flown by faster than Tim has seen the big improvements come! He's working hard to have some solo steps so he can walk down the ramp when Bethany comes home! We ask You to give him encouragement and show him something big this week that he can see, and give him the 'eyes' to see it! Matt 17:20 "If you have faith as small as a mustard seed, you can say to this mountain, 'Move from here to there,' and it will move.

Nothing will be impossible to you." Tim doesn't always like to hear anything pertaining to the measurement of 'mustard seed' faith because he feels his faith is the size of the mountain in the verse! Tim 'moved one of the mountains' this week—he stood against a wall by himself for several minutes and was also able to lean forward from the waist and bring himself back to the wall! PTL! The therapist was very proud when Tim showed him on Friday—he and Howard had been practicing while I went to Cheyenne one day. They have had a few 'surprises' for me the days I have been gone—some not so good, but most of them are good. He stood against one of the walls at church today and it was an encouraging sight for many! Tim has let many know through his facebook page! He also has enjoyed his macroeconomics online class. We are seeing a little more movement in the left hand, but we ask you to continue with us asking God for full function (faster, Tim would add!) of that left hand and arm—being thankful and grateful for what He has done thus far and for what He is doing! We will be going to one of his sister's ballgames this week—good for him to watch and he did keep his shooting form (right form) and has almost made a few baskets when we go shoot at our community center, but it's hard to watch and know where he was with his basketball ability and see him struggle with the ball. We consider that another 'mountain' and we continue on this journey *standing* in His grace and *walking* in faith! We are working hard and praying God will let Tim take a few solo steps when Bethany comes home for Thanksgiving—will you join us with that prayer request? Thanks again for your words of encouragement and your prayer support—it is greatly felt! PRAY & BELIEVE!

Week of November 7-13, 2011—We worked on the ROM machine several times this week and he is improving with strength (at least he can see that on his chart!) still on the upper body, legs aren't there yet. Tim was able to push-up off the balance ball! Tim went and voted with us at the Comm. Center—there was a school bond issue special election on Tuesday. Went to the wedding of the friend that we prayed for that had the fall a couple of weeks ago—so good to see how You answered that prayer especially with all the wedding plans! Saturday, our pastoral candidate and wife met with the different committees/

boards in the church, and he will preach tomorrow. Tim loves potlucks and we had one after the service with a Q & A time with the Morrison's afterwards. Great Day! 2 Tim 2:1 "You then, my son, be strong in the grace that is in Christ Jesus." We have asked and have seen different ways of strength this week . . . Tim is walking, still with assistance, but getting stronger in his left leg everyday, with both balance and coordination improving! PTL! He has stood against the wall several times this week and as he put on his facebook page, he stood during the singing and greeting time at church today with his back against the wall along with us 'standing by'—but he stood by himself most of the time!!PTL!! He spoke during praise and prayer time about him standing on his own during the week! Another sign of strength. The daily strength He gives us not only physically, but emotionally and mentally shows His immense love, grace, and mercy! Tim has done well on his macroeconomics online class (which only he and Howard understand!) and is holding a good grade with his quizzes and tests. He completed ten sit-ups which is another strength blessing! Worked some cattle this week which he so enjoys and what huge strength strides in the ability to work the chute both sitting in his chair and then standing with someone just holding a hand behind him for hours!—especially in the cold! In church today he walked (with two by his sides) up and down the stairs to our auditorium and then down and back up the stairs from our church basement! Looking forward to Bethany's coming home this weekend for Thanksgiving—continue to pray for some solo steps while she is here! PRAY & BELIEVE!

Week of November 14-20, 2011—Went to Cheyenne to get Bethany from the airport shuttle! Tim was excited to see her, even though he couldn't walk by himself, she saw lots of improvement. It was good for Tim to hear of the improvements other than from the ones who live with him every day! (He asks us every day what we thought the improvements were today) The highlight of the week was when Bethany finally got here, our kids, along with other family members, had a 25th Wedding Anniversary Celebration at the community center for Howard and me! Had about sixty friends and family, even some from out-of-town! We are so blessed! Thank You, Lord, for the week with all its safety with the girls here, Bethany travels to Tulsa, Denver, and home, for daily strengthening Tim, and for life itself! Prayin'—Believin'-Trustin'!

Week of November 21-27, 2011—Tim had a really good workout on the ROM—and can now push and pull the left arm by itself! Tim had another ROM times on Wednesday and getting stronger! Had our Malm Thanksgiving at Martha's house this year! Took pictures and Tim stood against a tree with all of us around him for a family picture! Played games after the 'feast'. So very thankful for Your overflowing of blessings and 'good gifts' from You, our Heavenly Father! We thank You for the improvement, healing, and faith growth with this year in not only Tim's life, but the lives of many family and friends! All praise and glory to You, Our Father, Savior, Lord, and Healer!!! Thank You, for a great week! Job 8:20-22 "He will yet fill your mouth with laughter and your lips with shouts of joy." We've had a wonderful week with Bethany home and spending time with family (had a cousin sleepover!) with Thanksgiving! It was so good to see and hear Tim laugh so hard at times, he almost lost his breath! Hope all ya'll had a great time with your family and friends! So blessed and thankful for God's blessings, miracles, graces, promises, and above all, knowing-trusting-believing Him! Looking back at Thanksgiving last year when Tim was just able to barely stand out of his chair and with lots of assistance, barely take two steps to doing a great job up and down the stairs at church with two people helping on the sides for balance! PTL! He is getting stronger with the balance and coordination improving daily! We still see a little improvement with the function of his left hand so we ask you to continue to pray specifically for God to restore the function very soon—seeing something—however small it may seem—is encouraging to Tim! He is doing quite well with the online class and hopes to finish it by Dec. 15th!

We ask for prayers this week as the NFR (National Finals Rodeo) starts on Thursday and Tim will be watching and recording all the calf-roping! The emotional roller-coaster of wanting to watch it, but allowing the 'drain' on his 'broken' heart to go along with it—only God knows and we pray that He will either restore Tim to that passion or give Tim another passion. Those of you who knew Tim knew of his passion for calf-roping—I know of very few people who ever have that kind of passion or work ethic. Take a look at the uploaded photos . . . I hope the pictures will be on the photo page and you will see Tim standing against the tree and then again beside the slide. Continue to pray for eye alignment! We are a asking God for a huge Christmas present in that Tim will take some solo steps this month—Bethany will be home in three weeks and he would love to walk down the ramp to greet her! With God, nothing is impossible! We thank God for each and every one of you and for your continued prayers and encouraging words! PRAY & BELIEVE!!!

Week of November 28-December 4, 2011—Another goal set to walk by my birthday—Tim says that would be a great bday gift! AMEN to that! We had a ROM session before I left for Cheyenne (Jessica's game) and he is getting very consistent with the left arm/ shoulder motion! We continue to believe as we watch & wait in Your timing! Speech came on Tuesday, and will only come for once a week for the next two months, so the girls and I will be his therapists!! Howard and Tim have worked really hard on his macroeconomics class and their goal is to be finished by the 15th! I think the ROM has strengthened Tim's arms and he did three (with very little assistance except holding the left hand down flat) push-ups in PT!!! The therapist said more weight bearing on that left shoulder/arm will be good! (I think Jessica could sit on him while he is doing them!—Tim said "Not!") Nanny took pictures during PT when Tim was on his saddle. Church was great and Tim 'walked' each stair step individually with each foot/leg for the first time, YEA! Lord, we thank You for that, and it's so good to overhear people behind us say, "Hey, look at Tim!" or "Way to go, Tim!" What an encouraging week, Lord! Thank You!!

Numbers 6: 24-26 "The Lord bless you and keep you, the Lord make His face shine upon you, and be gracious to you; the Lord turn His face toward you and give you peace". One of my favorite passages—a huge "promise" sandwich with BLESS & KEEP on one side with GIVE PEACE on the other with all the rest in the middle! We have had snow this week along with low temps and two word pictures come along with that—one, the 'washing us white as snow' and the peacefulness with the snow (even though all of the feeding and caring of animals doesn't always carry that picture with the snow!) It has been a chore pushing Tim with his chair in the snow—Howard says we may have to 'chain it up'! Getting stronger and praying daily for more and more balance control! His prayer request today in church was to take a few solo steps on his own by Christmas for his present! The 'keep & peace' part of the verse has proven faithful as Tim has watched the NFR—good to watch, but a lot of talking and prayer afterwards. We continue to ask Him for the emotional strength during the NFR and for your prayer support also for physical and emotional requests of Tim. Thank you again and again. He is doing well with the online class and hopes to do four chapters, quizzes, and tests this week! Keep warm and keep in His Word. Have a week of blessings and peace!

Week of December 5-11, 2011—Tim got some ROM sessions in this week! Had good therapies with Tim improving in daily little ways in different ways—we see it, but Tim wants 'bigger' ones! People at church or who come visit every week or so really notice things like hand grip (some have their weekly left-hand shake at church to work on it!) and eye alignment improving! Have to bundle up 'wheeling' Tim to church and clean off the tires before coming into church and our house, but that's winter and we thank You for the moisture! Church was good—kinda feels like 'something' is missing without a music cantata! Thank You again for the time Mom (Nanny) is here—she's a huge help and we enjoy our time together! We continue to pray for Tim's birthday present to me tomorrow—I still get up every morning with an expectancy to walk in his room and see him up and ready to walk!

John 1:16 From the fullness of His grace we have all received one blessing after another. As believers and followers of Christ, we have the awesome privilege of knowing where and thanking whom for where our blessings come from—unlike the 'world' when they have to sometimes consider them as luck! Again, we have had a week of blessings—some 'small', some 'big', but only we with our earthly minds consider size when they come from a big Father God who wants to give good things to His children. Tim has enjoyed the NFR (Nationals Finals Rodeo) every night, but it was emotionally spent at the end of the evening. He gives it all to the Lord and we live in that trust to be back in his saddle roping for Him! We have increased strength and movement with the left arm/shoulder, a little more movement with left hand/fingers, stronger vision in right eye with more alignment between the eyes, walking with less and less assistance without any brace on the left foot/ankle, and good grades with his online class! His grandma from Oklahoma has been here all week and what a huge blessing and gift—thank you, Lord! Some dear friends secretly put lights up and down the 'runway' (ramp) for Tim to maybe take a few steps when Bethany comes home (this weekend!) Please pray for these steps to come as a Christmas present from God! Tim was able to completely stand against the wall and shake hands this morning in church without Howard or I touching him—PTL! He also did very well on the stairs-stronger, faster, and individually with each foot!! Merry CHRISTmas to each and every one of you. We are going to try to put our family Christmas letter on here hopefully next week.

Week of December 12-18, 2011—The week started off with my birthday on Monday! I turned 50! It would have been Mom & Dad's 57th Anniversary—it's been special to have been born on their anniversary, but now has a little 'sting' with him being gone. Sure thank You again and again for their example of their Christian friendship, marriage, and family life—what a gift from and them! I have noticed how hard prayer time is at times. Hearing Tim pray for his friends, for the chance to go back to school, to walk, and to rope again is sometimes terribly tough to pray after him! We pray for good rest, sweet dreams, and encouraging words from You through the night as Tim prays for You to touch him with Your healing hand while he sleeps to surprise him in the morning! Still praying for 'steps' by Christmas! Beth was able to catch an early flight so we picked her up on Saturday morning in Cheyenne. After her week of finals, Bethany enjoyed a little sleep-in time! Tim wanted to walk when she came home, but now praying for Christmas! Even though it's winter, Tim still sweats when working on the ROM machine, and how we like to see that as he is working so hard! Enjoyed our week with baking, playing games, watching some

Christmas movies, therapy sessions, and taking 'neighbor' gifts around! Enjoyed our little Christmas with our writing down some memories and blessings that I will keep!

I love it when Christmas falls on a Sunday!!! We had our traditional Julotta (Swedish) at 6:30 a.m. Had lots of people do specials. I sang *You're Here* off stage while Chaurisse dressed as 'Mary' and held her newest grandson dressed in 'swaddling' clothes! Tim drove the navigator out and did better than when he drove on T-Day. Only in Albin, can you drive to the Ranch and not have any traffic! Had a Christmas meal with Montgomery's out at Grpa & Grma's—will have the Malm get-together on the 30th. Thank You, Lord for the 'family' at the manger and our families, but mostly for time, memories, and Your Word—From cradle to cross and living in our hearts. I am sending to you our family letter and our picture is already posted on the top left. We have had a great week of therapy and now have an OT (occupational therapist) working with Tim. He stated his prayer request today that God would give/allow him a couple of steps this week! Please join us for that specific prayer—who knows, we all might see God give Tim a huge miracle (He gives us 'little' ones everyday!) this week!?! Bethany made it home safely—PTL! Hope to hear from ya'll.

> HAPPY MOMENTS . . . . **PRAISE** GOD
> DIFFICULT MOMENTS . . . . **SEEK** GOD
> QUIET MOMENTS . . . . **WORSHIP** GOD
> PAINFUL MOMENTS . . . . . . **TRUST** GOD
> EVERY MOMENT . . . . **THANK** GOD

"**Trust** in the Lord with all your heart and **lean** not on your own understanding, but in all your ways **acknowledge** Him, and He will **direct** your paths." Proverbs 3:5-6

We wish all ya'll a **Merry Christmas** and pray that you have health, humor, and feel our hugs as our thanks for your continued prayers and love. We pray that as you have 'walked' with us on this journey that you have either come to know Jesus Christ as Lord and Savior, have renewed your relationship with Him, and/or you and your family/friends have grown closer together because of Tim's accident. We are still trusting, leaning, acknowledging, and waiting as He directs. Yes, we are weary on this journey, but God has been faithful to sustain us each day with His amazing love, grace, mercy, strength, and peace as we praise-seek-worship-trust-and thank Him through all our moments! We are closing the year 19 months from the accident and oh, what a journey it has been and continues to be! We still see and hear improvements everyday and we are so thankful for that—PTL! If you have been reading caringbridge.org (timmalm) I've tried to update weekly with his progress and prayer requests, and we have so enjoyed reading all your replies. Tim's theme (goal words) are "Walk, Ride, Run, Rope, and Win" (these have also helped in speech therapy!) so the words pretty well sum up his drive, work ethic, and determination! He has amazing trust and faith as he waits in God's timetable for healing and restoration! He has spoken at college rodeo church services, uses his telephone and computer (text, email, & facebook), will complete an online course (macroeconomics) from his college this week, and is very close in taking some solo steps!

December 25, 2011—Merry Christmas! Christmas still amazes me—guess because He is so amazing! I wrote and sang a song a few years back (*Is There Any Room?*) which tells that we are innkeepers—our hearts. Just like the innkeeper, we have to make room after we have 'opened' the Christmas gift of Jesus—our salvation. To trust Him as we walk with Him in a relationship that started in the manger and will be for eternity—Amazing!

Tim has had a busy week with therapies, ROM machine workouts, and time in the pool—what HUGE improvements from the last time we were in! We are thankful that he continues to have improvements from his hard work. With a platform walker and Howard barely holding on from behind (I was in front holding the walker down), Tim took two steps, not totally solo, but we'll keep saying it again and again—We're close! Continue to pray for balance, strength, and coordination and maybe we'll see God give a belated gift to Tim this week!?! Thank you for all the cards, emails, and texts. As we are, we pray that each of you will take this week to look inside and look back to look forward as we continue this journey! We ask nightly for renewed, refreshed, and Tim asks for refueled strength and grace for our daily walk—it gets tiring especially emotionally for Tim. God is so faithful and gracious for that strength and grace. We are excited and anxious to watch and be a part of God's healing and restoring of Tim's body and broken heart in 2012. Thank you again and again for your continued prayers and encouragement. PRAY and BELIEVE!!

Week of December 26, 2011-January 1, 2012—Girls slept in a bit and even Tim stayed in his bed until 7! (Even though he talked to everyone in the house at different times!) "Cooper" Christmas was at Cheryl & Chuck's—they made 'Merry Christmas Malm's' letter signs and took a family picture and sent it to us over the internet and then we skyped with everyone! Miss being there and know it was hard not having Shena there—remember us girls sleeping on our hide-a-bed couch with the Christmas tree lights on all night, just something about that glow! Hard to think about being in Oklahoma this day last year singing at Shena's memorial service in Walters. Talked with Candra about life changes with Dad and Shena with You—knowing we'll all be together someday, and with Tim's journey—believing in Your healing and restoration of him. Still wishing for someday to have enough room to have Christmas up here with the Coopers and Malms together.

    Tim had a good PT session starting to use the walker with the upright handles! We had a swim session and Bethany and Jessica went with us. Friday was our Malm Christmas which started off with family pics with everyone dressed in white or black around Grma's fence. Jillian (McL) took them and they turned out good! Had a great meal, good food, and lots of fun. Last year—they carried Tim in in his chair, this year—he 'walked' in with assistance, hopefully next year—he walks in on his own! Tim could sit in a regular chair at the table this year! We shared New Year's Eve with Dwayne & Chaurisse with food and a long movie! Sunday was just a 10:00 service, so people came in at different times, not everybody knowing or remembering! Have lots of prayers, wishes, & goals all wrapped up in Your will, Your plans, &Your timing! Thank You for another 'mile' (year) on this journey and in the chapter of our life story! Deut. 10:12&13 "And now, O Israel (put in your name in place of Israel), what does the LORD your God ask of you but to

fear the LORD your God, to **walk** in all His ways, to **love** Him, to **serve** the LORD your God with all your heart and with all your soul, and to **observe** the LORD'S commands and decrees that I am giving you today for your own good.

HAPPY 2012!! What a year it has been and what a year it can be!—especially if we discipline ourselves to follow and apply the Lord's resolutions in the verse in our daily walk for the year! We pray blessings for each of you for this year and thank you again and again for your continued prayers and encouragement on this site, facebook, emails, cards, visits, and hugs! I hope each of you will view the movie, *Utopia*, soon—it's very good. I'll try not to ruin it for you before you see it, but for those of you who have seen it . . . "SFT" We will be standing on these letters and their meaning from the movie as Tim is really close to those solo steps (maybe the first times with the walker)—his physical therapist said he was very close!! It does Tim good to hear those encouraging words from all his therapists rather than always from his family! Like the word, 'yonder', that we use in the South . . . the words 'close' and 'soon' have become measurement words with different meanings for different situations. We thought and used the words for over a year now truly thinking that the progress and improvement was 'close' and 'soon' . . . I look back and thank God for keeping us in that mode that even today (even though we get weary along the journey) we still have the excitement and expectancy of seeing Him fully heal and totally restore Tim. Sometimes it causes me to wonder if the Christians had the same word thoughts ('close' and 'soon') after Jesus ascended to Heaven as they awaited for His Return. Hundreds of years later, we still await with excitement and expectancy for His Return, for He is coming 'soon'! We look forward to our therapy sessions and some time in the pool. We ask for your continued prayer for full function of the left hand/arm and God to grant full balance, strength, and coordination for Tim to take those long-awaited solo steps within these next few days or couple of weeks . . . and be watching for an update or hear us shouting when he does!!! Thank you, Lord, for another year along this journey, but most of all, for being there leading, holding, and loving us every breath, every step, and every day!

Chapter Seven

Home in Albin (2012)

Week of January 2-8, 2012—Tim had a doctor appointment with Dr. Beer in Cheyenne on Wednesday. Didn't get to spend very much time with him because we had our initial eye appointment with Dr. Cotton—she is a developmental optometrist. She spent from 3:40-5:20 with Tim! The other patients were so kind and just said they would come back on Friday, so the office was able to reschedule everyone for us. Very excited to be watching her work with Tim! Tim had good therapies this week, working the hardest on balance! Lord, thank You again for the time that Bethany was here and for her safe trip back to Branson to start this semester. We pray You will strengthen Cassady as she returns to the team to play bball. God, You know use of Tim's left hand would help greatly in so many areas, how we plead for full function of it and to start this year with some solo steps this next week!

Week of January 9-15, 2012—It was nice enough to rope outside for some of the PT session (it could be freezing and be 'nice enough' for Tim to rope!). Had a pool time on Wednesday and Tim improving all the time 'walking' with both of us down the stairs, in the water, and then back up the stairs! Tim's highlight of the week was to have Coach Cullen come up on Friday to spend the day before NJC started school back up. Tim did really well in PT—we had it over at the church and he 'walked' with us beside him down the aisle and then back again with the second time using the walker! Another week of Your blessings, protection, strength, & encouragement, and we are so thankful. Forgive us of our greediness to ask for more and faster healing? It's hard to hear of Tom not doing good—Tim prays for You to heal Tom first and that he can wait a little longer if need be. Isaiah 40:29-31 "He gives strength to the weary and increases the power of the weak. Even youths grow tired and weary, and even young men stumble and fall; but those who hope in the Lord will renew their strength. They will soar on wings like eagles, they will run, and not grow weary, they will walk and not be faint." We are reading through this book and this familiar verse came on a day we were extremely tired—God has amazing timing! Most of the time you just see the 'soar-run-walk' part, but the first of Him giving strength and increasing the power—what 'food' and encouragement that is! I've always wondered why He chose to use the flow of 'soar-run-walk' and not the other way of walk-run-soar?

In church, Tim told of one of his praises of the week: Tim was able to stand in the pool all by himself without either one of us of touching him, nor was he against anything! He did it twice for a few seconds each time. He is becoming quite the checkers player—his grandpa, dad, and Jess give him the toughest competition! Coach C didn't fare too well, and Aunt Lynette is still in the beginner stage! He sure enjoys the visits! He had a good day and the weather cooperated for him to rope outside with the calf head dummy! He told one of his friends (after his friend had said he'd had a not so good day at roping) that any day you get to rope is a good day and never take it for granted! Had a very good therapy on Friday using stairs with Howard and his therapist, using the walker with just Howard holding the walker in front and his therapist using minimal assistance, working with trunk control in an armless chair, and standing against a wall by himself. I'm here and there with 'encouraging' instructions! (Not sure Tim would word them as such, but he has told me that I can 'push') We keep praying for quicker improvements, but God has and is holding us as we watch, work, and wait—on Him, through Him, and for Him to show Himself through the healing and restoration of Tim. To God be the Glory! So thankful for His daily grace and strength that keeps us expecting a miracle—keep your eyes and ears open!! PRAY & BELIEVE

Week of January 16-22, 2012—Along with the other therapies, Tim also worked on the vision therapy exercises/games. Tim "walked" (with us and the rail) down the hot tub steps after swimming in the pool—we all enjoyed that! Went to Cheyenne to finish the eye exam with the doctor-Tim will be getting some glasses that will progress as the alignment and focus progresses. Tim finished the week on Friday with really good therapies, especially PT in the church and on the ROM machine! Always praying that within Your timing, that it might be at church when You allow Tim to 'walk' in by himself some Sunday. Tim did great on the stairs with only Howard and the banister (I was busy and they started without me, so I just stood behind and 'verbally' helped with an extra little lift of his left foot to get the toes of his shoes up and over that extra 'lip' on the carpeted stairs it gets caught on) He stood for 'mini-seconds' during the songs, but it's a start! Had a short mini-blizzard, but we made it over to church We continue to plead for Tim's full healing and restoration here and that we may see huge improvements this month! John 16:24 "Ask and you will receive and your joy will be complete" Again, this is a struggle verse for Tim and us—probably because we are a 'now' society and patience is a lesson God is teaching all the time to us. The verse reminds me to obey (ASK) and leave the results and timing to Him. It also reminds me to be joyful; it states that your joy . . . so I take it to mean that there is already joy there and that joy will be complete. I pray our kids truly know the difference between joy and happiness; happiness can be a response to your joy, but joy comes from Him and within when your heart and soul 'smiles' whatever or whenever. Continue to pray for balance and coordination to come together and for full-function of the left hand/arm! Thank God for all He has done, is doing, and going to do! Have a joyful week!

Week of January 23-30, 2012—Snow on the ground on Monday and Tuesday, but our therapists were able to still make it out! Worked sitting in an armless chair and also in the saddle with balance and strength, even able to sit a few minutes by himself with making adjustments however to 'stay' in the saddle! Chris gave Tim a haircut this week—what improvement there from the first time she cut his hair!!!

Lord, Tim's prayers are sometimes getting too hard for me to pray after him, I may need to go before! He is so genuine and honest with You. How we pray for You to restore him to Your fullness of the 'plans' You have for him. Been a lot of medical prayers this week, and we are so thankful that we can rely on You for guidance, patience, and trust in Your care. January has flown by, and yes, Lord, I really thought we would see Tim take some steps. I keep using the word 'close' with writing on Caringbridge and talking with people, but evidently the meaning and timing is different between us. Tim had a frustrating PT therapy even though he pushed through it, but seeing his body not respond the way he 'tells' it to makes him mad. Made it to both Friday and Saturday games at Burns—the teams are so encouraging to Tim! The Men's Breakfast Group (last Saturday of the month) sent over the pancakes, eggs, and bacon so we had a breakfast brunch! Right after the varsity games, I took them on in to Cheyenne for a weekend of child care with the Jessen's. Always look forward to our Sundays, especially with our church family and the encouragement they are to Tim and our whole family! Maybe a small church, but they have huge hearts and such prayers warriors for us! Thank You again for bringing the Morrison's to this church body out here on the 'prairie'! Tim sure enjoys and learns from him, especially likes his jokes and sense of humor! You start our week off right! Psalm 31:2-4 "Since You are my rock and fortress, for the sake of Your name lead and guide me.' This verse is a standing deal; since you give your reason (the first phrase) and then ask Him to lead and guide—your part of the 'deal' is that you are agreeing to follow Him, His lead, and His guidance. We continue every day to thank Him for His strength, leading/guiding, and perseverance along this journey. Tim displays it the most, and it is a constant effort because being very cognitive of this injury, he focuses on trusting God with the healing and restoration, along with God's timing. Everyone sees improvement in all areas—Tim sees it as very slow and keeps asking God to pick up His pace! Our biggest prayer concern still centers around his left hand/arm, but we are seeing a little more each day! PRAY & BELIEVE!!

Week of January 30-February 5, 2012—Gal 6:9 "And let us not grow weary while doing good, for in due season we shall reap if we do not lose heart." Ecclesiastes also talks about the times and seasons for everything. Watching the Giants win the Super Bowl after the season they had, but they hung in there and it brought them to tonight and the championship—this was their season, their time. after a long and hard journey. We are trying not to get weary and trusting God along each step on this journey trusting in this time and season according to God and His timing with His healing and restoring Tim. We thank each of you again and again for the prayer support you have been and are for us. Tim continues to work very hard and improvements are seen every day (still small in Tim's eyes) but we are so grateful to Him for each and every one of them. Tim prays even harder for some of his friends. With schools being in full swing, he really misses the 'busyness' of school with the classes, roping practice, friends, 'talking' on the phone and texting with them. He tries to keep busy with other things and focusing on his rehab! The hot tub time after swimming really feels good this time of year and we are so thankful for them both being indoors! Tim trying to get some use out of the 'ski-pole' walker (what I call it!) but for some reason, the tone sets in when trying to walk with it. He did great on the stairs and we are seeing more strength in that left quad! Lord, How we thank You for Tim's eye improvement—he tells us of being able to read some of the smaller print and clearer picture on the tv and using smaller font sizes on his computer and phone! (He's reading smaller font size than I can with my glasses!)

We were so excited on Thursday that Tim rolled over on his left side, could move his head smoother from the right and to the left, PTL! We all got Tim down on his stomach using the big wedges hopefully to get some weight bearing on that left shoulder, arm, and hand. We are still very close to those solo steps, I know we keep saying that, but continue praying that we will see them SOON! The anticipation reminds me of '09 National High School Rodeo Finals when Tim came in to the final round in 11th place—he had a great run and we sat there keeping the averages and as his time on three calves kept holding up, our stomachs were churning . . . then when it was finished, Tim was National Reserve Champion! Tim has made it through the first round, and this second round is rough and slow, but in God's time and in His strength, Tim will make it to the next round!

My stomach still churns and my heart yearns each morning thinking 'this might be the day'! Tim displays great perseverance and keeps a positive attitude . . . but the other day someone asked him if he hurt anywhere? Tim pointed to his heart—please pray for Tim's broken heart. He misses roping and his horses beyond words and not being able to work on the ranch alongside his grandpa is terribly tough. Tim wants so badly to climb up in the tractors, grease and work on machinery, hay with the windrower, tag calves, etc.—we are thankful that even though it's tough right now, those desires are motivational to him. Thank God, along with us, for his attitude and trust in God, and continue to uphold him before God that He might display His power with His healing and restoring Tim, and moves a little faster! Tim is on Facebook and he writes on it so let me know if most of ya'll have or you would rather switch to it, then we could do that. I enjoy writing—it keeps me 'connected' with you, but many enjoy reading Tim's posts and I am so thankful he can do that now! Let me know . . . Expect a miracle and we PRAY & BELIEVE!!!

Praying for February to be a month of miracles!! Goodnight, Lord, we love You!

Week of February 6-12, 2012—The week started off cold so we didn't get to go do ROM, but had a good OT session on Monday. Had a pool day on Wednesday, and Tim did well. He has taken a few steps in the pool! Tim worked sitting in different chairs and standing up out of them, did some squats, and 'walked' up and down the stairs. Howard did all the feeding out at the Ranch since Fanny and Gordon went to a cattle sale up in North Dakota. With the snow, Howard and Tim decided to stay home while I drove the girls over for their bball on Saturday evening. It was a cold ride over for Tim, so church felt warm when they got there! It was good and we set up the table and chairs after church for the Valentine Banquet that we had tonight. Everyone had a good time! Thank You for these friends, good food, and good times in Your House! Pray & Believe to WALK!

Proverbs 4:10-12 "Listen, my son, accept what I say, and the years of your life will be many. I guide you in the way of wisdom and lead you along straight paths. When you walk, your steps will not be hampered;

when you run, you will not stumble." We love Proverbs—daily food to really chew on! Pretty simple . . . He guides and leads and we walk and run and in that order. It sure seems like you see a lot of people walking and running before they know Him or let Him do the guiding and leading! Tim has had another steady (slow to him) week of daily small improvements as he builds strength, balance, and staying emotionally strong. He hit one of his goals this week on the ROM machine we work on—he finally hit 80 on his numbers!! Won't mean much to most of ya'll, but I'm barely in the 80's so he's about to past me in the upper body work numbers! We ask you to add to your prayers that God will heal/restore/rid Tim of any 'tone' spasms (kind of like major yawns/stretches/cramps for a moment for you and me). Continue to pray for God to show His power in this week in Tim's journey! Expect a Miracle as we PRAY & BELIEVE!!!

Week of February 13-19, 2012—I am running on 'empty' and need refueled with full tank of strength, rest. Tim did get his new glasses which is taking some getting used to them! We watched one of Tim's favorite movies, "Facing the Giants "with a friend of his. We all went down for the season's last game at Pine Bluffs. Tim visited with several people in between games. We watched the movie, "Courageous" and it was GREAT!!! Tim really enjoyed it. I'm so very grateful that Howard is the 'courageous' dad that he is to our kids. Many of you have seen the friendship/bond Howard and Tim had before his accident, and many of you have seen and watch Howard with Tim now—pretty tough, but special and Tim thanks God for him all the time 'cause he knows his rehab has progressed and continues to progress because of him (Howard) and Him (Jesus Christ) Lord, we made it through this long week and long season! Thank You again and again for all the protection with the miles we put on going here and there, Cass' injury, Tim's improvements, and giving us good nights of rest and renewed strength! You are an amazing God, Father, Healer, & Savior! Waiting & Watching You.

Proverbs 10:9a "The man of integrity walks securely . . ." Again, His Word tells us how one walks is first characterized by the inside then on the outside. This journey of Tim's has strengthened and encouraged

Tim, us, his sisters, his family, his friends, and many others as He has strengthened and lengthened our steps in the inside and the outside as we walk securely with Him. Tim is so ready to receive all of God's healing and restoring of his physical body so all can know and see that Tim walks securely because of his Lord, Savior, and Healer. We continue and know ya'll do also pray for his steps to come soon and to keep trusting God for His perfect timing. Phil 4:13!!! Thanks again and again for your prayers and encouragement. PRAY & BELIEVE!!!

Week of February 20-26, 2012—Tim increasing his breathing capacity to hold his 'ah' sound to 20 seconds! Therapies went well with working on the yellow balance ball, timing with speaking and breathing, and began working/walking with the hemi-walker. The therapist said this was about three times harder to walk with than the 'pole-ski' walker. Tim struggles with it but we are using it a little every day to try to get the 'hang' of it! In the pool this week, Tim 'walked' a little with us, but without the life vest on so it wouldn't float him up too much—he did great with trusting himself (and us!) Tim did a great job with the hemi-walker in church today—kind of 'dangerous' with it when not using it as a walker! [With Howard and I (and the hemi), we walked up the aisle when Carl asked everyone to gather around Tim for a special prayer time with our church family. We thank You for all of them; they are so supportive, encouraging, and loving!] Lord, we thank You for this 'new page' of a long 'chapter' on this journey with the improvements You gave this week and the encouragement it gave Tim. Praying for more—forgive our greediness and impatience with wanting more and quicker. Thank You that we can bring our desires to You, even though You already know our hearts—I guess that's the 'child' in us, thank You, Father! Looking forward to a great week! Prov 16:9 "In his heart a man plans his course, but the Lord determines his steps." This verse keeps coming into our devotions and/or daily readings. It gives us the motivation to make goals and plans, but also because of the privilege of being His children—through accepting salvation because of His Son and the cross—we have the choice to walk in His control and timing as He determines our steps. To daily make that choice is a daily battle; but oh, what a comfort and relief to be able to walk in that trust, holding

His hand, and feeling His hug! We go to the vision doctor this week to show her the improvement there. Continue to pray for that left-hand function as we watch God work this week. Thank you again for your prayers!!

Week of February 27-March 4, 2012—The week started off with giving the OT a "pound" with the left hand and arm! Thank You for the movement and the message to get there! In speech, the therapist had Tim stand (with our help) and tell the accident story—he recalled quite a bit and we filled in when he needed us to. It was interesting watching someone who doesn't know rodeo/roping lingo try to picture or understand what was said! PT sessions had Tim on the yellow ball and we could see improvement with balance and strength! We thank You and continue to ask for more! Had a vision appt in Cheyenne for Tim and a follow-up med appt for Cassady. Tim "walked" really well up the ramp with us! Waiting and Watching for those steps! We went swimming on Friday and we continue to see improvement—amazing what water can do! Also had a ROM session and gaining strength and coordination there every time! Lord, we thank You for the improvements we saw this week, keeps our excitement and anticipation up! Looking forward to someday that we walk in, see him sitting on the edge of his bed, waving at us with his left hand, & saying, "What's up?"

John 3:27 To this John replied, "A man can receive only what is given him from Heaven." A little picture of Tim's perseverance . . . hardly a night goes by that Tim doesn't reply to God that he is ready to receive His healing and restoration, that maybe this will be the Luke 23—Several verses starting with 32 through 43 were presented today by our pastor (preacher, for the South folks!) in a series of "Seven Sayings of the Savior on the Cross"—the first two dealt with the word of Forgiveness and the word of Salvation. Everyone can have a 'head-faith' because we have the Word, but it takes a 'heart-faith'—a relationship with Jesus Christ to be one of His Children. It's hard to put in words how knowing Him as Lord, Savior, Healer, Comforter, etc. has kept us through this journey. I truly don't know how the world deals with situations in life without God-Jesus-Holy Spirit!?! We are excited for the month to see where and how God strengthens, heals, and restores

Timothy! Even though they are small to Tim, he has improvements daily that he knows are building steps to those solo steps that will lead to walking—we just ask God to allow us to live in His timing when we are anxious for quicker healing and restoration. We still believe that if God so chooses, He could totally touch Tim and we could see him walk and rope any day . . . but we also believe in His Sovereignty—even though we don't understand it—and will depend on His daily grace to 'walk' this journey at His pace and be so thankful for what He has done, is doing, and is going to do! Thank you again for all the prayers you have offered up for us. Continue to pray for others to see Him and His power through all 'this' journey of faith and persistence! Tim asked God the other night "how long was persistence?" In His time, we'll be shown! Have a Blessed Week

Week of March 5-11, 2012—OT session had Tim using left hand/arm hitting the dangling (Tim says "dang") ball given as one of the vision exercises. He still has that competitiveness! Weather was beautiful for PT and after inside work, Tim was 'in the saddle' roping the dummy—did well! Tim 'stood' with us for thirty minutes in speech doing breathing and his 'ah' timing sounds! Enjoyed our visit with our home health care program coordinator (Laura, from Boston originally)—when she saw one of Tim's roping pictures, she asked "why do you carry a rope in your mouth!" Tim really laughed, and Howard explained it politely while Tim was laughing! Grpa & Grma came by after Wed. night prayer meeting and Bible Study. Howard and I sure miss that, but this is just a 'season', and we will get back to going. Was able to go swimming again this week. While I was at Music Festival with Jessica held here at Albin, Howard and Jason worked with Tim on the sidewalks outside of church and then inside on the stairs. Howard said he did really well! I will be excited to see his progress on Sunday. Maybe March, we will see steps!

With the nice weather, Howard, Tim, and Jessica went shooting on Saturday and they all did well! Good day in Your House today with family and friends (Bennie came out from Cheyenne) and Tim 'walked' well! Fanny & Gordon drove in from their Montana trip and visited with us before going home. Took a 4-hr nap today—little tired!! Thank

You for the rest, and Howard & Tim resting some today! Gearing up for a great week, watching & trusting You! It is encouragement and motivation coming from that perseverance, trust, and believing in His Word and in Him. We were given more exercises from the vision doctor on Wednesday where, when asked to lift his left arm/hand to tap the ball hanging from the ceiling, he could not do it. As many of you know Tim and his work ethic—Thursday didn't come fast enough to start working on that! He was able to raise it up and almost touch the ball, but not quite yet. With working on the ROM machine and swimming on Friday (again, he is showing improvement with all the exercises and movement in the pool!!), he had to wait for Saturday to work on the ball exercises, especially the tapping. He worked up a sweat and finally tapped the ball two times!! He is using the hemi-walker with more and more smoothness and consistency. Walked up the stairs (using the banister and with Howard in front) better than ever today! He brought his left foot and leg up and on the next step without any assistance from me! He stood with the walker without Howard or me for about ten seconds at one time! PTL! Continue to pray for his balance, it is improving just not at the rate that Tim wants. We are seeing more movement with the left hand . . . Tim is able to lift his wrist/hand to the straight, neutral position from the relaxed downward position—maybe more finger movement this week!?! Please pray also for God to grant Tim the emotional strength during the upcoming spring rodeo season—many of his friends will be at a rodeo in Cheyenne this weekend and the college rodeos will be starting soon. He misses the practices and the performances terribly—only God knows how his heart is broken and only God can fill, heal, and restore his heart in His timing and in His ways. Have a great week!!

Week of March 12-18, 2012—Monday started off with us having a ROM machine session and Tim did well, especially with the left hand crossover! He was also able to work a little on the back of the machine which is for the legs! He's only been able to help hold himself up while 'stepping & walking', but it takes all three of us to even do 10 steps, but it's a huge accomplishment! We also had swimming time and it went well. Howard turned 55 this week on his birthday Saturday. Tim did well in church—he could stand totally on his own for about five seconds at a time.

Lord, how we pray for steps soon—he's praying that he won't have to take his wheelchair to the Torrington College Rodeo the first weekend in April. I pray we see rewards for his faith and perseverance, he's working so hard! We thank You for our week, we saw improvements in several little areas and things—we know they are the 'building blocks' of rebuilding, recovery, and restoration. We pray for a strong end for the month! "Without even knowing it, your faith is a shining light touching those close to you and even those who do not know your name. Without realizing it, your faith is the topic of conversations. Your perseverance and strength could only come from God who lifts and sustains you in this time and shows up in amazing ways when you are discouraged. Yes, your light is brightly shining and warming the hearts of all who are near." Matt 5: 14-16 was also printed on this card Tim received this last week and we wanted to share it with you. It was and is great encouragement. Tim had really good therapy sessions—especially, as many of you may have seen on Tim's facebook, the short video of him sitting in his saddle on the special rack made by his college rodeo friends from NJC outside roping the calf dummy!! He roped it several times and I thought we were never going to get him out of the saddle! His core strength and balance is improving—we didn't have to hardly hold him very much. We thank God for the warm weather outside to be able to do this. Our warm weather and no moisture is very unusual for this time of year! Had a great vision appointment with new exercises to work on these two weeks before we go back—PTL! Tim set a new record of his on the ROM machine this week—hoping to break the '90' number this week!

Had a great worship service this morning—wrote down the following statement . . . "Can't be prepared to live until you're prepared to die!" Our prayer is for all to look inside these next two weeks preparing for Palm Sunday, Good Friday, and Resurrection Sunday (Easter) and make sure of your preparations with our Lord and Savior! Continue to pray for Tim's left fingers and hand—we are seeing more and more everyday, and we are so grateful. The slowness of the healing and function being restored is what Tim struggles with, but continues to trust Him with His timing and His purpose and plans. PRAY for a miracle, EXPECT a miracle, and WAIT for a miracle—PRAY & BELIEVE!!!

Week of March 19-25, 2012—Matt 21:1-22 Today was Palm Sunday and with this whole week we challenge each of you to read these passages every day and thank Him everyday His week for His gift of salvation! If you haven't seen The Passion of the Christ, maybe that could be included in your week. We had a good day in church—Tim 'walks' better every week across the foyer and up/down the stairs with assistance. He is standing with his hemi-walker totally by himself for 5-10 seconds at a time and that will be increasing everyday I believe. We still had unbelievable weather and were able to rope on the saddle rack in physical therapy on Friday—Tim even added a little 'standing in the saddle' with only one person holding for extra balance!! He has worked really hard on the ROM machine and is surpassing me! Tim was able to do a few (bent-knee)push-ups with his left hand out flat, along with help, to make him go slow. He had a really good day shooting and didn't get sunburned on Saturday! Continue to specifically pray for function and restoration of his left hand/arm and for balance—it is improving, but not fast enough for Tim. He works really hard and stays very positive, but does struggle at times when talking to God about 'picking up his mat and walking', 'if two or more . . . ', 'asking and believing', 'faith to move this mountain', 'faith as a mustard seed', etc so ask for encouragement and gifts of mobility and healing toward restoration! Again, we thank you for your prayers and support as we ask for emotional strength this week as we go the college rodeo on Fri/Sat and Tim gets to see, visit, hug, and watch (through a tear-stained, broken heart) many friends, and enjoy the sport he loves and asks God to let him rope again. Good times . . . tough times, but God is Good! Focus on the Cross and His unbelievable love this week

Week of March 26-April 1, 2012—The manure spreaders came today, so Howard had to move cattle round to different pens for Larry to get his loader and truck in and out. Felt so good to be able to walk almost two miles and pray like I used to before Tim's accident. Haven't made the time to get back in the routine of that, hopefully sometime soon. I had so hoped to push Tim around our school track, and then to progress to 'walk' with him around it this spring. Been a while since Tim was on the yellow ball and he did push-ups without it underneath him! Thank you for the increased strength and allowing more function with the left hand in order to do those! Tim's balance has so improved on the saddle; I just help stabilize him from behind him (less chance of getting roped, also!) Tim so enjoyed the Chipotle burritos Grpa brought home from Cheyenne! Thank You for providing these 'treats' from them! Went to Scottsbluff and Mitchell for errands and picked up all twenty bags of our beef to fit in the navigator! Thanks for the safety and strength with all the travel and lifting, plus plenty of air in the tires with that much weight of the meat! Watched some Final Four NCAA bball! Hard to believe that April is here! So thought we would see steps in March—we try not to let Tim see any 'down' moments, but encourage him to "Press On" and keep trusting! He knows more than anyone the intense slowness and hardness of this recovery and restoration. Praying for Torrington next week, physically, especially emotionally!

Week of April 2-8, 2012—Tim got on the 'shaker' machine that belonged to the Martin's and used the left hand some by itself!! We sang "Happy Birthday" to Bethany on the phone on Tuesday! Can't believe she is 20—now we have two teenagers and two young adults! Had good therapies, with a surprise meeting of the fill-in for our regular PT, Jason. She is from Alabama and her name is Angie—what a neat God-thing to bring in someone (from the South!) that can also validate the other therapists, but bring added encouragement! We really enjoyed her for the week! Tim worked on the ROM machine and slept in chair on Tuesday 'cause his leg ached a bit, praying for a good night's rest! Pray it'll be one of those 'good' hurts from working and awakened some muscles. Had to reschedule our vision apt because Howard had to take heifers to Torrington. Pastor John came over for a visit—Tim always enjoys and is encouraged when he comes. Fixed all the food to feed the NJC rodeo team and other friends on Thursday night. Getting emotionally ready to go to Torrington this year was extremely hard for Tim. He so wanted to not take his chair, but not in Your timing this year, hopefully next year! My hearts breaks for him, watching him this whole weekend in the arena and eating with the team and his friends, and all the visiting. Thank You for supplying the emotional strength that You did and for being our Rock! Fed about forty and enjoyed meeting some of Coach Cullen's friends and the parents of some of the kids.

We slept in the Navigator for a couple of hours waiting for the night performances to start. I was able to have a few minutes just to stand by myself—smelling the arena, hearing the announcer, watching the rodeo . . . one of those moments in life where you're there, but 'not there'. I watched Tim mostly from where I was standing praying while wondering what was going on inside of him. You have given Howard and Tim a special bond that I am so very thankful for, especially for Howard to be that spiritual leader, support, and friend for Tim. He is a great picture of the balance he has with being Dad and friend to all our kids, but especially with Tim. My heart is overflowing with tears (I think probably from Tim's heart), but holding them back from the outside and I thank You for helping me go through that—I can hold his tears . . . . With this being Easter weekend, the finals were on Saturday, so we went back up for them. Easter, "Resurrection Day!" and had a great celebration in our hearts and with everyone in church! The focus totally on You and thankfulness for what You did on the Cross for our salvation! Thank You again and again! He also drove the navigator out better to the Ranch—that's even hard for me remembering how young he started driving and what a good driver he was with all the vehicles, trucks, & machinery. Praise Your name and we anxiously await for April miracles! Hope ya'll read the passage we challenged ya'll to read and keep praying for this 'mountain' to move! Tim told the Lord he'd be happy with a few more 'pebbles' to be moved out of the way on the journey of healing and restoration!

We thank you for praying for the rodeo weekend (Th/Fr/Sa). Tim struggled the night before we went on Friday with the emotional side of watching his passion in an arena that he did well in about two months before the accident! He did amazingly well and hides his hurting heart behind his smile, laugh, hugs & handshakes to all the friends. He encourages them, but all the time, words, hugs, & handshakes really encourage him! Thanks to so many of you who took the time, and we understand how hard it is for some of you who just can't bring your self up to Tim because you hurt so bad for him, don't know what to say, or whatever . . . in time, when you are ready. We have prayed that the Lord will give us and show us a new outlook on the word TIME! This small word can take on so many meanings for all situations, good and bad . . . Tim feels the weight of this word and the loud 'ticking' is a struggle for him when he so badly wants to be on his horses and roping. We love you and Jesus loves you, too!

Week of April 9-15, 2012—We had our monthly visit with our home care coordinator that Tim always looks forward to and enjoys! In PT, Tim worked on the yellow ball and his left hand was the best we had seen with more relaxation to be able to hold it down for some push-ups! How we beg for full-function for that left hand and arm! Sunday, we started a series, Contagious Christian—hope we display what some would want to 'catch'! Tim 'walked' very good today—looking forward to Your miracle of steps, SOON!Tim received a 'Soul Card' from a friend and wanted to share some thoughts from it. It talked about life lessons in which we are called to overcome them when we would rather avoid them. Answering five questions—"what should you do, what will you do, what won't you do, what can't you do, and what can He do through you?" can allow you to achieve a more genuine experience of God and His grace in overcoming the lesson in His strength (Phil 4:13). From birth, life puts us in the school of soul where the curriculum is not our choice—but the choice is to choose Jesus Christ as Lord and Savior and have a relationship with Him! Then as we 'walk' through life's lessons and journey, because of Him—we can be and are overcomers! In the Greek New Testament, the word "overcome" bears special nuance and its meaning is "Nike". The term was used for athletes who competed and excelled in Olympic games and was used as empowerment connected with the choice to overcome rather than avoid life lessons. The card encourages one to pay the price for personal growth—which sometime can be messy, and even embarrassing at times to struggle with negative feelings, fears, and upsets, Give them all to Jesus as you face them and beware of the easy path. Allow these feelings, fears, and upsets to be teachers as God strengthens you to overcome the lesson.

In Romans 8:35 it says ★ . . . "nothing can separate us form the love of Christ. In all things you will be more than overcomers." The friend now refers to Tim as "Nike" man! This encouragement goes along with our reading in 1 Samuel with David and Goliath, the Philistines, and all his travels and troubles with Saul. What a friend Jonathon was to David, and how we are so thankful for all our family and friends! Tim had good sessions in therapy—we are down to just one speech and one physical a week for the rest of April and then we will be off the home care list for awhile—will try to re-apply in the fall. He has had his highest numbers on the ROM machine and looks to better them this week. I gave a praise in church this morning the I hesitate to leave Howard and Tim at home at times because they sometimes attempt things without me . . . I went to a track meet to watch Jessica and when I came home, Tim asks his usual question, "Mom, want to know what we did?" I reply, "Do I want to know?" When Tim first began to get on his saddle and the iron rack that was made for him, it took four adults to get him on, hold him up, and the get him off—usually with everyone sweating! The facebook videos of Tim roping in the saddle have shown Howard and I assisting him and the last on, I was holding him from behind the saddle, BUT yesterday Howard held Tim while Tim was able to pull his left knee and leg up, around, and in the saddle by himself! PTL!!

We will be going to his vision doctor this week and I think she will be pleased with his progress! We ask you to pray and ask God for full-function of that left hand/arm and balance—we still see daily progress, but the slowness of His healing and restoration is hard, especially for Tim, to see His perfect timing. Even though Tim struggles with his physical frustrations, what a joy to hear him end his prayer time with the Lord with a positive tone of trust, thankfulness, and expectedness to hear Him say, "Tim, pick up your mat and walk!" and be granted that miracle of walking . . . maybe in the morning! Thank you again and again for your prayers and encouragement. Praying for weather safety this spring for everyone and thanking Him for restful nights and strength for the days!

Week of April 16-22, 2012—Have been noticing my journal entries have shortened, especially when I look back at last year's. It seems I am give out at night and think I will write in the morning . . . pretty soon it's the end of the week and I'm catching up, sometimes with looking on the calendar as to where our week went? I thank You because I see it as progress with working with Tim in a different way than last year—which seems to take up our time and move it in a different way! Now it's as much therapy as we can get in rather than last year was more physically doing so much taking care of him in the physical ways he has improved in now! Does that even make sense? I just know it's different, and GOOD! We are planning on Tim riding this week!?! I will have to let You work on me these next few days gearing me up for this. I've mentioned to Tim that maybe the reason God hasn't had him back on a horse quite yet is that his momma might not be ready to see her boy back on a horse? Well, I guess I'll have to be ready! Lord, thank You again and again for our prayer time, my quiet time, and the prayers of the thousands of people holding us up 'cause I know it's their prayers and You being a gracious Father that's holding me and our family together on this journey. I pray many will really experience the Power of Prayer! 1 Thes 2:12 "That you would walk worthy of God who calls you into His own kingdom and glory." Our prayer and instruction for our walk with Him and for Tim's physical walk in this journey—we are praying for God's hand of healing and restoration to his left hand, neck/head, and to take steps this week! We are, our family is, our church family is, and we ask each of you to pray specifically for left hand, head/neck, steps, horse, and rodeo church this week. Tim will be speaking for some of the rodeo church service this next Sunday, April 29th, so along with the verse . . . this accident and journey is all about Him, His kingdom, and His glory. We pray for Tim's awareness for him to know when and how to straighten his neck and head (it tilts to the right when he strains to use other muscles) so I don't have to 'ride' him about straightening it so much. I'm sure of his love, but the other day he told me to take off my 'spurs' since I was riding him so much about his head/neck! He also thanks me for those verbal clues. How we thank the Lord for his humor! Have a great week!

Week of April 23-29, 2012—Wednesday went beyond words . . . Bandit was so calm with Tim! We had this special two-level step that Jerry & Howard helped Tim on, then I brought Bandit up right beside Tim, and with Michael and Josh (thank goodness they are both about 6'4" ish!) we all could get Tim on and in the saddle! Howard led Bandit around in the pen while I filmed! They did great, but I think I was holding my breath the whole time! To see Tim's body relax and him smiling with his big smile was pretty amazing! It was a great time! The day progressed with vaccinating cattle (Howard, Tim, Martha, and a vet in the big building) and Gordon, Fanny, Andy, and I loading bulls for the truck that Grpa & Grma were taking to Omaha and the two trailers that a couple of bull buyers had come to pick up their bulls. A very long day full of emotions all over the place! How we thank You for safety with all the animals, with Tim & Bandit, and girls driving back and forth to school this week! Even though it was windy on Thursday, Tim still roped! Laramie was an experience! Had a great time with Coach Cullen and his family! Tim didn't want to use their elevator like he had to last year, so we went to the end where he could walk up the stairs (I think about twenty-three stairs!) As we were 'walking' a little crowd had gathered. When Tim made it to the top, they all started clapping! I wanted to cry, both for joy at what he had accomplished, but overwhelmed with the thoughts/memories of a year ago when he spoke, two years ago when he finished his first college season one place out of going to college nationals, '07-'08-'09 high school rodeos, and six years ago when they called us up at Laramie to tell us about Dad! He did really good and many told us afterward how much he had improved with his speaking since they had last heard him. We pray lives were changed, people were encouraged, and above all, God was glorified! Praise the Lord!! Already planning this week what days we will ride! Hugging and visiting with friends kept me strong, so I don't think anyone noticed how heavy my heart was! Thank You for holding it in Your hands. About 250-300 people showed up for church! PTL!! Everyone laughed when after helping Tim to stand, hold on to the rail, he asked Howard to 'step away'! He stood pretty good, got a little tired at the end, but finished it! Several told us how much more they could understand him and what improvement they saw—encouragement for Tim! Stayed for Finals and then for the

Awards. Coach wanted pictures of Tim with Shay (C) and Hayden (S) and their belt buckles and saddles they'd won for their events and all-around titles. Tim did great standing on the arena floor—he has a smile, but I know his heart was crying! Tim wanted to ride in by himself and speak at Laramie . . . we will keep trusting and waiting! Thank You for a GREAT week! Romans 8:26-39 with emphasis on 31b "If God is for us, who is against us?" and 37 "But in all these things we overwhelmingly conquer through Him who loved us". Tim had his last week of speech and physical therapy for the summer—looking forward to more time outside with therapy! Will head in for another vision therapy appointment and hopefully, his bifocals will be in! Again, we are so thankful for God answering our prayers for emotional strength as Tim relied on Him to hold him together to watch the rodeo, speak at church and with friends. It was such an encouragement and honor for him to be included in the picture with the champions and coaches from his college—thank you! Wasn't it good to see his big smile? Thank you, God, and all of you who shared this weekend with Tim and his family. Have a great week!

Week of April 30-May 6, 2012—Thank You for this week with all the changes and trying to set up our direction and schedule with Tim and his therapy with us! We pray that we have major changes and major improvements! We are so thankful and continue to see 'little' ones each day, but I guess we are greedy and we ask for more! We are closing out this month with two years since the 'accident'—starting year number three will need a huge dose of encouragement—the word picture that comes to mind is just after getting over one hill and you lay down for just a moment out of exhaustion. You raise your head to see the next mountain that you couldn't see from climbing this side—You take that big breath, gather yourself up, and start again with the first step! That filling 'breath' gives us Your strength, renewed focus, and because of the prayers of so many, a renewed energy! Thank You.

Another card we received this week that I would like to share with you. 1 Peter 4:1-2 in the verse it is centered around with the reading that during times of suffering, you will long for someone to share your journey. Strangers you meet during your treatment time, will become friends who encourage you through the day to day struggles. Family members will always linger near to comfort you. And Christ, who suffered himself, has promised never to leave your side. He will hear every prayer, weeps with you when you weep, and stay to dry the tears when you cannot sleep. *Today, find hope* in the knowledge that you are deeply loved and that many prayers with your name are ascending to heaven. *Today, find comfort* in the promises that you are not alone for God is walking every step of the journey with you. There's hardly a week goes by that we find out someone, some family, or some church that we haven't met or didn't even know about that has been praying for Tim and us! Strangers maybe to us, but not to God, and we know that some of you who read and respond here on caringbridge or Tim's facebook page are friends we haven't met, but know and thank you for you upholding us in prayer! Keep Tim and Howard in your prayers this week as the girls and I head to Branson to be with Beth then drive home together in two cars!! I get to spend Mother's Day with my mom (first time in 26 years!). You never know what Tim will talk Howard into trying while I'm gone . . . so I could use your prayers to trust them!! Continue to pray for FULL FUNCTION of Tim's left hand/arm and BALANCE to walk by himself!!!

Week of May 7-13, 2012—The week started off with the yellow ball! That's going to be the first thing Tim wants to shoot when he's up, walking and working! We remember when it took both PT and OT therapists along with Howard and me to work on the sitting and push-ups, and now it's just Tim and us! Our week was FULL! I picked up Cassady and Jessica from school on Thursday driving Cassady's car for our trip to Branson to pack up Bethany from school and drive both cars home together! Stopped by a cemetery where Rosie (W) was buried and then went to Johnny's house at Trenton, NE for a long visit—so enjoyed meeting his new wife, Nel. Thank You for all those memories with them! Our twenty hour trip ended with a short nap in Donnie & Bonnie's yard about 5:00 in the morning. Cleaned up there and was so good laughing and visiting with them! Mom drove in mid-morning, and Beth came over when she had a break, and then Sug and Joe took us all out to eat the largest Golden Corral! "A good time was had by all" as the saying goes! Bethany gave the girls and me a college tour and then we helped pack up and load the cars! We slept really well and we needed it! Went to Silver Dollar City on their 'student-friend' tickets and it was fun with Bethany and her friends. Wearing Shena's bracelet takes me back when we four girls and Mom & Dad all met there with our families one summer—what memories! Went to couple of shows, Mom even on stage at one of them! A great Mother's Day weekend!

We left about 7:00 and finally stopped in North Platte! We had three drivers and we rotated between cars so we thank You for the safe trip to and back home again! Talked with Howard and they 'managed' without us—even up the 'stairs' at the church today! Will head home first thing in the morning so they girls can hopefully get to school! Thank You again for a successful year with Bethany at college—it's really hard on her being away from Tim, she is excited for her summer working with him, now that she changed her direction and headed toward being a speech therapist! Thank You for the financial means for our trip. Looking forward to the week! Today in church we were given the message on how to pray bold prayers and to dream big things and to ask God for big things while trusting him whole heartedly because that's what He wants for us.

Amanda Welsh posted on Tim's facebook page: "The first person that came to mind was you, the times we've talk you have always said you'd rope again & you have asked God for big things, you have never doubted a day that you were asking too much or not believing you couldn't do it. I just want to thank you for being such a bold man for God. You have changed people's lives & have encouraged many other believers that God DOES want BIG things to happen with us while trusting him with our whole heart. You will do BIG things Tim! Looking forward to the day you step off your horse & tie a calf again, while every step you'll be praising the Lord! have a great Sunday.

(Another card) God's Promises to You . . . "I will protect you . . . (Acts 24:17), I will listen to you . . . (Jer 29:12), I will be with you . . . (Gen 31:3), I will give you rest . . . (Matt 11:28)" We have all really felt His promises literally cover us. Many, many miles and His angels hung on the whole way!! We are planning our therapy for this week, praying and working hard for this to be the month for those solo steps!! We would like to beat the two-year mark (June 6th)!!! Isn't it still hard to believe . . . Only God knew and only God knows, and we will continue to hold on tight to His hand as we WALK this journey—thanks for walking with us!!

Beth wrote, "I hate how every time I hear sirens it takes me back to the arena, sitting on the ground watching the ambulance pull in. It has been close to two years since the day that changed my life in so many ways, some good and some bad. I love you so much and am so glad you are still here with us. I miss you like crazy but love you even more! Keep on working hard and I can't wait till the day I get the text/call when you take your first solo step without any assistance! You are my hero."

Week of May 14-20, 2012—We worked with Tim on various things, working hard and praying we will have steps by June and he wants to walk in to CNFR this year! Tim is showing great numbers on the ROM machine! He even did about twelve steps on the back of it, YEA, Lord! We also roped this week and we see improvement there. Had a great day in church! Tim standing a few seconds by himself during the songs! Thank You again for this wild week and for protection for us and improvement with Tim!

Week of May 21-27, 2012—Another big and long week, but glad to have Bethany home! Bethany filmed some of Tim's workouts! Howard and Tim out all day working heifers in the big building—Howard said he did great that long and stayed warm enough! Bethany went out on Saturday with Tim and Dad to ultrasound some bulls. He even stood about five seconds by himself at the chute, then got to work the chute for the last five bulls! PTL!! We all went to church and Tim did well with the stairs—seeing improvement makes me even more anxious and excited to see him walk those by himself! Tim is praying hard about the college national finals at Casper in June. The president of the NIRA (Nat'l Intercollegiate Rodeo Assoc) had talked with Tim last year, and Tim had told him he would be back for this year, but 'in the box', not in this wheelchair! It would have to be a big miracle, but you are a big God . . . please start preparing him for the emotional side of going to the rodeo he so badly wanted to be back for!

The second year mark is around the corner, so we pray for all that entails for all of us! Thank You for the improvement we are seeing with Tim and his therapy, and we pray for more and emotional strength for the upcoming weeks! Thank you, again and again, for having our whole family home for our summer of 'home therapy'! Prayin' & Believin'! Cor 3:3 "You show you are a letter from Christ, the result of our ministry, written not with ink but with the Spirit of the Living God, not on tablets of stone, but on tablets of human hearts." If you have not seen 'Letters to God"—this is the verse from the movie! We watched it this week and WOW—brought tears (doesn't take much to bring me to tears!) At the end, Tim asked if we had ever said 'good-bye to him in the hospital? We never did—God's peace and trust in Him kept us believing . . . and we still believe today in that total restoration and healing of Tim. We continue to see daily progress! PTL! We would love For God to allow Tim to take his solo steps before the two-year date of the accident (June 6, 2010) We have stated how "*close*" he is to walking for about a year—it's amazing how far and close "*close*" can be and is, and how frustrating that can be! We thank you again and again for you being a part of this journey as prayer partners!! PRAY & BELIEVE!!!

Week of May 28-June 3, 2012—One of the few, but 'weird' nights for Tim . . . woke up at 1:40 hungry, and couldn't believe why Bethany wouldn't go get him some 'Dirt' dessert at that time! He and Bethany had slept out in the living room, so Howard moved him to his bed and he watched three episodes of McGyver! THEN, he tells us at 5:30 that he is tired! Tim started off the week of therapy with doing two minutes of the lower part of the ROM machine!!! We took Tim to the chiro—his jaw was 'out'—we will do exercises to help strengthen the other side to hold it in better. Mainly bothers him when he yawns and chews a lot (thank goodness for his Body by Vi shakes). Howard and Tim had a road trip with Gordon up to Upton to look at some calves—Howard said Tim did great with the travel and the time. Hopefully, we can all ride in one vehicle to Casper when we go to CNFR and to Oklahoma in July for Shiloh's wedding! Everybody home about 6:00, thank You for protection the many miles we all went this weekend!

Mentioned in church that this was the Sunday, two years ago, that Tim had the accident that affected us all, and how much everyone has meant to us with their prayers, encouragement, love, and support. We asked for them to pray for us as we start another year, another 'chapter, another 'season, on this journey with Tim. Even though Wednesday is the actual date, June 6, we look at it today as it seems like it was just yesterday in some ways, and then in other ways it seems like it's been forever! Again, TIME has taken on all different meanings and amounts, not just with Tim, but in all aspects of our lives now. Learning to live in His timetable has been and continues to be one of the many lessons I have been learning and continue to learn, live in, and depend on. Lord, I really can't put in the words what this journey has been or will be with You and our faith and trust in You, individually, and as a family. It truly is a "God-thing" and "This is all about You"! I pray that people have seen You, come to know You, and/or are just walking closer with You because of this accident and this journey. I pray You will reward Tim with full healing and restoration for his faith, trust, commitment, and perseverance with his testimony for Your glory! You have given him opportunities with speaking at the college rodeos, state high school finals rodeo, churches, and with friends, and what a blessing that has been! Coming from hardly a chance of making it through that night, restoring his mental capacities (and more!), and daily giving him the strength—Phil 4:13 to work so hard to get back physically to where he was has shown us, what an incredible God and Father You are! Tim has won and is winning many of life's "belt buckles"! With this coming year, or whatever timetable You have, we PRAY & BELIEVE we will see Tim "WALK, RUN, RIDE, ROPE, and WIN" in the 'arenas' of life! June 3, 2012—Today marks the actual day of Tim's accident with Wednesday marking the date (June 6th, 2010) Two years . . . and our journey of faith continues with both weariness and eagerness. God has been and is beyond words. I shared this morning in church the words (someday they will have music and I will sing it) God gave it to me and I wrote it down about a year ago on a piece of paper. It was laying in my journal when I glanced through it this morning.

> "In a second life can change
> And all your plans are rearranged
> All your dreams and goals seem to vanish far away
> As you wait in that space of time
> Praying God will help you climb
> This mountain of faith and give you another day
> We Pray and Believe in another day
> We believe in His healing hand
> We believe with Him we will stand
> Amen . . . Amen
> Only God knows when the time will be
> We give Him all the praise and glory
> Philippians 4:13 . . . Pray and Believe
> As we travel along this road
> We read and feed on His Word
> That a touch, a word, a mustard seed of faith can heal
> And as we work and pray everyday
> Try to stand and walk in His way
> We continue to wait for Him and give Him praise
> We Pray and Believe in another day
> We believe in His healing hand
> We believe with Him we will stand
> Amen . . . Amen"

Thank you all for remembering Tim and our family today. I asked him if he wanted to go to the arena and stand and pray where "it" happened? He said he didn't want to go to the arena until he can ride and rope! In God's hands and in His time . . . We do thank God for the little rainstorm that came through even though it hindered me to go to the arena (haven't been in the arena for about a year). We will be headed to the College National Finals Rodeo next week so I will try to write from Casper, Wyoming—please pray for Tim as he again emotionally gears up to go—how or why he wants to go is too tough for me to know, but we go in His strength and with Tim's strength!
PRAY & BELIEVE

Beth posted this on June 3 as well.

"It's hard to believe that two years ago today (it is the day, but not the date) and this time that my parents and sisters, and other family and friends were crowded into the tiny waiting room, waiting on the first round of tests and learned the extent of Tim's accident. I never thought my family would have to go through something like this, but we are truly blessed to have the family and friends that have walked with us through this tough time. So, I personally want to thank everyone who came to the hospital that night and any other time, and Thanks for all the visits, cards and prayers! It's funny how God works. One of Tim's best friends (who was in the arena when the accident happened) is with our family tonight also. Please continue to keep our family in your prayers, Wednesday, since that will mark the actual date our lives were changed. Sometimes it seems like it was just yesterday and sometimes it seems like it was a lifetime ago, that our lives were forever changed. June 6, 2010 will always stick out in my mind. It started as a typical Sunday at our house. We went to church, ate lunch, rested and then went to the arena. The girls and I warmed up and rode horses and ran some pole runs, just like normal. After getting kicked I went to lie down and ice my hip for a while until I heard those words "Call 911, Tim's not breathing". However, it didn't really hit me until we heard the doctors say "the next two hours will tell". I thought that I would never get to see those big blue eyes, or shake those big hands, or receive that gentle hug, but God was not and is not done with Tim yet. I thought I was about to lose not just my only brother, but one of my best friends. God is truly and awesome God we serve as we started witnessing miracles that very night and continue to see them. It has been an extremely long and difficult road but I we have been blessed with those who have traveled along with us. We truly cannot say thank you enough. Our family is blessed with you all, but my siblings and I are also blessed with the parents that we have going through all of this. Their faith nor has my brother's faith diminished at all, and mine has grown tremendously. Tim I am so proud of you and can't even describe the impact you have in my life. Continue to work as hard as you do! Phil. 4:13 Keep Praying and Believing!" Love ya, Bethany.

Tim's aunt Lynette wrote:

"Through Tim's experience, God has taught me great things. As Tim recently stated in his testimony, things like belt buckles, accomplishments, etc. will all collect dust. The only thing that really matters is the Lord and that if we allow him to he can use us in whatever circumstances we find ourselves in if we have a willing and heart. I thank God for both Dixie and Howard's parents and for the spiritual legacy both have instilled in all their children, grandchildren, and great-grandchildren. In this life if we have left our children treasures on earth, but have not introduced them to Jesus Christ and lived out or fail in front of them when we really have left them with nothing of value. The true test of successful parenting is not that our children will never make mistakes or get hurt but that they get back up and make the best of the situation and become God—fearing people walking daily with Him."

Cheryl Baber wrote,

"It's been a year and a half since Shena's funeral, and two years since Timothy's accident. I continue to read Dixie's blog and I marvel at her strength and faithfulness. The emotional, financial, physical, mental and spiritual toll have been enormous for her and Howard, but their love for Tim and all of their children is even greater. My prayers for them are for strength just as my prayers for Tim are for healing. My prayers for all of us who love Tim and his family are that we will use this experience, whether we have watched from nearby or far away, day-by-day or every now and then, for the glory of God and to advance His kingdom.

In His Time

Dixie's thoughts—Our 'accident-anniversary' week went well—hard to imagine it all again! We recalled improvements from last year and actually spent the day in Cheyenne with a chiro appt—still working on Tim's left mouth/jaw muscle development—it was weaker and Tim had started eating most of his food on his right, so the doctor is having us do exercises with Tim along with him checking to see if everything is staying in place with the jaw! We are excitingly awaiting for Second Step (I'll describe it as an adult 'walker') where Tim will be able to sit and stand as he develops his walk without Howard assisting him!! Even though you all know about insurance fights . . . we, along with Tim, felt it was something needed—so please pray that this will be used by God toward Tim's walking!! (with or without the insurance—it's their loss of a blessing!) Tim did extremely well with the lightweight travel wheelchair that folds up and we were all able to go to Casper for the College National Finals Rodeo in one vehicle! Little crowded—kinda reminded me of the days before four-door pickups with Elroy Cooper & Daughters (with Mom also) and our trips to the wheat fields!!! We sat through two morning slacks and one evening performance (about fifteen hours of rodeo!) It was great seeing, hugging, shaking hands, and visiting with friends! Thank you all for your time with us. Tim did really well emotionally (sometimes better than I do!) with it all (friends, teammates, horses, ropes, the smell of the arena dirt and horses, etc, etc) We told 'hospital' stories from when and what the girls did from when we left with the ambulance and Tim to the hospital and who all and what all took place those first few days of ICU, waiting rooms, friends sleeping in the chapel, etc. We had many laughs and Tim would just ask for more 'stories'—guess we all forgot we had not told him many of them before! It was a real "Walton" family time in our hotel room!!

    They (Corey Ross) have Rodeo Church after the night performances (from about 9:30ish to close to 11:00) and Tim just spoke a few minutes about God has a plan—it's his job to keep living each day, finding out the plan, and trusting Him! Thanks to all who prayed for us this past week and for the time at the Rodeo. We pray God will show His amazing ways with Tim's left fingers/hand, jaw muscles, and continue to encourage him with His hand of healing and restoration—We ask you to pray for this coming Sunday—Tim has been asked to speak at the Wyoming High School Finals Rodeo in Douglas! The seniors there were all freshmen when Tim was a senior. The emotional side of returning to the arena where he was State runner-up (2 yrs. '07 & '08) and State Champion ('09) Calf Roper and where we attended Rodeo Church for four years during the Finals—I pray will be an encouragement and God will be glorified through it all! We are looking forward to seeing many friends. Thank you again and again for your prayers—we feel them daily as we are held up to Him by all ya'll.

Jim McNamee sees an overwhelming effect on the high school and college-age rodeo young men and women. He said, "Tim is showing them what faith is all about and also why it is so important to appreciate life more. When my son's high school basketball team from Burns (some of the same kids Tim had played with a few years earlier) went to state this year, Tim inspired them through a letter he wrote to encourage them but also to tell them to enjoy the experience and live for God. Tim sends out similar texts each morning to family and friends. That's just a small part of his influence."

(Words from the speech given when presenting the Tim Malm Cowboy Spirit Award which is a cash scholarship awarded to a LCCC Rodeo Student)
"The patch on the NJC rodeo vests is Phil. 4:13 which Tim stands on—"I can do all things through Christ who strengthens me!" Tim looks forward to being back in the arena, ready to "Nod his head!" His faith and trust in God for full healing and restoration, the prayers and encouragement of thousands of people, and his love for life keeps him going on this journey. His goals are to Walk, Ride, and Rope."

> **With this entry marking the second year anniversary of Tim's accident, we conclude this portion of the journaling account of Tim's recovery. I know that all the Malms sincerely ask for your continued prayers for Tim's full recovery. Dixie will still be journaling on Caringbridge.com if possible and you can keep up with Tim's progress on his Facebook page as well.**

We all believe in God's time, he will be healed and we will all be witnesses to another of God's miracles. As Grandma Shirley said, "God is not through with Tim yet." I also truly believe all those who read Dixie's weekly journal entries will continue to be inspired by her words, God's words, and the Malm's continuing display of their amazing faith.

Final Thoughts

I remember a poem with the line "shot heard round the world" where it talks about moments in history that will be remembered forever. There are times in our lives when things happen that change our lives forever: the death of a loved one, hearing the diagnosis of cancer, etc. These seconds in time change us forever. Just when we think we have life all figured out, it happens. Things happen that are not in our plan. We have to change course and none of us like change. Only when you have lived through these seconds do you realize that life has no plan. All we are asked to do is live it one day, one second at a time. There is a verse in the Bible that says something about we can make our plans but God directs our paths. What we think at the time are roadblocks or detours are really all a part of God's route for our lives.

I remember talking to Dixie about two days after the accident. She was so positive, like she always is, and was talking about taking Tim home in a few days and everything would be back to normal. She was always trying to fix everything. I wanted to tell her things would never be normal again, no matter what. Also what is normal? I remember telling Danny that I prayed that Dixie would be able to handle it when God did not answer her prayers the way she wanted Him to and in the time frame she wanted Him to. Accepting God's plan and God's timing is the most important thing we can do when going through these moments in our lives. June 6, 2010 was truly a shot heard round the world, a day none of us will ever forget.

Fanny Malm, Tim's grandmother shared her thoughts:

"How to begin? Where to begin?—I've had a hard time deciding. I remember June 6, 2010 like it was yesterday! Jessie came running from the arena screaming, "Grandma, call the ambulance! Tim is hurt!" It's been a journey of ups and downs since then. My memory goes back to when Tim would get through with his work on the Ranch at night and then would always stop and visit us before he went home. How we miss those visits! When he and Grandpa Gordon would go to Lagrange to work cows, Tim would always be text messaging someone. After about four days in ICU, his right thumb began to move—I said he was text messaging again! Tim has taught me so many things. I've learned to appreciate the simpler things in life I always took for granted. He never complains and still has a marvelous sense of humor. He has a deep love for the Lord and such a determination to get well. I never visit him but come away feeling very blessed to have such a wonderful grandson! Tim is a blessing and an inspiration to all he comes in contact with. God is using him in a mighty way! His entire family has been such a testimony for the Lord. I'm praying God will allow Tim to walk one of these days real soon. In the meantime, I cherish every visit and time spent with him!"

As I think about how all this is affecting me, I have come to the conclusion that never again will I complain. I think back over the trivial and selfish things I have worried over and complained about in the past. Both of my boys played collegiate baseball. I would get so upset when they lost a game or struck out at the plate, etc. I now realize I should have been so excited to just watch them play. They were blessed with the ability and opportunity to play and I was blessed to be able to watch them live their dreams. Such trivial things to complain about. They are nothing compared to what the Malms are facing. Every time I am tempted to complain, my mind races to Tim and his family and I suddenly realize I have absolutely nothing to complain about. I am so blessed and should be thanking God every minute of every day for those blessings instead of complaining. One day my students were complaining about having to get up that morning and come to school. I said, "Shame on you for complaining. My nephew Tim would love to be able to get out of bed by himself and go to school or work." One story Tim tells will stick in my mind forever. One of his rodeo friends was telling Tim of a recent competition. He told Tim he had a bad day of roping. Tim shook his head and said, "No, you didn't. ANY day that you CAN rope is a good day." Tragedies always have a way of putting things in perspective for us.

After reading through several pages of thoughts sent to me from Dixie that she had gathered from family and friends of Tim, so many of them talked about the inspiration Tim has been to them through this accident. Tim's coach said, "It is always super neat when Tim blesses us with a sermon at the college rodeos. The improvement I see in him every time we get together is awesome. I am sure it is not fast enough for Tim but the devil tried to steal, kill, and destroy this young man and it backfired because Tim is sharing the good news with everyone.'

Katelin Malm wrote, "Anyone Tim has come in contact with, he has touched their life. Tim's journey has led people to the Lord, strengthened or renewed some people's faith, but for me Tim has shown me how truly fragile life really is. Timothy looks fear in the eye and endures hardship and adversity without complaining. He lives each day with courage. Because of Tim's courage and faith, his time here on earth was not completed. Timothy is bold in his faith and uses his accident as a testament that and pick up on his passion where he left off is what counts the most."

JD Ellis, Tim's cousin, wrote, "To see you shift your focus and determination to getting better makes me know that you will keep progressing. As well as re-cooping, you decided to take up public speaking which about 99% of the population would never think of doing."

Kaden Malm, age 12, wrote, "Tim has taught me that hard work pays off. He has taught me this through how hard he has worked after his accident."

Karissa Malm wrote, "I realized what life was all about when someone I loved the most was almost taken away from me.
Kelsay Scott wrote,

"When I think inspiration, the first thing that comes to my mind is Tim. I have never met someone with the drive and determination that Tim has. He pushes himself every day to overcome something that would cause most people to give up, that would leave most people saying why me, that would make most people bitter towards everything and everyone. Not Tim. His faith in the Lord and his courage to accept what has happened as a gift is something that could turn a non believer into a believer. He talks about how God has a plan for him and how this is just a new challenge for him. He explains to everyone that he doesn't want us to feel sorry for him but to pray for him to have the strength to overcome this. Tim doesn't feel sorry for himself like most people would; instead he smiles and goes on with life and his new challenge."

Joe and Katherine Nance said, "Tim Malm has shown others the faith, strength and courage to face life challenges. He is turning tragedy into something beautiful, into blessings bringing light into darkness in others' lives. We thank God every day for Tim's witness in the midst of his tragedy."

Cimarron Boardman PRCA Calf Roper—"I could always tell that he was a winner and he carried himself in that manner all the time. You can still see it today; he will always be that way."

Cole Glover—"Tim, you remind me daily that He loves me and to keep my head held high. I thank you for being such an inspiration in my life."

Jack Tyner wrote, "I believe that his accident just proves how tough Tim Malm is. His faith and try are what allowed him to survive an accident that would have killed most people. He wouldn't give up. But that's just Tim; he's always been that way."

I can not imagine what Dixie and Howard must be going through. I know what it was like to see my dad lying there in the hospital room, but not my child. As parents, we want to fix everything and don't want to see our children in pain or disappointed. We want life to be wonderful for them and for them to dream big and reach all their goals.

So many times we get all wrapped up in them succeeding in what the world views as success. When circumstances get in the way of their hopes and dreams, we hurt with them. When they are passionate about an area of their life, so are we. Tim and his family were passionate about rodeo. When the accident changed Tim's goals, it changed all their lives as well. Through all of the disappointment, pain, and daily struggles, their strength and faith are inspirational. How many of us would stay this positive for three days—much less three years or more? How many of us would turn angry and bitter? How many of us would simply give up? We watch how they are totally trusting God and His plan for Tim's life. They know their lives will never be the same, but we all learn at some time in our lives that "normal" takes on many different definitions as we go through the ups and downs of life. We are scarred by the tragedies but we live on. The scars are daily reminders of what God brought us through.

Faith means trusting God—with everything. Not an easy thing to do, especially in this day and time when we as a society want to have control over everything that happens in our lives. We plan our lives and want God to bless our plans. I am so guilty of this. As I said earlier, we want our children to be successful and happy. We want all their dreams to come true. We need to be careful about this. Being successful is not about making money but making a difference. Doing what God plans for us to do. Only then we will be truly successful and truly happy. I am only now trying to understand what giving all our lives—all our plans and dreams—all our plans and dreams for our children and grandchildren—everything to God. They are His anyway and He has a perfect plan for each one of us. Martha, Tim's aunt, said it wonderfully when she wrote, "When God promises that He 'causes all things to work together for good to those who love God . . ." He is the only one who can determine what that "good" is. I am tempted to question what God is doing because I want to define good according to my own ideas and limited perspective. I came to understand that our Good God would never have spared Tim's life just because of the words we did or did not pray as our hearts ached and we asked God to let Tim live. God spared Tim's life because it truly was His best for Tim. God spared Tim so He could use Tim and his injury for His good. He left Tim here on earth because He still has work for Tim to do. I praise God for all the good He has done and continues to do in and through Tim."

Tim and his family want more than anything for him to be able to rope competitively again. That is his dream. BUT Tim is willing to give that life up for Jesus if that is what Jesus wants. Tim lives for Jesus- not for Tim. That is what giving our lives for Jesus really means. Most Christians have no problem giving their life, dying, for Jesus. He died for us. BUT many Christians have a problem giving up their perception of life and their dreams and plans for what Jesus wants for them to do with their lives. There is a big difference. We are getting the privilege of watching this kind of faith in action with the Malms. Tim is doing what God wants him to do right now. He is affecting people through his sacrifice of his own dreams for God's plan. Joni Eareckson Tada wrote, "Even though we've never met, Tim's story has traveled far and wide. After 43 years living as a quadriplegic in a wheel chair, there are still mornings I wake up and think, 'I don't have the strength.' It's the way the apostle Paul felt in II Corinthians 1:8-9 when he said, "We were under great pressure far beyond our ability to endure . . ." But then the next verse says, "But this happened that we might not rely on ourselves, but on God." What a powerful reminder that things happen so that we might rely on God and not our own understanding. Perhaps Tim is learning that the weaker we are, the harder we lean on Jesus and the harder we lean on Him, the stronger we discover Him to be."

Ernest Hemingway in his book "The Old Man and the Sea" talks about being defeated but not destroyed. As an athlete, Tim understands what victory and defeat are all about. He knows you can't truly understand one without experiencing the other. What makes a true competitor is not whether you lose or not, but what you do when you do lose. What do you do when you strike out, miss the shot, or fall from the horse? You dust yourself off and step up to the plate again, take the court again, or get back on the horse again. You keep fighting in the arena. This is what Tim is doing now. He is dusting himself off and in the process of getting back in the saddle. The life lesson in this analogy is so important. We will all fail at some time in our lives. When we are faced with difficult circumstances, we don't give up. We work harder than ever to get back in the race. We may be defeated, but not destroyed. As you follow Tim's recovery, you will realize there is no quit in him. Ultimately, he will come out on top.

Tim's journey is not over. He is still recovering and making daily progress to full restoration. His daily entries with scripture verses on Facebook are so inspiring. The last time I saw Tim and his family was in July 2012 when they traveled to Oklahoma for a family wedding. I was amazed at the progress he had made since October. I am still amazed at his quick wit. He was a joy to visit with and brought tears of laughter to our eyes. As we talked about past memories and looked at pictures, he remembered it all. It was heartwarming to see his contagious smile. At one time Tim asked me what I needed him to do for the book. I told him, "You're doing it, Tim. You are the book!" As I watched his dad carrying him and holding him when he stood, it reminded me that this is just like our Heavenly Father does for us. Even though Tim is bigger and outweighs Howard, Howard has the strength to do this. As I have said numerous times throughout this book, I know Tim will be healed. God will choose to heal him here on earth, or He may choose to call him home to heaven for his complete healing there as He did with my sister Shena. No one knows but God. Tomorrow is not promised to any of us. I truly believe that if it is God's will and purpose for Tim's life, he will be "Back in the Saddle" again. I encourage you to continue to share this walk of faith with Tim and his family through their journaling on Caringbridge.com and Facebook. Every day that you read Tim's devotion along with his recovery update and watch his videos you too will be encouraged and motivated in your walk of faith. Continue to pray for Tim and be a part of his recovery. Experience the miracle. I guarantee you will be blessed and your life will never be the same again. I chose to end this book with the speech given by Tim in June of 2012:

> *For those of you who don't know me, I'm Tim Malm. Three years ago, 2009, I was right where you're at—getting ready to 'nod my head' for the last time in this arena as a high school competitor. I was pretty successful and had been blessed with some great accomplishments. I was not only recognized as a calf roper, but also for my horsemanship. I was State Runner-up Calf Roper in '07 and '08 with being State Champion in '09. I was proud to represent Wyoming as a*

3-time National Qualifier. After winning at State, I went to the National High School Finals in July and was the National Reserve Champion Calf Roper! I attended Northeastern Junior College on a rodeo scholarship and ended up fifth in the college region. I had and still have a passion for roping calves. I loved practicing as much as competing and I believe that passion was used by God to develop dedication. I'm 6th generation on our family ranch so I've always worked hard. I miss working with my family, my horses, and the cattle very much. Today I'm here to tell you all the belt buckles and accomplishments in the world will only gain dust and fade away so I want to ask a question today—"Why are we here then?" I believe we were put here to bring God glory—that's really the only thing that matters! AND if He uses us with horses and ropes, all the better! So why do this—why rodeo or anything else we do in life? Is it for personal glory or God's glory? I'm not saying we should quit rodeo and become pastors or that God doesn't care about rodeo . . . No-No He cares about our faith and if that's what we use to live out our faith then great. In 1st Corinthians 10:31 it says, "So, whether you eat or drink, or whatever you do, do all to the glory of God." He loves us so much! I love my parents beyond words, and I know they love me, but I don't think they would ask me to die for other people. I know all you here love your parents. but that doesn't come close to God's love—He loves each of us a billion times more than that! He sent His Son to die for us. I can't wrap my mind around that, but I believe it and have accepted Him as Lord and Savior of my life. I would have a terrible time dying for people I love; I can't see any way that I would for complete strangers, and definitely no way for people that hated and called me names. Yet Jesus died for us all just as His Father planned. He just wants a personal relationship with each of us—to become His children and follow Him! That answers the question of today . . . and that is why I rodeo, to give God all the glory possible. I pray that is for you also. Preparation, good advice, time, and practice all took me to State, to Nationals, To college, and to PRCA rodeos. I see all those in my relationship with my Lord as they take me through this journey of life. Preparation is asking, believing, and accepting Him as Lord and Savior to begin your walk with Him. Good advice is *the Bible and we need to be spending time in prayer and reading His Word. Practice is the daily lifestyle of living out the faith—"Walk the Talk". You never know what tomorrow holds. Just look at me—that Sunday evening on June 6, 2010 was gonna be like any other roping practice. I wasn't thinking anything like this would happen. The first hours were critical and the first couple of days were nip and tuck. The doctors didn't give me any chance to even make it through the first night. The word they gave my parents and the 40-plus people praying on the knees in the ICU waiting room was a "glimmer" of hope. Praise God I'm here and living each day in God's will, You never know what tomorrow holds, but I know the Guy who holds tomorrow, and I totally trust that He's got my best interest in mind. He says in Jeremiah 29:11 that 'He knows the plans that He has for me' and for you, so I'm standing on His Word and promise. Don't feel sorry for me because God is using me in big ways and in ways I never thought. God will never put you through anything more than you can handle. So, I just look at this as a challenge to make it back. One of my favorite verses is Philippians 4:13 "I can do all things through Christ who gives me strength!" Yeah, it's taken longer than I would have hoped, but Lord willing, I will be back! Keep Praying and Believing! Thank you for letting me come and speak to you this morning. In the words of my good friend, Derek Barton, "Let's Go, Let's Show, Let's Rodeo!" Thank you and God Bless!*

Yes, Tim, your light is brightly shining and warming the hearts of all who are near. Matt 5:14-16 "Ye are the light of the world. A city that is set on a hill cannot be hid. Neither do men light a candle, and put it under a bushel, but on a candlestick; and it giveth light unto all that are in the house. Let your light so shine before men, that they may see your good works, and glorify your Father which is in Heaven."

When Tim gets through this and on the other side, his testimony for Christ will be indescribable. When all this is a thing of the past and we are on the other side of this valley, I will make it a point to tell Tim and his family how they changed my life and the lives of so many other people. Thank you Tim for letting us share in your journey back in the saddle. Thank you Jesus for Tim.

Appendix

(Bible verses used in the book were either NIV or NAS Bible versions unless otherwise stated.)

God gave these verses to these friends to share with the Malms as a means of support and encouragement.

"Praise to the Lord, to God our Savior, who daily bears our burdens" Ps. 68:19

". . . I will rain down bread from heaven for you . . . ." Ex. 16:4

"Then your light will break forth like the dawn, and your healing will quickly appear; then your righteousness will go before you, and the glory of the Lord will be your rear guard." Isaiah 58:8

Jeremiah 29:11 "For I know the plans I have for you," declares the Lord, "Plans to prosper you and not to harm you, plans to give you hope and a future."

Phil. 1:6 "I am convinced and sure that He who began a good work in me will continue until the day of Jesus Christ, developing and perfecting and bringing it to full completion in me."

"With God all things are possible!!" Matthew 19:26

John 9:1-4 . . . his disciples asked him, saying, Master, who did sin, this man, or his parents . . . ? Jesus answered, Neither hath this man sinned, nor his parents: but that the works of God should be made manifest in him. I must work the works of him that sent me, while it is day: the night cometh, when no man can work."

Phil. 4:6 "Be anxious for nothing, but in everything by prayers and supplication, with thanksgiving let your requests be made known to God!"

Matt.18:20 "For where two or three have gathered together in My name, there I am in the midst!"

"Find rest, O my soul, in God alone: my hope comes from Him" Ps. 62:5

"The Lord is good, A stronghold in the day of trouble, And He knows those who take refuge in Him." Nahum 1:7

Jeremiah 33:[2-3]& [10a-11] "Thus saith the LORD the maker thereof, the LORD that formed it, to establish it; the LORD is his name; Call unto me, and I will answer thee, and shew thee great and mighty things, which thou knowest not."

[10-11] "Thus saith the LORD; Again there shall be heard in this place, . . . The voice of joy, and the voice of gladness, . . . the voice of them that shall say, Praise the LORD of hosts: for the LORD is good; for his mercy endureth for ever: and of them that shall bring the sacrifice of praise into the house of the LORD. For I will cause to return the captivity of the land, as at the first, saith the LORD"

Jeremiah 17:14 NKJV "Heal me, O LORD, and I shall be healed; Save me, and I shall be saved, For You are my praise."

"But for those who revere my name, the sun of righteousness will rise with healing in its wings. And you will go out and leap like calves released from the stall" Malachi 4:2

Psalm 18:16 . . . "He reached down from on high and took hold of me; he drew me out of deep waters."

Proverbs 4:20-22 "My son, pay attention to what I say; listen closely to my words. Do not let them out of your sight, keep them within your heart; for they are life to those who find them and health to a man's whole body."

"Now, my God, may your eyes be open and your ears attentive to the prayers offered in this place" 2 Chronicles 6:40

"But He knows the way that I take; When He has tried me, I shall come forth as gold." Job 23:10

CPSIA information can be obtained at www.ICGtesting.com
Printed in the USA
LVOW130759040613

336783LV00002B/5/P